English Grammar

An Introduction

Peter Collins and Carmella Hollo

First published 2000 by
MACMILLAN PRESS LTD
Houndmills, Basingstoke, Hampshire RG21 6XS
and London
Companies and representatives
throughout the world

ISBN 0–333–69600–X hardcover
ISBN 0–333–69601–8 paperback✓

A catalogue record for this book is available
from the British Library.

This book is printed on paper suitable for recycling and made from fully managed and sustained forest sources.

10   9   8   7   6   5   4   3   2   1
09   08   07   06   05   04   03   02   01   00

Copy edited and typeset by Password, Norwich, UK.
Printed in Hong Kong

English Grammar

An Introduction

From the same Publishers

A Coursebook in English Grammar 2nd edition
Dennis Freeborn

Meaning in English
Lesley Jeffries

An Introduction to English Language
John Peck and Martin Coyle

Contents

Preface

This book is intended as an introduction to English grammar for secondary and tertiary students. It is divided into two sections. Part A, 'Grammatical Description', begins by locating the study of grammar within its broader context and explaining general aspects of the approach adopted in this book, and then presents in step-by-step fashion the various categories that are used in analysing the grammatical structure of sentences. Part B, 'Looking at Language in Context', applies the methods developed in Part A to the analysis of texts of various kinds.

The aim is not only to equip students with a set of tools for critically analysing texts, but also to make students aware that there are often different ways of analysing a set of grammatical data. In various places throughout the book we shall pause to draw attention to, and argue against, analyses that have been adopted by a number of grammarians, but which we have decided not to follow.

The type of grammatical analysis used is influenced strongly by Rodney Huddleston's (1984, 1988) structuralist model of grammar, but it also draws insights from the work of Randolph Quirk and associates (Quirk et al. 1972, 1985; Leech et al. 1982; Greenbaum and Quirk 1990). While the approach we adopt builds on the work of contemporary linguists, it nevertheless retains the familiar terms and categories of traditional grammar wherever possible. Recognising that there will be a number of users of this book who will have some knowledge of traditional grammar, we shall draw attention to aspects of our description that differ significantly from those found there.

Exercises are presented at the end of each chapter, and answers are provided at the end of the book (pp. 239–46). Following the answers you will find a glossary and a list of books and articles for further reading.

Acknowledgements

The editors and publishers wish to thank the following for permission to use copyright material:

Tim Flannery for an extract from 'Creature Features', *Sydney Morning Herald*, 30.12.97; W. W. Norton & Company for e. e. cummings, 'anyone lived in a pretty how town' from *Complete Poems* 1904–1962 by e. e. cummings, edited by George James Firmage. Copyright © 1991 by the Trustees for the e. e. cummings Trust and George James Firmage; Margaret Connolly & Associates Pty Ltd on behalf of the author for an extract from Christopher Koch, 'Mysteries' from *Crossing the Gap*, Chatto & Windus (1987) and Angus & Robertson (1993).

Every effort has been made to trace copyright holders, but if any have been inadvertently overlooked the publishers will be pleased to make the necessary arrangement at the first opportunity.

Symbols and conventions

Many of the symbols and notational conventions are as used by Huddleston, *English grammar: An Outline* (CUP, 1988), and by Leech et al., *English Grammar for Today: A New Introduction* (Macmillan, 1982).

Bold for technical terms at points where they are first discussed

Italics are used for citing words, sentences and other expressions

( ) parentheses are used to enclose phrases

[ ] square brackets are used to enclose clauses

⌐⎯⎯⎯⎤ a horizontal line is used to link discontinuous elements

(e.g. *Have you been there?*)

< > angle brackets are used to enclose a coordination of elements (e.g. *She ran <down the road and over the bridge>*)

+ a plus symbol is used to represent any coordinator

* an asterisk is used for an ungrammatical expression
? is used for an expression of questionable grammaticality

Abbreviated labels

Function labels

A	Adjunct
Ax	Axis
C	Complement
Cx	Non-central complement
Dr	Determiner
H	Head
M	Modifier
O	Object
Od	Direct object

Oi   Indirect object
P   Predicator
PC   Predicative complement
PCo   Objective predicative complement
PCs   Subjective predicative complement
PD   Peripheral dependent
Pred   Predicate
Rel   Relator
S   Subject

Class labels

ACl   Adverbial clause
Adj   Adjective
AdjP   Adjective phrase
Adv   Adverb
AdvP   Adverb phrase
Aux   Auxiliary verb
CCl   Comparative clause
Cl   Clause
Clen   Past participial clause
Cli   Infinitival clause
Cling   Present participial clause
Coord   Coordinator
Dv   Determinative
DvP   Determinative phrase
GP   Genitive phrase
MCl   Main clause
Mv   Main verb
N   Noun
NCl   Noun clause
NP   Noun phrase
Pcle   Particle
Pn   Pronoun
PP   Prepositional phrase
PredP   Predicate phrase
Prep   Preposition
RCl   Relative clause
SCl   Subordinate clause
Se   Sentence
Subord Subordinator
Ved   Past tense form of verb
Ven   Past participial form of verb
Vi   Infinitival (base) form of verb
Ving   Present participial form of verb
Vo   General 'other' present form of verb
VP   Verb phrase
Vs   Third person singular present tense form of verb

Part A | Grammatical Description

1 | Introduction

1.1 Grammar and the description of language

What is grammar and where does it fit into the description of a language? According to most contemporary linguists, we can divide the description of any language into three major areas: grammar (comprising two sub-fields, morphology and syntax), phonology and lexicon. Sometimes grammar is understood to encompass all three areas.

Grammar
> *Morphology*   deals with the form of words
> *Syntax*   deals with the arrangement of words to form sentences

Phonology   deals with the sound system (involving sounds, stress and intonation)

Lexicon   provides information about the individual items of the vocabulary (words, and idioms such as *kick the bucket*)

In each of the three major areas we may distinguish between the study of form and the study of meanings (the term **semantics** often being applied to the latter, the study of linguistic meanings). Thus, for example, the study of grammatical form will deal with grammatical categories such as past tense and interrogative clause, while the study of grammatical meaning will be concerned with the meanings associated with these categories (past time, question, and the like).

Traditional grammarians have tended to assume that the relationship between form and meaning is straightforward. However, in many cases it is not. For example, traditional grammars commonly describe the past tense simply as a form of the verb which expresses the meaning 'past time'. Such a claim accurately captures the meaning of the past tense verb form *left* in:

> John **left** at three o'clock yesterday

However, the relationship between form and meaning is less direct in:

> It would be better if you **left** tomorrow

Here the past tense form *left* indicates a time which is not in the past, but in the future.

As a second example, consider the familiar traditional definition of interrogative clauses as clauses that are used to ask questions. This definition is valid for a clause such as:

> Will it rain tomorrow?

However, the 'meaning' associated with the following interrogatives is quite different (respectively 'command' and 'offer'):

> Will you sit down!
> Will you have another sandwich?

In the next section we shall explore further the complexity of the relationship between form and meaning as we begin to explain the type of approach adopted in the present grammar.

1.2 Defining grammatical categories

One of the reasons why modern grammarians have reacted against traditional grammar is that traditional grammarians commonly invoke meaning rather than form when defining grammatical categories. When you attempt to use meaning-based definitions (sometimes called 'notional' definitions) to identify the items associated with a particular category, you will often obtain results that are misleading, or even plainly wrong.

Consider as an example the category of 'subject'. There are in fact two types of meaning-based definition that one finds applied to the subject in traditional grammar. One is that the subject represents the 'doer' or 'actor', and the other is that the subject represents the 'topic' or 'what the sentence is about'. There are problems with both definitions. Consider:

John injured the goalkeeper

John was the goalkeeper

In both sentences we would presumably want to analyse *John* as the subject, but it is only in the first sentence that John is understood to have performed an action. The second sentence does not express an activity, but rather a state of affairs. Consider another pair of sentences:

The rain was pouring down

It was raining

Here we would presumably want to treat *the rain* and *it* respectively as subjects. However, while we may regard *the rain* as the topic of the first sentence, what it is about, it would be odd to say that the second sentence is about *it*, since *it* is here merely a grammatical item which does not convey any meaning. Presumably, a sentence can only 'be about' something that has an existence, real or imaginary.

In order to correctly identify the subject of a sentence we must rely on formal grammatical properties rather than meaning. For instance, one important formal property of subjects is their role in the formation of question tags: the subject of a sentence in English is the element which is either 'proformed' (i.e. replaced by a pronoun) or copied in a question tag, as in:

John was the goalkeeper, wasn't he?

It was raining, wasn't it?

Notice that this formal criterion clearly reveals the weakness of the traditional definition in some cases. Consider:

Tom was telephoned by Mary

The traditional definition of the subject as actor would suggest, counter-intuitively, that *Mary* is the subject. However, we can confirm that *Mary* is not in fact the subject, but rather it is *Tom* (even though Tom is not the performer of the action) by applying the 'tag-test':

Tom was telephoned by Mary, wasn't he?

As a second illustration of the inadequacy of notional definitions, consider the traditional treatment of nouns in English. Traditional grammars generally define a noun as 'the name of a person, place or thing'. This definition is unproblematical when applied to words denoting concrete objects such as *tree*, *ocean* and *bicycle*. Unfortunately, however, there are many words which we readily recognise as nouns, but which are not covered by the traditional notional definition, including such intangibles as *stupidity*, *rejection* and *deafness*. Some may seek to argue that the latter would be covered by the definition if we simply allowed the meaning of the word 'thing' to be extended so that it applied not simply to concrete objects, but also to abstractions. But such an interpretation of the word 'thing' would surely make the traditional definition of nouns unacceptably circular. For instance, the word *stupidity*, which refers to something intangible, a property or characteristic, would legitimately be classified as a noun, but why then should we not apply the same criterion and treat *stupid* as a noun? Why should we accept *suggestion* but not *suggest*? Why accept *deafness* but not *deaf*? The problem would be that in order to know whether or not a word fitted the traditional definition, we would need to know in advance whether or not that word was a noun.

As in the case of the subject, so with nouns, it seems clear that we need to appeal to formal grammatical criteria in order to provide an adequate definition. For instance, nouns are distinctive in the types of dependents that they may take: compare *such stupidity* and **such stupid*; *his deafness* and **his deaf*.

1.3 Grammatical categories and 'prototypes'

We have demonstrated that semantically based definitions are inadequate, and that if we are to correctly identify the parts of speech, we shall need to consider how they differ in terms of their formal properties rather than in terms of their meanings. Does this mean that the traditional definitions have no role to play in a grammar? No, not at all. The traditional meaning-based definitions do have an important role to play, in so far as they may be applied to the **prototypical** members of a category.

Thus the most typical nouns of English are precisely those that refer to people and things. For example, *car, tree* and *girl* are prototypical nouns, whereas the abstract noun *deafness* is not (notice that it differs from prototypical nouns in not having a plural form: **deafnesses* is ungrammatical). Prototypical nouns are the most frequently occurring in the language. They include the first nouns to be learnt by most children, and they share the same properties that are relevant to defining the category of nouns across the world's languages.

Similarly, the most typical subjects of English are precisely those that represent the actor and topic, and not surprisingly these notions also tend to be associated with the subject in those languages of the world which have such a category. Those subjects in English which are associated with only one of the two notions of actor or topic (or with neither, such as the *it* in *It is raining*) are more peripheral members of the category.

We shall thus conceive of grammatical categories as indeterminate or 'fuzzy'. Each category comprises a central core of instances, which share a number of grammatical properties and can generally be identified via a traditional meaning-based definition, and shades off into non-central members which exhibit some, but not all of the properties.

1.4 Morphology: words and lexemes

In this section we shall attempt some clarification of what is meant by the term 'word', and introduce some basic concepts of morphology, the study of the forms of words. Consider the following:

> *If he seeks to* **qualify**, *and* **qualifies** *fairly, then you must accept him as a legitimate* **qualifier**

The only difference between *qualify* and *qualifies* is that *qualifies* has a suffix (*-es*) not present in *qualify*. Similarly, the only difference between *qualify* and *qualifier* is that *qualifier* has a suffix (*-er*) not present in *qualify*. And yet the two pairs are not quite the same. Whereas most people would probably regard *qualify* and *qualifies* as in some sense 'forms of the same word', *qualify* and *qualifier* would be regarded by most as different words.

It is helpful to have a term other than 'word' to clarify the differences between the two pairs: we shall say that *qualify* and *qualifies* are different words, but that they are associated with a single **lexeme** (a more abstract unit than a word). By contrast, *qualify* and *qualifier* are associated with different lexemes.

The words associated with a lexeme are said to be related to each other by means of **inflection**: in this case, *qualify* is the 'infinitive' and *qualifies* (which carries the present tense -*es* inflection) is related to it as a present tense form. The words associated with a lexeme are sometimes said to constitute a 'paradigm'. The paradigm for the verb lexeme *qualify* contains the words *qualify*, *qualifies*, *qualified* and *qualifying*.

Consider some further examples: the paradigm for the adjective lexeme *slow* contains *slow*, *slower* and *slowest*; that for the noun lexeme *uncle* contains *uncle*, *uncles*, *uncle's* and *uncles'*; that for the demonstrative *this* contains *this* and *these*. The most complex paradigm is that for the verb *be*: it consists not only of the positive forms *be*, *is*, *am*, *are*, *was*, *were*, *been* and *being*, but also the negative forms *isn't*, *aren't*, *wasn't* and *weren't*.

We close this section by noting that there are two main branches of morphology: inflectional morphology and lexical morphology. When, in introducing morphology in the prelude to this chapter, we treated it as a sub-field of grammar we were oversimplifying matters. It is actually only the first branch of morphology, **inflectional morphology**, that falls within the domain of grammar. Inflectional morphology deals with the processes which give rise to inflectional forms, and it interacts with syntax, in so far as it is the rules of syntax that determine whether a lexeme can or must carry a particular inflectional property. Consider the verb form *forgotten* in:

> *I have forgotten your name*

It is a rule of syntax which dictates that the verb following *have* must carry the past participial inflection, while the rules of inflectional morphology determine that the past participle form of *forget* is *forgotten*.

Lexical morphology is dealt with in the lexicon, and is thus, strictly speaking, outside the concerns of grammar. It deals with the processes by which lexical items (the basic units of the vocabulary, or 'lexicon') are derived. These processes include **affixation** (the addition of *prefixes* to a stem, as in **un***equal*, **dis***agree*, and **extra***marital*; and of suffixes, as in *equality*, *informant*, and *careless*), **compounding** (the adding together of stems, as in *blackberry*, *fireplace* and *postmodern*), and **conversion** (the change of a word from one part of speech to another, as in the conversion of the adjective *even* to the verb *even*, and of the verb *act* to the noun *act*).

1.5 Constituent structure

Syntax, we have said, is concerned with how words combine to form sentences. Sentences have a hierarchical structure, with the larger units consisting of successively smaller units. Thus we might analyse the sentence *Some people collect old Australian stamps as a hobby* informally as follows (in the form of what is generally called a 'tree diagram'):

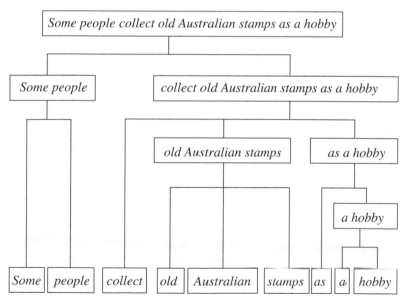

Each unit that is at the end of a line, or 'branch', and thus is part of a higher unit is called a **constituent** (so there are 14 constituents: *some people*, *collect old Australian stamps as a hobby*, *old Australian stamps, as a hobby, a hobby, some, people, collect, old, Australian, stamps, as, a* and *hobby*). Complementary to the notion of constituent is that of **construction**. For example *some* and *people* are constituents of the construction *some people*. In the tree diagram above there are six constructions: *some people collect old Australian stamps as a hobby, some people, collect old Australian stamps as a hobby, old Australian stamps, as a hobby* and *a hobby*. Thus constituents make up constructions and, conversely, constructions are made up of constituents. It follows that the topmost unit, the whole sentence, can only be a construction and not a constituent since it is not a part of a higher grammatical unit, and that the bottom-most units can only be constituents since they are not made up of further constituents. *Some people* will be both a constituent and a construction: it is a constituent of the sentence and it is also a construction since it is made up of the constituents *some* and *people*.

One further term that we shall introduce is **immediate constituent**. The immediate constituents of a construction are those which are directly below it in the hierarchy, those that it is firstly – 'immediately' – divided into. For example, *as* and *a hobby* are the immediate constituents of *as a hobby* (*a* and *hobby* are constituents – but not the immediate constituents – of *as a hobby*; *a* and *hobby* are the immediate constituents of *a hobby*).

There is a good deal of redundancy in the tree diagram above. A more economical way of representing the same constituent structure information is presented below:

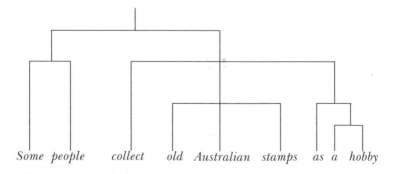

How do we know how to analyse a sentence into its constituents? Ultimately the answer to this question will depend on the sort of grammatical knowledge about sentence structure that this book seeks to provide you with. At this stage, suffice it to say that there are several rules of thumb which will be of assistance.

- 'Substitution' is one such rule of thumb. If a sequence of words can be substituted by a single word, then it can generally be assumed that the sequence is a constituent. For instance the status of *some people* as a constituent is suggested by the possibility of substituting a single word for it, such as *they* (*They collect old Australian stamps as a hobby*). It is possible to apply a similar test to confirm the status of *collects old Australian stamps as a hobby* as a constituent. Notice that if someone had queried the proposition, asking *Is it really true that they collect old Australian stamps as a hobby?*, and in reply you sought to affirm it, saying *They do!*, then *do* would be a substitute for the constituent *collect old Australian stamps as a hobby*.
- 'Movement' – the possibility of moving a constituent to another position – is a second test for constituency. Thus there is evidence for the status of *old Australian stamps* as a constituent in the fact that it can be moved to another position as in *Old Australian stamps they collect*. Consider several further examples. We can confirm that *in late July* is a constituent of the sentence *Aunt Gertrude arrived in late July* by noting the possibility of moving it as in *In late July Aunt Gertrude arrived*. Again, we can confirm the status of *the American stockmarket* as a constituent of *The American stockmarket is very robust*, by comparing it with *Is the American stockmarket very robust?*

Below are several further examples of sentences analysed in terms of their constituent structure:

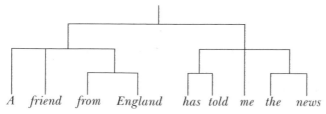

A   friend   from   England   has   told   me   the   news

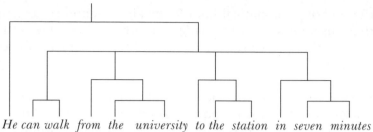

He can walk from the university to the station in seven minutes

As a final point in this section, it may be noted that the type of constituent structure analyses we have been discussing can sometimes be used to shed light on ambiguous sentences, each different interpretation corresponding to a separate constituent analysis, as in:

They are French history students

This sentence can mean either that 'They are students of French history' (as reflected in (a) below, where *students* and *French history* are constituents), or alternatively, 'They are history students of French nationality' (as reflected in (b), where *French* and *history students* are constituents).

(a)   (b)

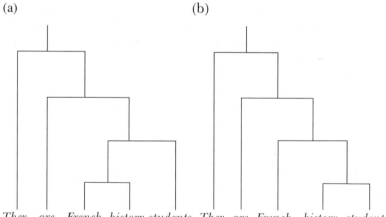

They are French history students   They are French history students

As a second example of an ambiguous sentence, consider the two interpretations of:

We discussed our victory in Italy

This sentence can mean either 'We discussed our victory that took place in Italy' (as reflected in (a), where *our victory in Italy* is a single constituent), or 'It was in Italy that we discussed our victory' (as reflected in (b), where *our victory* and *in Italy* are separate constituents).

(a)   (b)

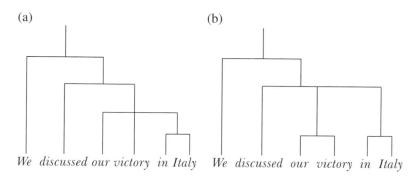

We discussed our victory in Italy   We discussed our victory in Italy

1.6 Classes and functions

The tree diagrams that we have presented so far identify the syntactic units in a sentence, but they do not supply any descriptions of these units. For each unit we may assign two types of description, one relating to its **syntactic class**, and the other to its **syntactic function**.

The syntactic class of a unit is determined by the grammatical properties that it shares with other forms, while the syntactic function is the grammatical role of a unit within the construction that contains it. The labelled tree diagram below demonstrates how we can assign a syntactic class and function to every constituent of a sentence (with the function label presented first, followed by the class label, and the two labels separated by a colon). It would be putting the cart before the horse to attempt to explain every label here: this is the task of subsequent chapters. We shall merely make some selective comments:

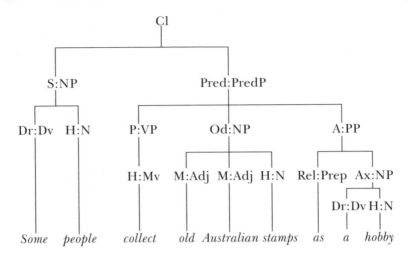

Some people and *old Australian stamps* belong to the class of 'noun phrases' ('NP'), grammatical units with a noun as the 'head' element (the head of *some people* is the noun *people*, and the head of *old Australian stamps* is the noun *stamps*). Further evidence that *some people* and *old Australian stamps* belong to the NP class is their function within the clause: *some people* is the subject (notice that it can be proformed in a tag, as in *Some people collect old Australian stamps as a hobby, don't they?*); *old Australian stamps* is the object (notice that it can be substituted by *them* but not by *they*, as in *Some people collect them as a hobby*). In turn *people* and *stamps* are classed as nouns because of the properties that they share with other members of that class (such as the capacity to express contrasts of number – *person* vs *people* and *stamp* vs *stamps* – and to take adjectives as dependents), and because they have the 'head' function within their NPs. Notice that the topmost unit, the clause, has no function assigned to it because it is not a constituent, not part of any larger grammatical unit.

In order to reduce the amount of 'vertical complexity' in our constituent analyses we will from this point onwards omit the Predicate as a constituent. Below is another sentence analysed in this way. Notice that P and A are now immediate constituents of the clause.

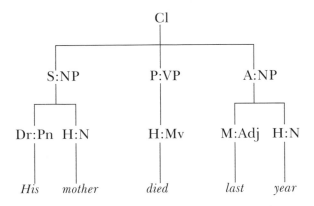

Finally, we note that an alternative method of notation to the tree diagram that we shall sometimes use is **labelled bracketing**. While bracketing does not show constituent structure as transparently as do tree diagrams, its 'flatness' gives it an advantage if you are engaged in analysing a succession of sentences in discourse. The main features of this method are:

* clauses are enclosed in square brackets [ ]
* phrases are enclosed in round brackets ( )
* function labels are represented as superscripts placed before brackets and individual constituents
* class labels are represented as subscripts placed before brackets and individual constituents

Here is a labelled bracketing analysis that presents the same information – except for the omission of the Predicate – as in the labelled tree diagram above:

$$[\ ^{S}(\ ^{Dr}Some\ ^{H}people)\ (^{P}\ ^{H}collect)\ (^{Od}\ ^{M}old\ ^{M}Australian\ ^{H}stamps)$$
NP Dv   N   VP Mv   NP Adj   Adj   N

$$(^{A}\ ^{Rel}as\ (^{Ax}\ ^{Dt}a\ ^{H}hobby))]$$
PP Prep   NP Dv   N

Here is a labelled version of the tree diagram we presented earlier, along with the corresponding version with labelled bracketing (again, we have simplified the analysis slightly by omitting the Predicate):

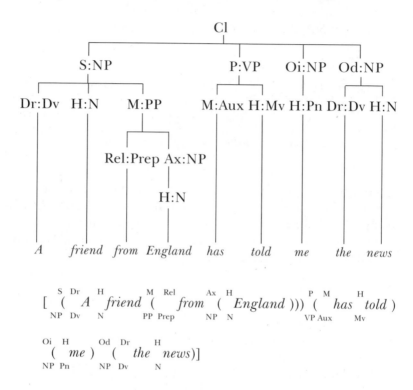

1.7 Descriptive and prescriptive grammar

A popular view of the role of grammar, one which is reflected in many school grammars, is that it should present a set of rules for speaking and writing 'correctly'. This approach may be described as **prescriptive**; that is, concerned with prescribing the ways in which – according to the grammarian – language should be used. Modern linguistics is, by contrast, **descriptive** in orientation: its concern is with describing how language *is* used rather than pre-scribing how it *should* be used. Thus, for example, we may find a 'rule' in a traditional prescriptive grammar of the type: 'A sentence should not end with a preposition', (according to which, sentence (1) below would be considered 'incorrect', the 'correct' version being (2)).

1. *This is the house which he lives in*
2. *This is the house in which he lives*

Such a rule would not be found in a descriptive grammar, where the grammarian's interest lies in the question of whether sentence-final prepositions do or do not occur in modern English (and, more specifically, if they do, what types of contexts favour their occurrence). In this particular case it would be important for the descriptive grammarian to distinguish between formal contexts (which are more likely to favour the occurrence of a sentence such as *This is the house in which he lives*) and informal contexts (where *This is the house (which) he lives in* is more likely).

Whereas prescriptive accounts tend to operate with a simple contrast between correct and incorrect, descriptive accounts recognise the existence of different varieties of language: formal vs informal, written vs spoken, standard vs nonstandard, and so on. The point is that both *This is the house in which he lives* and *This is the house he lives in* are constructed according to valid principles of grammar: the first sentence is not inherently better than the second and, in fact, it would create an effect of aloofness or stiffness if produced in an informal context.

Prescriptive grammar and descriptive grammar are not necessarily in conflict: they simply have different goals. Prescriptive grammarians present rules that they intend their readers to follow, while descriptive grammarians aim to account for the grammatical system that underlies our use of language. Prescriptive grammar is in a sense logically dependent on descriptive grammar: only prescriptive rules that are based on a sound description of the facts should merit our attention. This is the problem with, for instance, the traditional prescriptive rule forbidding the 'splitting' of infinitives (that is, the interposing of a word or phrase between the infinitival marker *to* and its verb) as exemplified in:

She used **to** deliberately **annoy** the neighbours

Despite the prescriptive rule, such a sentence is, in fact, as likely to be heard in contemporary usage as *She used to annoy the neighbours deliberately* and *She used deliberately to annoy the neighbours*: the rule is out of step with what a descriptive grammar would recognise to be the facts of usage.

Or again, it seems unreasonable to insist on the prescriptive rule that *may*, rather than *can*, should be used in requesting and granting permission, in view of the fact that (1) below is a more natural-sounding interchange than (2), at least in a typically informal, family environment.

1. *Can I have a lemonade please? Yes, you can*
2. *May I have a lemonade please? Yes, you may*

An important distinction that it is relevant to invoke in this section is that between *rules of grammar* and *rules of style*. A sentence may conform to the rules of (descriptive) grammar and yet contravene rules of style (those which dictate whether sentences are stylistically acceptable; in other words, easy to follow, unambiguous and clear). For example:

Did you see the man near the table with the hairy legs?

This sentence does not break any rule of grammar, but is stylistically flawed insofar as it allows for an unintended interpretation in which it is the table rather than the man that has hairy legs. Further examples of stylistically awkward – but not ungrammatical – sentences are:

Here is a photograph that a boy that my sister met in France last year took

Mary has handed all the goods currently in her possession over

These sentences do not break any grammatical rule of English, but they do break rules for effective communication. The first is difficult to follow, and may require several readings before the message is understood (it could be more felicitously expressed as *Here is a photograph taken by a boy that my sister met in France last year*). In the second, the position of *over* disrupts the balance of the sentence, a problem that could be solved by moving it closer to the verb *handed*, as in *Mary has handed over all the goods currently in her possession*.

Using language effectively is a skill that can be developed and improved. An increased knowledge of the grammatical resources of the language will provide the language user with

conscious mastery over a range of possibilities for construct-
ing sentences effectively. This is undoubtedly one of the most
important reasons for learning about grammar.

Exercises

1a. For each lexeme (boldfaced) write out all the inflectional
     ·word forms that are possible in the given context.

   Example:

He	***be***	*the*	*one*	***who***	*I*	***want***	*to*	***come***
	is			*who*		*want*		*come*
	was			*whom*		*wanted*		
	isn't							
	wasn't							

   1. *Our **friend** will be **leave** on the 3 o'clock train*
   2. *We **have be** trying to find a **good** price*
   3. *Some of **they be** in the mood for a party*
   4. *We were **encourage** to find a **simple** solution*
   5. *Mary **be be** harassed by her boss*
   6. ***Do** you support the local **team**?*

1b. Answer the questions based on the following constituen-
     cy 'tree diagrams'. (You should assume that the analysis
     given is correct.)

   1.

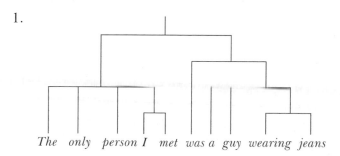

   The   only   person I   met   was a   guy   wearing   jeans

   a. Is *the only person* a constituent?
   b. Is *was a guy wearing jeans* a constituent?
   c. What are the immediate constituents of *a guy wear-
      ing jeans*?

2.

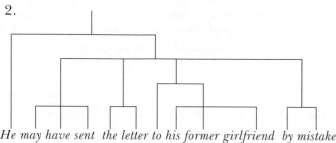

He may have sent the letter to his former girlfriend by mistake

a. Is *He may have sent the letter* a constituent?
b. Is *his former girlfriend* a constituent?
c. What are the immediate constituents of *to his former girlfriend*?

1c. Each of the sentences analysed below has two structural interpretations, as represented in the two tree diagrams provided. In each case explain the ambiguity, indicating which interpretation corresponds to which tree diagram.

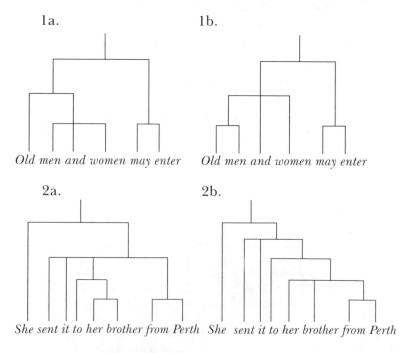

1a.

Old men and women may enter

1b.

Old men and women may enter

2a.

She sent it to her brother from Perth

2b.

She sent it to her brother from Perth

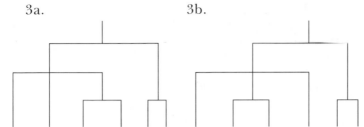

3a.   3b.

The Japanese car salesman is here   The Japanese car salesman is here

1d. Convert the following labelled tree diagram into a labelled bracketing.
     Note: this is merely a mechanical exercise; you are not required to understand the labels in order to complete it.

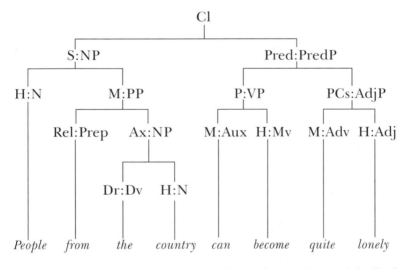

1e. Convert the following labelled bracketing into a labelled tree diagram.
     Note: this is merely a mechanical exercise; you are not required to understand the labels in order to complete it.

[^S^ (^Dr^ ^H^ *The teacher*) ^Pred^ (^P^ (^M^ *has* ^H^ *given*) ^Oi^ (^H^ *her*)
  NP Dv   N   PredP VP Aux   Mv   NP Pn

(^Od^ ^Dr^ ^M^ *the highest* ^H^ *mark* (^M^ ^Rel^ *in* (^Ax^ ^Dr^ *the* ^H^ *class*))))]
  NP Dv Adj   N   PP Prep   NP Dv   N

1f. The following sentences would be rejected by some speakers as breaking various 'rules' of prescriptive grammar. Try to find out what the rule is in each case. Do you consider that the rule has any validity in Modern English?

1. *None of the children have finished their homework*
2. *There should be no ill feeling between you and I*
3. *We were surprised at them being absent*
4. *It would be unwise to completely ignore him*
5. *Which room were you hiding in?*
6. *They have been monitoring our progress more closely than it has ever been before*
7. *Sonia is taller than him*

2 | A preliminary overview

In presenting the grammar of a language we are inevitably confronted with a paradox: the categories of grammar are closely interrelated (e.g. preposition and prepositional phrase, noun and subject, adjective and complement) and yet we can only introduce them in a linear fashion. Our strategy will be to begin by presenting an overview of the basic components of grammar, one which will be expanded and refined in subsequent chapters. Our plan is to work up from the parts of speech, which are the elementary building blocks of grammar, through phrases and clauses, to the largest units of grammar, sentences. The 'intermediate' units, phrases and clauses, are structurally quite different from one another. As we shall see in this chapter, most phrases are constructed around a 'head' word, while clauses have a subject-predicate structure.

2.1 The parts of speech

Traditional grammars generally distinguish eight 'parts of speech', or 'word classes': noun, pronoun, verb, adjective, adverb, preposition, conjunction and interjection. There is much in this classification that is sound and that has, not surprisingly, stood the test of time. Nevertheless, there is also much that can be improved upon.

For a start, interjections have little significant role to play in the grammar of English. They include emotive expressions (*ouch, oh, phew*, etc.), swear words (*shit, damn*, etc.), greetings (*hi, bye*, etc.), and certain 'discourse particles' (*yeah, okay, well*, etc.). They are peripheral to the language system and are better handled in the context of a discussion of spoken discourse (notice that some even lack the recognisable phonological form of words: *hmm, psst*, etc.).

Another point is that the differences between nouns and pronouns are not sufficient to warrant treating them as separate primary classes: rather, we shall regard pronouns – as they are regarded in many modern grammars – as being a subclass of nouns.

Let us begin by distinguishing eight primary classes (presented below with examples), a number of which have subclasses that we shall examine later. Notice that the traditional class of conjunctions has been replaced by the two primary classes of subordinators (corresponding to the traditional subclass of 'subordinating conjunctions') and coordinators (corresponding to the traditional subclass of 'coordinating conjunctions'), in recognition of their quite distinct grammatical roles (see further Section 2.4 and Chapter 7). Note also that determinatives are more commonly referred to as 'determiners' in modern grammars: in this book the term 'determinative' is used for a grammatical class and 'determiner' for the grammatical function associated with that class (see further Section 3.5).

Noun ('N')	*Many **people** own **yachts** in **Monaco***
Verb ('V')	***Have** you **organised** the farewell party yet?*
Adjective ('Adj')	*The **red** apples are more **expensive***
Adverb ('Adv')	*You should **never** treat us **rudely***
Preposition ('Prep')	*Bill is **in** trouble **over** his decision*
Subordinator ('Subord')	*He says **that** he'll leave **when** he's ready*
Coordinator ('Coord')	*Do you **and** Joe prefer red wine **or** white?*
Determinative ('Dv')	***The** poor woman has suffered **a** tragic loss*

A number of general points may be made about this classification:

• **Subsidiary role of semantics:** The classification is based on distinctions of grammatical behaviour, with semantic considerations playing a merely subsidiary role. Thus, for example, *explode* and *explosion* are very similar in the meanings that they express, but we regard them as belonging to the verb and noun classes respectively on the basis of the way they behave in the structure of clauses and their morphological form (these are discussed in Section 2.3 below).

• **Multiple class membership:** Words may belong to more than one word class. *Down*, for example, may be a preposition (e.g. *She ran* **down** *the road*), an adverb (e.g. *She fell* **down**), an adjective (e.g. *She's feeling very* **down** *today*), a noun (e.g. *My doona is filled with* **down**) or a verb (e.g. *Watch him* **down** *this schooner*).

Normally, a sentence will provide enough context to indicate which part of speech is involved, but occasionally ambiguities can occur, as in *She looked down*, where *down* could be interpreted either as the adjective ('She looked dejected') or the adverb ('She looked downwards'). Since the defining criteria for word classes are grammatical, in cases where we have overlapping classes the only way to determine which class a word belongs to is to consider the grammatical context. For example *kindly* is an adjective in *He's a kindly person* because it modifies the noun *person*, but an adverb in *He behaved kindly* because it modifies the verb *behaved*; *hammer* is a noun in *Pass me the hammer* because it takes the article *the* as a dependent, but a verb in *You should hammer that nail right in* because it has an object, *that nail*.

- **Subclasses:** As we have already noted in Section 1.3 above, grammatical classes will have not only prototypical, but also non-prototypical members. Furthermore, the eight parts of speech that we have identified are 'primary' classes, intended to capture the grammatical similarities and differences between words at a very general level only. For many of the eight primary classes there are subclasses that are widely recognised, and which we must explore in subsequent chapters; for example common vs proper nouns, transitive vs intransitive verbs, and attributive vs predicative adjectives.

- **Open versus closed classes:** The eight word classes may be subdivided broadly into **open classes** (the first four above) and **closed classes** (the second four). The open classes have a comparatively large membership, one that is 'open' to the admission of new items. New members may be formed by means of the processes of lexical morphology, some of which we have referred to in Section 1.4 (as with the verb *prioritise*, which is derived from the noun *priority* by suffixation), or by borrowing from another language (as with the noun *restaurant*, from French).

The closed classes are by contrast relatively fixed in their membership (for example the demonstratives *this*, *that*, *these* and *those*, a subclass of determinatives, have remained the same since about the time of Shakespeare, when the form *yon* was lost from Standard English).

It is not just the primary word classes that may be classified as open or closed, but also subclasses of them. For instance the three subclasses of nouns, common nouns, proper nouns and pronouns, are respectively open, open and closed; verbs are classifiable into the open subclass of main verbs and the closed subclass of auxiliaries.

2.2 Words and phrases

The four open word classes have phrases associated with them, and in turn these phrases are classified according to the word functioning as their head. Thus noun phrases are phrases headed by nouns, verb phrases by verbs, adjective phrases by adjectives, and adverb phrases by adverbs. There are two major properties associated with the head function:

- **Obligatoriness:** The head is obligatory, but dependents are usually optional. Compare:

1. $\underset{\text{NP}}{(}\ \underset{\text{Adj}}{\overset{\text{M}}{Cool}}\ \underset{\text{N}}{\overset{\text{H}}{drinks}})\ are\ available$

2. $\underset{\text{NP}}{(}\ \underset{\text{N}}{\overset{\text{H}}{Drinks}})\ are\ available$

3. * $\underset{\text{NP}}{(}\ \underset{\text{Adj}}{\overset{\text{M}}{Cool}})\ are\ available$

Cool drinks in (1) is an NP in which the head noun *drinks* is accompanied by a dependent, the adjective *cool*. It is possible to omit the dependent, as we see in (2) where the subject, *drinks*, is an acceptable 'head-only' phrase. However, as we can see from the unacceptability of (3), it is not possible to omit the head *drinks* from the subject NP.

There follow some further examples of phrases (with the

obligatory head word in bold type):

NP: *all his **attempts**, **cars** from Japan, the only **chance** left*
VP: *has been **singing**, will **feel**, should have **phoned***
AdjP: *quite **expensive**, very **reliable***
AdvP: *very **rudely**, **fast** enough*

- **Distribution:** It is not just the obligatoriness of the head that makes it dominant. It is also its role in determining the distribution, or 'combinatorial potential' of the phrase; that is, how the phrase combines with other elements of the larger construction (namely, in most cases, the clause). For example in the NP *cool drinks*, it is the head word *drinks* rather than the dependent *cool* that accounts for the capacity of the NP to function as the subject and object respectively in:

$$^{S}(Cool\ drinks)\ are\ available$$
$$\text{NP}$$

$$They\ prefer\ ^{O}(cool\ drinks)$$
$$\text{NP}$$

In the following sentence it is the presence of *lost* as head of the VP *may have lost* that determines the capacity of *may have lost* to combine with *their way* as the object (if an 'intransitive' verb such as *escape* had been selected as the head word, then it would not have been possible to select an object: **They may have escaped their way*):

$$They\ ^{P}(\ ^{M}may\ ^{M}have\ ^{H}lost)\ their\ way$$
$$\text{VP Aux}\quad\text{Aux}\quad\text{Mv}$$

Not all phrases have a head-dependent structure. Prepositional phrases ('PP') and genitive phrases ('GP'), exemplified below in round brackets, belong to a general class of constructions called **relator-axis constructions** (which are discussed further in Section 2.4.3 below.

$$I\ sent\ it\ ^{Cx}(\ ^{Rel}to\ ^{Ax}(\ my\ brother))\ ^{A}(\ ^{Rel}on\ ^{Ax}(Thursday))\qquad\text{(PP)}$$
$$\text{PP Prep}\quad\text{NP}\qquad\qquad\text{PP Prep}\quad\text{NP}$$

```
    S   Dr  Ax                      Rel   H
   (  (   (The secretary)  's  )  computer)  is quite old        (GP)
   NP  GP  NP                        'S   N
```

In order to encapsulate the distinction between head-dependent phrases and relator-axis phrases, we introduce the terms 'endocentric' and 'exocentric' (borrowed from a model of grammar called *Tagmemics*, as are the terms *relator* and *axis*). **Endocentric** (or 'inwardly focused') constructions such as NP and VP are organised around their syntactically central element, the head, which determines the types of dependent elements that may or may not occur with it. By contrast, relator/axis constructions are **exocentic** ('outwardly focused'): the role of the relator, which is structurally somewhat extrinsic to the construction, is to 'relate' the axis constituent to the larger construction. Thus, for example, the relator *to* in *She gave the job to Ken* serves not only to introduce the phrase *to Ken,* but also to relate *Ken* to the verb *gave* as the 'recipient' (a traditional grammarian would say that *to* serves to mark the status of *Ken* as that of 'oblique object').

GPs differ from PPs in two ways: the relator in a GP (namely *'s*) is positioned at the end of the phrase, and it is not a word but a **clitic**. (A clitic is an element that differs from a normal word in so far as it does not contain a vowel, and is attached to another word: for example, *'ll* as in *she'll* and *'ve* as in *we've*). The most characteristic function of GPs is as determiner within the structure of NPs (see Section 3.5 below).

2.3 The open classes

In this section we shall briefly consider the most salient properties of the open part of speech classes: verbs, nouns, adjectives and adverbs (followed by the closed classes in Section 2.4 below). The account given will be cursory, intended merely to provide you with some appreciation of the differences between the primary classes: a number of concepts and categories introduced here will be discussed in greater detail in subsequent chapters. Since all basic clauses (see Section 2.5 for a discussion of basic clauses) contain at least a noun

and a verb (as in *She died* and *Charles smokes*) we shall begin
with these, turning then to adjectives and adverbs, whose most
characteristic function is to modify nouns and verbs respectively. For each of these four classes, we shall consider three
general types of properties:

(a) **External syntax:** The 'external' syntactic properties of
the parts of speech include their *function* within the associated phrase and their *distribution* (specifically, the kinds of
dependent items that they may combine with in phrases).

(b) **Internal morphology:** The 'internal' properties of the
parts of speech include their *inflectional morphology* (the types
of inflectional properties they exhibit) and their *lexical morphology* (the morphological processes used for forming
members of this part of speech from other parts of speech).

(c) **Semantic:** The types of meaning associated with each part
of speech, you will recall, are often given prominence in traditional definitions. While such semantic considerations
typically apply to the central members of a class, they are
generally insufficient in enabling us to identify all and only
the members of the class.

2.3.1 Nouns

(a) **External:** Nouns characteristically function as the head
of noun phrases, and these in turn may function as subject,
object, predicative complement or adjunct (see further Section 2.6 below):

$\underset{\text{NP}}{\overset{\text{S}}{(\textbf{\textit{My best friend}})}}$ *has arrived*   (subject)

I contacted $\underset{\text{NP}}{\overset{\text{O}}{(\textbf{\textit{my best friend}})}}$ (object)

She is $\underset{\text{NP}}{\overset{\text{PC}}{(\textbf{\textit{my best friend}})}}$ (predicative complement)

My best friend left $\underset{\text{NP}}{\overset{\text{A}}{(\textbf{\textit{last Friday}})}}$ (adjunct)

Within noun phrases, nouns take a range of dependents different from those taken by the other parts of speech; most distinctively, nouns are the only part of speech to take adjectives and determinatives as dependents (see Section 3.5 below). Nouns are also the only class to take relative clauses (see Section 3.6 below) as dependents.

(b) **Internal**: Most nouns have separate inflectional forms for number (singular and plural) and for possessive (or 'genitive') case (e.g. *table/tables/table's/tables', horse/horses/horse's/horses'*). Pronouns have a comparatively wide array of inflectional case forms: for details, see Section 3.3 below.

Nouns are commonly derived from other word classes by suffixes such as *-ness* and *-(i)ty* (usually used to derive nouns from adjectives, as in *thickness* and *royalty*) and *-er, -ment* and *-ion* (usually used to derive nouns from verbs, as in *helper, retirement* and *inflation*).

(c) **Semantic**: Prototypical nouns denote persons and concrete objects. A distinction is often drawn between nouns of this type, called 'concrete' nouns, and 'abstract' nouns, those denoting states, activities, occasions, and the like (e.g. *decadence, retirement, sadness*). This is a semantic distinction rather than a grammatical distinction, and for this reason we shall not explore it further in this grammar book.

2.3.2 Verbs

(a) **External**: The vast majority of verbs have the distinctive property of functioning as the head of verb phrases (which in turn function as the predicator within the clause). Auxiliaries (e.g. *will, must, have*) are a closed subclass of verbs which function as dependents within verb phrases, as in *will sing* and *must have gone*.

(b) **Internal**: It is the inflectional morphology of verbs that is their most characteristic feature. Prototypically, verbs have six inflectional forms, including a contrast of tense, as discussed in Section 4.1 below. Thus, for example, the tensed forms of *take* are *takes, take* and *took*, and the non-tensed forms are *take, taking* and *taken*.

There are some verbs that display distinctive features of lexical morphology (notably verb-forming suffixes such as -*ise/-ize* as in *industrialise* and *terrorise*, and *-ify* as in *falsify* and *purify*).

(c) **Semantic**: Verbs characteristically express actions, activities and events (which explains why they are traditionally defined as 'doing words'), but the class also includes members which denote states and relationships (e.g. *be, seem, resemble*), sensory perceptions (e.g. *hear, see*), cognitive processes (e.g. *think, believe*), and the like.

2.3.3 Adjectives

(a) **External**: Adjectives function as the head of adjective phrases ('AdjPs'). AdjPs in turn have a very characteristic distribution: traditionally, they are subclassified as **attributive** (occupying the pre-head modifier slot in an NP, as in *A **dark** cloud appeared*) or **predicative** (occupying the predicative complement slot in the predicate of a clause, as in *The cloud was **dark***).

Most adjectives may take degree expressions as dependents: *very large, quite upset, absolutely fabulous*.

(b) **Internal:** Many adjectives inflect to express degrees of 'comparison' (e.g. *short/shorter/shortest*; *good/better/best*).

Many adjectives have characteristic features of lexical morphology: a large number are derived from nouns by means of such suffixes as *-less* (e.g. *penniless*), *-ful* (e.g. *dreadful*), *-al* (e.g. *comical*), *-ous* (e.g. *pompous*) and *-ese* (e.g. *Japanese*). A common means of deriving adjectives from verbs is via the suffix *-able* (e.g. *enjoyable, agreeable*).

(c) **Semantic:** Adjectives typically denote a quality or property, including physical properties (e.g. *short, heavy*), psychological qualities (e.g. *sad, cowardly*) and evaluations (e.g. *cheap, silly*).

2.3.4 Adverbs

(a) **External:** Adverbs characteristically modify verbs (e.g.

speak **loudly**, *enter* **gracefully**), but some may modify adjectives
(e.g. **inexcusably** *late*), adverbs (e.g. **quite** *slowly*) and even
entire clauses (e.g. **Surprisingly**, *the kitten emerged without a
scratch*).

(b) **Internal:** A small number of adverbs can, like adjectives,
inflect for comparison (e.g. *hard/harder/hardest*), but perhaps
the most distinctive feature of adverbs is to be found in their
lexical morphology: a large number are derived by adding
the suffix *-ly* to an adjective (e.g. *frankly, quickly, happily*). Two
things should be noted with regard to this feature of adverbs,
however. One is that not all *-ly* suffixed words are adverbs: a
number of adjectives also carry this suffix (e.g. *a* **sickly** *child,
a* **cowardly** *act, a* **deadly** *virus*). The second is that by no means
all adverbs are derived in this way (e.g. *rather, fast, well, furthermore*).

(c) **Semantic:** Adverbs express various kinds of meaning,
especially those which function as adjuncts (see Section 2.6
below). Amongst the most common types of meaning here
are manner (e.g. *carefully, leniently, well*), place (e.g. *there, locally*), direction (e.g. *away, home*) and time (e.g. *now, afterwards*).
Adverbs which function as modifiers in AdjPs or AdvPs (e.g.
very, slightly, quite) express degree. Adverbs which modify
whole clauses either express a connection with what precedes
(e.g. *therefore, however*) or express an aspect of the speaker's
attitude towards the content of the clause (e.g. *frankly, importantly*).

2.4 The closed classes

The only criterion that is consistently relevant to defining the four closed classes is the external syntactic one of
distribution. With only one or two closed-class items is
there any inflection (some determinatives inflect for
number) and there are no widely employed processes of
lexical morphology to speak of. Furthermore, unlike open-
class items, closed-class items (with the single exception of
determinatives) do not function as the head of a phrase.

2.4.1 Determinatives

Determinatives have the distinctive feature of functioning as determiner in the structure of NPs (see Section 3.5). The most central members of the class are the articles *the* and *a(n)*; other determinatives include *this, some, which,* and so on. Some determinatives can be combined (***all our** possessions,* **both those** *paintings,* **the three** *kittens,* etc.). Only very occasionally do determinatives take dependents, as in the determinative phrase ('DvP') *very many people* (where *very* must be interpreted as a dependent of *many* and not *people,* as we see from the ungrammaticality of **very people*).

2.4.2 Prepositions

Prepositions function as the relator in prepositional phrases. They commonly express meanings that reflect the contextual circumstances of a situation or activity, especially those relating to time and place (e.g. **in** *Perth,* **to** *the brink,* **after** *your party*), and role-related meanings such as agency (e.g. *It was written* **by** *Shakespeare*) and recipience (e.g. *He handed them* **to** *his sister*).

2.4.3 Subordinators

The term 'subordinator' is a simpler expression used here for the traditional grammarians' label 'subordinating conjunction': for example *that, whether, because, unless, whereas* and *although.* Like prepositions, subordinators function as relators in relator-axis constructions. The difference is that in the case of subordinators, the axis slot is filled by a clause rather than a phrase.

Many subordinators express circumstantial meanings, including time (e.g. **before** *you enrol*), condition (e.g. **if** *Tom succeeds*), cause (e.g. **because** *the train was delayed*) and concession (e.g. **although** *she prefers coffee*).

There is considerable overlap between the classes of preposition and subordinator. In the following paired examples *after* is respectively preposition and subordinator:

> The party ended (after Mary's departure)
> A Rel Ax
> PP Prep NP

$$\textit{The party ended} \quad \overset{\text{A}}{\underset{\text{ACl}}{[}} \quad \overset{\text{Rel}}{\underset{\text{Subord}}{\textit{after}}} \quad \overset{\text{Ax}}{\underset{\text{Cl}}{\textit{Mary departed}}}]$$

Similar in their capacity to function as either preposition or subordinator are *as, before, since, than* and *until*.

Note: Some modern grammarians recognise a separate class of subordinators called 'complementisers', including *that, whether, if* (the *if* that alternates with *whether*, not 'conditional' *if*) and *for* (as in *It would be good for you to join*). *For* is used only when the axis clause is non-finite. *That, whether* and *if* occur with finite noun clauses (see Section 7.3), *that* if the mood of the clause is declarative and *if* or *whether* if the mood is interrogative. A special feature of the subordinator *that* is that it can often be omitted; for example it can be omitted from *He said that he was the champion*, but not from *That he was the champion is unlikely*).

2.4.4 Coordinators

Traditionally called 'coordinating conjunctions', coordinators are words which can conjoin clauses (e.g. *Mary is a lawyer **and** her husband is a surgeon*) and phrases (e.g. *Pass me a pencil **or** a pen*) or words (e.g. *He ran up **and** down the hallway*). Correlative coordinators are those which do not occur as the sole marker of a coordination, but rather each introduces a unit within the coordination (e.g. ***Both** Peter **and** Mary are looking for a spouse*; ***Either** she has lost her way **or** she has forgotten to phone*).

2.5 Basic and non-basic clauses

In this section we shall introduce the concept of **basic clauses**; that is, structurally elementary, descriptively straightforward clauses which we can use as a type of benchmark for describing the diversity of clause types in English. The concept of the basic clause thus enables us to achieve a degree of economy and simplification in our grammatical description. In the early chapters of this book our focus will be on basic clauses: not until Chapter 6 will we begin the systematic description of non-basic clauses.

In basic clauses there is no rearrangement of the 'unmarked' order of elements (thus *John has finished his homework* is a basic clause, but not the 'interrogative' clause *Has John finished his homework?*, where the auxiliary verb *has* is positioned before the subject *John*, nor the so-called 'cleft' sentence *It is his homework that John has finished*, in which not only does the object *his homework* precede the subject, but there are additional elements as well).

The properties of basic clauses are listed in the following table. It would be out of place in this introductory chapter to explain these properties in full: each property is further discussed in a subsequent chapter. Basic clauses display all the properties listed in the left-hand column, while non-basic clauses have one or more of the properties listed in the right-hand column.

BASIC CLAUSES	NON-BASIC CLAUSES
Declarative mood (e.g. *You are modest*)	Interrogative, imperative or exclamative mood (e.g. *Are you modest?*; *Be modest*; *How modest you are!*)
Positive (e.g. *He was home*)	Negative (e.g. *He wasn't home*; *No one was home*)
Independent (non-subordinate) (e.g. *She's leaving soon*)	Subordinate (e.g. *I believe **she's leaving soon***; *She wants **to leave soon***)
Simple (non-coordinate) (e.g. *He passed the exam*)	Coordinate (e.g. *He didn't study hard but **he passed the exam***)
Neutral with respect to information packaging (e.g. *Tom supplied the drinks*)	Marked for information packaging (e.g. *The drinks were supplied by Tom*; *It was Tom who supplied the drinks*; *The drinks Tom supplied*)

Notice that there is nothing preventing a basic clause from containing another clause (a subordinate clause) embedded in its structure. Thus *I believe she's leaving soon* is a basic clause, even though it contains within its structure the subordinate (and therefore non-basic) clause *she's leaving soon*.

2.6 The structure of basic clauses: a preview

In this section we will take a preliminary look at the structure of basic clauses. A more detailed treatment will be pursued in Chapter 6. The major division within the clause is between the subject and the predicate. The **subject** is prototypically an NP, but subordinate clauses are also possible. Compare (1) below, where *his confession* functions as the subject, with (2), where the clause *that he confessed* functions as the subject.

1. $\overset{\text{S}}{\underset{\text{NP}}{}}(His\ confession)\ was\ a\ surprise$

2. $\overset{\text{S}}{\underset{\text{Cl}}{}}[That\ he\ confessed]\ was\ a\ surprise$

Semantically, the subject is very often associated with the role of 'actor' (the performer of an action), as in *Bill ran a good race* (but not *Bill felt tired*). Very commonly, too, the subject corresponds to the 'topic' (what the clause is primarily about). Thus the most likely motivation for selecting, an active clause such as *Disraeli repealed the Act* instead of its passive counterpart, *The Act was repealed by Disraeli*, would be the speaker's desire to assert something about Disraeli rather than about the Act.

In Chapter 1 we noted the importance of using formal properties to define grammatical categories: in the case of the subject one such property mentioned in Chapter 1 is its use in interrogative tags. Some further formal properties of the subject in English are as follows:

• The subject in English can invert with the 'operator' (see

Section 4.2) to form interrogatives (as in *Was his confession a surprise?*).

- The subject can determine 'agreement' (see Section 3.1) with the verb (compare *His sister **is** ill*, where the singular subject *his sister* requires the singular verb *is*, with *His sisters **are** ill*, where the plural subject *his sisters* requires the plural verb *are*).

- The subject may be in the form of, or can often be substituted by, a pronoun in the nominative case (case is explained in Section 3.3 below). Thus in a sentence such as *Mary likes Jill*, we can confirm that *Mary* is the subject by noting the possibility of substituting *she* for it (*She likes Jill*), and by contrast, we can confirm that *Jill* is not the subject by noting the impossibility of substituting *she* for it (**Mary likes she*).

The **predicate** is quite simply what is left once the subject is removed from the clause. As this rather negative definition suggests, the predicate does not have a vital role to play in the grammatical description of basic clauses. Accordingly, we have used a makeshift term, the 'predicate phrase', for the class of element associated with the predicate function (note that the term 'verb phrase' is used in formal grammars for what we are referring to as the predicate phrase: we have reserved the term 'verb phrase' for the exclusively verbal part of the predicate phrase, that which functions as the **predicator**). Semantically, the predicate serves to say something about an activity performed by the subject-referent or about a property ascribed to the subject-referent. Thus in *Disraeli repealed the Act*, the predicate *repealed the Act* indicates that an activity in which Disraeli engaged was the repealing of an act.

A number of functions may be identified within the predicate phrase. They can be grouped broadly into two categories, complements and adjuncts. Whereas adjuncts can always be omitted, **complements** may or may not be omissible. Consider:

Bill became $\overset{\text{PC}}{(angry)}$ $\overset{\text{A}}{(yesterday)}$
$\qquad\quad\;\;\underset{\text{AdjP}}{}\qquad\;\underset{\text{AdvP}}{}$

Here the adjunct *yesterday* can be omitted (*Bill became angry*), but not the (predicative) complement *angry* (**Bill became yesterday*). We would similarly argue that *angry* is not omissible in *Bill grew angry* because there would be a significant change of meaning if it were. Furthermore verbs select, or 'subcategorise' for, particular types of complements, whereas the selection of adjuncts is not controlled in this way. Thus if we were to replace *became* in the sentence above with various other verbs, ungrammaticality would be produced because they do not select this type of complement: **Bill knew/washed/agreed angry*. By contrast, *yesterday*, as an adjunct, is compatible with any of these verbs.

The two main types of complement are object complement, or simply **object** ('O'), and **predicative complement** ('PC'). Compare:

1. $\overset{\text{S}}{Dave}\ \overset{\text{P}}{contacted}\ \overset{\text{O}}{a\ plumber}$
   $\ \ \text{NP}\quad\ \text{VP}\qquad\quad\text{NP}$

2. $\overset{\text{S}}{Dave}\ \overset{\text{P}}{was}\ \overset{\text{PC}}{a\ plumber}\ \sim\ \overset{\text{S}}{Dave}\ \overset{\text{P}}{was}\ \overset{\text{PC}}{handsome}$
   $\ \ \text{NP}\quad\text{VP}\quad\text{NP}\qquad\qquad\ \ \text{NP}\quad\text{VP}\quad\ \text{AdjP}$

Semantically there are two participants involved in (1), Dave (who, as the actor, performs the action) and the plumber (who, as the 'patient', undergoes the action). In (2) there is only one participant: the PC denotes a property that is predicated of him. Here the role of *was* is to serve as a link between the subject and the PC; in fact *be* is often referred to as a **copula** (along with other verbs that serve this 'linking' function with a PC, such as *seem, become, remain* and *appear*).

There are a number of syntactic differences between O and PC:

- O can normally undergo 'passivisation' (a process that reverses the position of the expressions representing the 'participants': see further Section 8.2), as in *A plumber was contacted by Dave*, the passive counterpart of (1) above. By contrast, (2), having only one participant, cannot undergo passivisation: **A plumber/handsome was been by Dave*.
- Another syntactic difference is that a PC can have the form

of an AdjP (as in *Dave was handsome*), but an O cannot (**Dave contacted handsome*).

- Finally, there is no requirement of number agreement between O and S (*Dave contacted a plumber/some plumbers*), but normally number agreement is required between S and PC (*Dave is a plumber/*plumbers; Dave's friends are *a plumber/ plumbers*).

In Chapter 6, where the structure of basic clauses is examined in greater detail, we shall see that there are subtypes of O and of PC, as well as other types of complement.

By contrast with complements, **adjuncts** are less closely integrated into the structure of the clause: they are less subject to grammatical requirements. Whereas complements are selected by particular classes of verb, adjuncts are entirely optional elements.

Another feature of adjuncts is their characteristic positional 'mobility'. Within the sentence below, the adjunct *very carefully* could be inserted in any one of the positions indicated by a caret mark:

$$\wedge \; \overset{S}{John} \; \wedge \; \overset{P}{lifted} \; \overset{O}{the \; injured \; bird} \; \wedge \; \overset{A}{from \; the \; sand} \; \wedge$$
$$\text{NP} \qquad \text{VP} \qquad \text{NP} \qquad\qquad \text{PP}$$

The various possible positions for adjuncts may be regarded as clustering around three 'zones':

- 'front zone', before the subject:

  e.g. $\overset{A}{However} \; \overset{A}{in \; Japan} \; \overset{S}{they} \; \overset{P}{eat} \; \overset{O}{raw \; fish}$
  $\quad\quad \text{AdvP} \qquad \text{PP} \qquad \text{NP} \quad \text{VP} \quad \text{NP}$

- 'central zone', usually before the VP:

  e.g. $\overset{S}{They} \; \overset{A}{often} \; \overset{P}{eat} \; \overset{O}{raw \; fish}$
  $\quad\quad \text{NP} \quad \text{AdvP} \; \text{VP} \quad \text{NP}$

or within the VP (the superscript horizontal bracket is used to link two discontinuous constituents):

  e.g. $\overset{S}{They} \; \overset{P}{(} \; \overset{M\text{-}}{will)} \; \overset{A}{often} \; (\; \overset{\text{-H}}{eat)} \; \overset{O}{raw \; fish}$
  $\quad\quad \text{NP} \quad \text{VP} \; \text{Aux} \quad \text{AdvP} \quad \text{Mv} \quad \text{NP}$

- 'end zone', after the VP, and if there are any complements, usually after these:

e.g. $\overset{S}{\underset{NP}{\textit{They}}}$ $\overset{P}{\underset{VP}{\textit{eat}}}$ $\overset{O}{\underset{NP}{\textit{raw fish}}}$ $\overset{A}{\underset{PP}{\textit{in Japan,}}}$ $\overset{A}{\underset{AdvP}{\textit{however}}}$

The classes of element that most commonly function as adjunct are AdvP (e.g. *quite happily, downwards, often*), PP (e.g. *with a smile, for them*), subordinate clause (e.g. *if I win, when the train arrives*), and less commonly, an NP (e.g. *this afternoon*).

The types of labels that are traditionally applied to different kinds of adjuncts are generally semantic. They include the following:

TYPE	EXAMPLE
Time	*at 7 o'clock*
Frequency	*every weekend*
Place	*on the corner*
Purpose	*in order to see clearly*
Reason	*because he had no friends*
Condition	*if you drive*
Manner	*quite brutally*
Degree	*totally*

In addition to these types of adjuncts, there are those that have a connective role (e.g. *however, moreover, in other words*) and those which express the speaker/writer's attitude (e.g. *unfortunately, to be fair*). These adjuncts have a parenthetical character; they are set off from the clause (by intonation in speech and usually by a comma in writing). We shall call them **peripheral dependents**. It is not uncommon for the domain, or 'scope', of a peripheral dependent to extend beyond the clause to the broader discourse.

There is a grammatical test which is often useful in distinguishing peripheral dependents: they cannot be highlighted in cleft sentences. For example, in the clause *Surprisingly, they* *were finished by midnight,* the peripheral dependent *surprisingly* cannot be cleft-highlighted (**It was surprisingly that they were finished by midnight*), but the time-adjunct *by midnight* can be (*It was by midnight that they were finished*).

Exercises

2a. The following sentences contain words (underlined) that can belong to more than one part of speech category. Identify the part of speech of each one.

1. *I must <u>perfect</u> the operation to make the <u>perfect</u> robot*
2. *<u>Disappointed</u> by Jane again, he left an even more <u>disappointed</u> man*
3. *If there's no <u>light</u> on the ceiling, <u>light</u> a lamp to make the room <u>light</u>*
4. *<u>Turn right</u> at the corner, then make another <u>right turn</u> at the police station.*
5. *A <u>kindly</u> person is one who behaves <u>kindly</u>*
6. *He is not normally a <u>fast</u> runner, but he runs <u>fast</u> in major events*
7. *The class behaved <u>worse</u> yesterday, making relations with the teacher even <u>worse</u>*
8. *It is described as a <u>quarterly</u> journal, even though it is not published <u>quarterly</u>*

2b. In the following sets of words there are some which belong to only one of the two classes specified and some which belong to both. Indicate which class or classes each word belongs to, and for those which belong to both classes, provide example sentences to illustrate the two uses.

1. Noun and verb:
   saucepan, knife, bottle, toothpick, pepper, spoon;
   father, cousin, mother, aunt, sister
2. Adjective and verb:
   even, slow, straight, narrow, high

3. Adjective and adverb:
   better, yellow, hardly, well, poorly

2c. Words that have no meaning ('nonsense words') can be assigned to a part of speech category if there are sufficient grammatical clues in the context. Consider the following passage:

Several mishful plodgers were flooming dribly past the gridge, when onto the brod plinged a strun. It vorled them, breening frowly, and mubbed their niddish toks. The plodgers were pidulous, and clandishly jipped at the snitchful strun.

Mishful is an adjective because it modifies the noun *plodgers* and has the adjectival suffix *-ful*. *Plodgers* is a noun because it has the plural suffix -*s*, is modified by the adjective *mishful*, has *several* as a determiner and agrees in number with the verb *were*.

Indicate the part of speech of the remaining nonsense words in the passage and for each one provide one piece of grammatical evidence to support your answer.

2d. Specify whether the following words belong to an open or closed class (or subclass). In some cases a word may be associated with two separate lexemes.

that, peach, he, will, mine, fine, hear, at, should, mist, undo, both, bath, green, in, over

2e. In the following sets, one and only one clause is basic. Which one is it?

1. a. *Did Bill insult her?*
   b. *It was Bill who insulted her*
   c. *She wasn't insulted by Bill*
   d. *Bill insulted her*

2. a. *I have noticed that the campus looks different*
   b. *The campus looks different*
   c. *Does the campus look different?*

3. a. *A ghost is in the cellar*
   b. *Mary believes a ghost is in the cellar*
   c. *There is a ghost in the cellar*

2f. What is the basic counterpart of each of the following non-basic clauses?

1. *Three more suggestions have been put forward by the treasurer*

2. *The rest of the money we put into an investment account*

3. *It was a mosquito that bit him*

4. *Haven't they noticed it?*

2g. Is the underlined expression an object or a predicative complement?

1. a. *She felt a sharp pain*
   b. *She felt a complete idiot*

2. a. *John grew a beard*
   b. *John grew angry*

3. a. *We are keeping calm*
   b. *We are keeping the jewellery*

2h. The following sentences are analysed into their constituents. Identify the function of each one as subject (S), predicator (P), object (O), predicative complement (PC) or adjunct (A).

1. *You | should heat | the olive oil | in a deep pot*

2. *She | seems | more depressed than ever*

3. *Football | she | can't stand*

4. *They | visit | us | here | every year*

5. *Unfortunately | the best players | sign | contracts | in Europe*

3 | Nouns and noun phrases

3.1 Subclasses of nouns

We have introduced the most important distinctive properties of nouns in the last chapter. Nouns can be divided into three subclasses. **Common nouns** are the largest and most central subclass, while **proper nouns** and **pronouns** are smaller subclasses with special features. In this section we shall discuss properties which are shared by the vast majority of common nouns, but less systematically by proper nouns and pronouns.

(a) **Number:** Common nouns are those to which the inflectional category of number applies directly, with noun lexemes having contrasting singular and plural inflectional forms (e.g. *road/roads*, *language/languages*, *mouse/mice*). There are, however, some exceptions to this generalisation, involving:

* invariable singular nouns, such as *ignorance*, *deafness* and *equipment* (compare **ignorances*, **deafnesses* and **equipments*), including words which look as if they are plural but are not, such as *news*, *ethics* and *politics*);

* invariable plural nouns, such as *tongs*, *clothes* and *pliers* (compare **tong*, **clothe* and **plier*), including words which look as if they are singular but are not, such as *people*, *police* and *cattle*).

The test that we use to determine what the number is in difficult cases is **agreement**. Since number applies not only to nouns in English, but also to verbs and determinatives, we may contrast examples such as (1) below (where the singular number of *equipment* matches – or, 'is in agreement with' – that of *this* and *is*) with examples such as (2) (where the plural number of *pliers* matches that of *these* and *are*):

1. **This** *equipment* **is** *faulty*
2. **These** *pliers* **are** *faulty*

The main distinction within the class of common nouns is between **count** and **mass** nouns. Compare:

3. *John likes beer*
4. *John would like another beer*

In (3) the beer is conceived of as a quantity, a substance, but in (4) as a separate item or portion. Strictly speaking, we should refer to the count and mass **uses** of nouns. Thus in (3) and (4) above we do not have two different nouns, but rather a single noun, *beer*, used in two different ways.

A plural noun can normally only carry a count interpretation. Exceptional cases are such invariable plurals as *winnings*, *dregs* and *remains*, which carry only a mass interpretation (thus you cannot ask *How many winnings did you receive?*). Some nouns, such as *furniture* and *information*, can only have a mass interpretation. These nouns have no plural counterparts and thus we can ask *How much furniture do you have?*, but not **How many furnitures do you have?*.

With singular nouns, certain types of determinative are compatible with a count interpretation (*a, one, another, each, every, either* and *neither*), and others with a mass interpretation (*most, much, enough, little,* and unstressed *some* or *any*). Thus in the following table, *stone* in the left-hand column can refer only to the geological matter of which rocks consist (as in *Most stone is very hard*), and in the right-hand column only to a detached or individual piece of this matter (as in *He threw another stone into the pond*):

MASS	COUNT
most stone	*a stone*
much stone	*one stone*
enough stone	*another stone*
little stone	*each stone*
some stone	*every stone*
any stone	*either stone*
	neither stone

There is another subclass of common nouns whose members disrupt the regular patterns of agreement between a singular noun and a singular verb, called **collective nouns**. As the name suggests, these are nouns which refer to a collection of items or individuals. Even when it is grammatically singular, a collective noun may occur with a plural verb. For example:

*The staff **are** discontented*

*The team **have** decided not to play*

Patterns of agreement with collective nouns tend to differ in British English, which prefers plural verb forms (as in the examples just given), and American English, which prefers singular verb forms, as in:

*The staff **is** discontented*

*The team **has** decided not to play*

(b) **Case:** A further inflectional distinction that applies systematically to common nouns is that of **genitive case** (or 'possessive' case). Case is a set of distinctions used in many of the world's languages for marking nouns or pronouns in such a way as to distinguish their grammatical /semantic functions (subject, object, possessor, and the like). With common nouns in English, case intersects with number in the following way:

	SINGULAR	PLURAL
COMMON	*cat*	*cats*
GENITIVE	*cat's*	*cats'*

The genitive is normally formed by adding *'s* to a singular noun; the apostrophe alone is added when the inflection is added to a plural noun ending in *s* (thus *the cats' tails*, but *the women's hats*). A further complication is that the simple apostrophe may also occur with certain singulars; specifically with singular proper nouns which end in the sound 'z' (e.g. *Jesus' teachings, Bill Jenkins' house*).

We prefer the term 'genitive' to 'possessive' because the latter may give rise to the misleading impression that the meaning expressed is always possession or ownership. While it may be true that this meaning is associated with the most central cases, the genitive case has a range of other semantic interpretations , including:

- 'duration' (e.g. *two years' work*)
- 'agency' (e.g. *Susan's victory*)
- 'type' (e.g. *a women's college*)
- 'attribute' (e.g. *Fiona's intelligence*)

The status of the genitive as an inflection is actually somewhat problematic, because the *'s* is sometimes attached at the end of an NP to an element other than the head noun. Compare:

> *the King's son*
>
> *the King of Norway's son*

In the first case the relationship of possession is indicated by means of a genitive case inflection on the head noun *King*, but in the second case by attaching the *'s* to the NP *the King of Norway*. In this second example the *'s* is less like a case inflection than a 'postposition' (i.e. an element comparable to the preposition *of*, as in *of the King of Norway*, but differing from it in being attached at the end rather than the beginning of an NP).

Some modern grammars of English analyse *'s* in this way as a postposition. An implication of this treatment would be that common and proper nouns in English would have no case inflection, only number inflection. However, we have opted for the more conservative treatment of *'s* as a genitive case inflection. Two of the reasons for this decision are that *'s* does not always attach to a full NP (as in *a retired people's club*, where it is attached to *retired people* but not *a retired people*), and that the postpositional analysis would mean that an entirely different treatment was applied to common and proper nouns on the one hand, and to pronouns (where only an inflectional analysis is possible) on the other.

3.2 Proper nouns

Proper nouns characteristically serve as proper names (i.e.

the formally conferred names of persons, places and institutions). The qualification 'characteristically' is necessary here because, in a sentence such as *I was referring to a different Jane*, the proper noun *Jane* is not serving as a proper name. Notice that a proper name need not be, or need not contain, a proper noun (for instance, all the nouns in the following names are common nouns: *The Opera House, Parliament House, Central Station*).

Proper nouns normally begin with a capital letter in writing, and when used as proper names generally have no plural form (**Janes*) and are incompatible with determiners (**the Jane*). Occasional exceptions occur, such as *the Alps*, which is both plural and requires a determiner.

3.3 Pronouns

Pronouns are treated as a separate primary class by many traditional grammarians. However, as the name suggests, they share features in common with other members of the noun class. They head NPs, which in turn may serve such functions as subject and object, and may take dependents of the type taken by common nouns, albeit with limitations (e.g. *all* in *all these*; *who wishes to try again* in *anyone who wishes to try again*). It is for these reasons that we shall regard pronouns as a subclass of nouns, a treatment adopted in most modern grammars.

When traditional grammars speak of a pronoun being used 'in place of a noun', they are referring to one of two main uses of pronouns which modern linguists describe as 'anaphoric'. **Anaphora**, which involves other classes as well as pronouns, occurs when an expression (the 'anaphor') depends for its interpretation on another expression (the 'antecedent') in the same text. Usually the antecedent precedes the anaphor, as in:

> *Mary burst in and she looked very upset*

In certain cases, however, the antecedent may follow its anaphor, as in:

> *Before they go to bed the children always say a prayer*

However, there is another use of pronouns that is not covered by the traditional definition. In the following sentence the pronouns *this* and *you* are not used anaphorically ('standing for' nouns), but rather **deictically** (i. e. with reference to particular features of the context in which the utterance occurs):

> ***This** is for **you***

More specifically, *this* refers to some physical object in the context, and *you* refers to the addressee.

There are a number of subclasses of pronouns. Several of these – 'personal', 'possessive', 'reflexive' and 'reciprocal' pronouns – are distinguishable in that their members identify different categories of **person** (that is, different parties involved in the speech act: see below). We shall begin with these, and then consider those pronoun classes to which the category of person does not apply.

(a) **Personal, possessive, reflexive, and reciprocal pronouns** The personal, possessive ('genitive') and reflexive pronouns of English, though they are usually presented in traditional accounts as separate classes, are inflectionally related as follows:

	1st person Sg	Pl	2nd person Sg / Pl	3rd person Sg Masc	Fem	Neuter	Pl
Nominative	*I*	*we*	*you*	*he*	*she*	*it*	*they*
Accusative	*me*	*us*	*you*	*him*	*her*	*it*	*them*
Genitive							
weak	*my*	*our*	*your*	*his*	*her*	*its*	*their*
strong	*mine*	*ours*	*yours*	*his*	*hers*	*its*	*theirs*
Reflexive	*myself*	*ourselves*	*yourself / yourselves*	*himself*	*herself*	*itself*	*themselves*

(Generic *one*, as in *One should always respect older family members*, is a peripheral member of the class.)

First person forms characteristically refer to the speaker/ writer or to a group of which the speaker/writer is a member, second person forms to the addressee(s) or a group including the addressee(s), and third person to people or others not involved in the speech act itself.

A distinctive property of personal pronouns is that they can occur in interrogative tags, as in:

The car hasn't broken down again, has it?

Aunt Mabel cooks lovely scones, doesn't she?

All the personal pronouns – except for *you* and *it*, as indicated in the table above – are inflected for either nominative case (sometimes called 'subjective case', because it is typically associated with the subject function) or accusative case (sometimes called 'objective case'). The terms 'subjective' and 'objective' are here avoided because they may imply that the two cases apply respectively to the subject and object functions only (when, in fact, this is not always the case; for instance, in *You can count on me being there* the accusative *me* is subject of the participial clause *me being there*).

Finally, *he, she* and *it* are differentiated in terms of **gender**, a set of distinctions applying characteristically to females, males and inanimate entities (with exceptions occurring, as for example when a pet animal is referred to as *it*, or an automobile as *she*).

Possessive pronouns (in other words, personal pronouns in the genitive case) have two forms. The 'weak' forms (*my, our, your, his, her, its, their*) typically carry no stress and the only syntactic function they serve is as dependents (more specifically, determiners) in NP structure. They are sometimes not analysed as pronouns at all, but rather as determinatives. However, the fact that weak possessive pronouns function as determiners does not require us to classify them as determinatives: they show the same alternation between non-genitive and genitive case forms as common nouns. Compare:

She regretted John/John's leaving

She regretted him/his leaving

Accordingly, we shall regard them as belonging to the class of personal pronouns. Strictly speaking, they should be analysed as constituting genitive phrases (consisting of a head only) which function as determiner within NP structure. However, for the sake of convenience, we shall simply analyse them as single words comparable to determinatives such as *the* and *two*.

Strong personal pronouns also constitute NPs, which serve the characteristic NP functions of subject, object, predicative complement and PP-axis. The symbol 'Cx' is explained in Section 6.3 below:

$$\underset{\text{NP Pn}}{(\ \overset{\text{S}\quad\text{H}}{\textit{\textbf{Mine}}})}\ \textit{is the red one} \qquad\qquad \text{(subject)}$$

$$\textit{They have chosen}\ \underset{\text{NP Pn}}{(\ \overset{\text{O}\quad\text{H}}{\textit{\textbf{yours}}})} \qquad\qquad \text{(object)}$$

$$\textit{It is}\ \underset{\text{NP Pn}}{(\ \overset{\text{PC}\quad\text{H}}{\textit{\textbf{hers}}})} \qquad \text{(predicative complement)}$$

$$\textit{It belongs}\ \underset{\text{PP Prep}}{\overset{\text{Cx}\quad\text{Rel}}{(\ \textit{with}}}\ \underset{\text{NP Pn}}{\overset{\text{Ax}\quad\text{H}}{(\ \textit{\textbf{hers}})})} \qquad \text{(PP-axis)}$$

Compare the analysis of weak *my* and strong *mine* in the following labelled tree diagrams:

Reflexive pronouns in English are those personal pronoun compounds with *-self* (*myself, yourself,* etc.) and *-selves* (*ourselves, themselves,* etc.) which 'reflect' some other NP. They have two uses:

- 'emphatic' (e.g. *Paul himself walks to work,* where *himself,* which is said to be 'in apposition to' *Paul,* emphasises that Paul as opposed to anyone else walks to work);
- 'basic' (e.g. *Paul injured himself,* where *himself* has a different syntactic function from *Paul,* namely object).

In their basic use the reflexive pronouns contrast with the

non-reflexive personal pronouns. Compare the different meanings of:

1.   *Paul injured himself*
2.   *Paul injured him*

In (1) *himself* is anaphoric to *Paul*, but in (2) *him* is not anaphoric to *Paul*.

The **reciprocal pronouns** *each other* and *one another* are like reflexive pronouns, in that they must normally occur in the same clause as their antecedent:

They were criticising **one another**

(b) **Other pronoun classes** The category of person does not apply to the remaining pronoun classes: demonstrative, interrogative/relative and indefinite. The **demonstrative pronouns** are *this* (which is normally used when the referent is close to the speaker) and *that* (which is normally used when the referent is further away from the speaker). Each has both a singular and plural form (*this, these; that, those*). *This* and *that* can also be determinatives: *that* is respectively pronoun and determinative in the following:

Look at **that!**   (pronoun)
That *cat has caught a rabbit*   (determinative)

Interrogative and **relative** pronouns are described in more detail in the discussion of interrogative clauses and relative clauses in Section 7.3 below. They are *who, whom, whose, what, which* (plus their *-ever* compounds, such as *whoever* and *whatever*) and *that* (relative only).

The membership of the class of **indefinite pronouns** is difficult to determine, because many items can be analysed either as pronouns or determinatives. Consider:

If you can't find your shoes, I'll lend you **some**

Here *some* would traditionally be regarded as a pronoun, but many contemporary grammarians would treat it as a determiner (with ellipsis of *shoes*). Similarly ambivalent are *any, many, several, much,* and so on. The same problems do not apply to the indefinite compound forms with *one, thing* or *body* (e.g. *someone, nothing, everybody*), nor to *none,* all of which are clearly pronouns.

We close this section with a summary of the various sub-classes of nouns discussed thus far in this chapter:

NOUNS

COMMON	PROPER	PRONOUNS
Count vs mass		Personal
Collective vs non-		Possessive
collective		Reflexive & reciprocal
		Demonstrative
		Interrogative & relative
		Indefinite

3.4 Noun phrase structure

NPs, phrases with a noun as head, may have dependents preceding the head and/or following the head. There are two types of 'pre-head' dependents: determiners ('Dr') and modifiers ('M'); and three types of 'post-head' dependents: complements ('C'), modifiers, and peripheral dependents ('PD'). NP dependents may be combined; in such cases the order will normally be as follows (i.e. before the head: determiners before modifiers; after the head: complements before modifiers before peripheral dependents):

$$Dr - M - H - C - M - PD$$

Some examples follow:

Dr M H
a red balloon
Dv Adj N

H C M
members of the committee from the western suburbs
N PP PP

Dr H PD
the storm, which we had been expecting
Dv N RCl

M H M
strange signals from outer space
Adj N PP

The different types of NP dependents listed here are discussed in more detail below.

3.5 Pre-head dependents

The class of items which most frequently serves the **determiner** function is the determinatives. Other possibilities include possessive pronouns and genitive phrases (e.g. *your, my*; *a dog's, the French Department's*) and cardinal numerals (e.g. *one, three, twenty-five*): see list below.

An NP may have as many as three determiners. The most basic type, which are sometimes called **central determiners**, may be preceded by another determiner (called a **predeterminer**) and/or followed by another determiner (called a **postdeterminer**). The most common determiners belonging to the three subclasses are as follows:

PREDETERMINERS
determinatives: *all, both, such, what* (exclamative, as in *What a superb view!*)
numerical expressions: *double, ten times, twice*, etc.
fractions: *half, one-quarter*, etc.

CENTRAL DETERMINERS —*can only have 1 at a time*
articles: *the, a/an*
demonstrative determinatives: *this, these, that, those*
possessive pronouns: *her, our*, etc.
genitive phrases: *the captain's, my family's*, etc.
quantifying determinatives: *some, any, no, either, neither, another, each, enough, much, more, most*
quantifying NPs: *a few, a little*
interrogative/relative determinatives: *which, what*

POSTDETERMINERS
cardinal numerals: *five, sixteen*, etc.
quantifiers: *every, little, few, many, several, (a) dozen*

There are restrictions on how the various items here may combine. Compare the following acceptable and unacceptable NPs:

only one from each class

both the boys ~ **both some boys*

his every success ~ **that every success*

Items from a single subclass cannot normally combine (e.g. **a his car* is ungrammatical because *a* and *his* are both central determiners).

Sometimes two NPs may look alike, but they will actually be quite different structurally. For example, notice the contrast between *these few pens* and *a few pens*. In the first case the head noun *pens* is preceded by two dependents, namely the determiner *these* and the postdeterminer *few*. In the second case there is only one dependent preceding the head, namely the phrase *a few*, which functions as a single determiner (*a* could not be a separate determiner here because it cannot be a dependent of *pens*, as we see from the ungrammaticality of **a pens*).

Two important categories associated with NPs, and typically expressed by determiners, are **definiteness** and **specificness**. The definite/indefinite distinction is most commonly expressed by the 'definite article' *the* and the 'indefinite article' *a(n)*. *The* is used in NPs which 'define' a referent; that is, it indicates that the description in the NP is sufficient to enable us to identify the referent. By contrast, *a* indicates that the following description is not 'defining' in this sense. Thus it would sound strange to say *a current Queen of England* rather than *the current Queen of England* because the description *current Queen of England* is all that is needed to identify the person in question. Normally the context will enable us to identify the referent and thus will 'legitimise' the use of *the*. Consider:

A man and a woman had been seen earlier outside the bank.

The man was carrying a dark leather briefcase.

Here the indefinite NP *a man* introduces a man into the discourse context, and he can subsequently be referred to by means of the definite NP *the man*.

The definite/indefinite distinction is independent of that between specific and non-specific NPs. Compare:

1. *John knows a good mechanic*
2. *John needs a good mechanic*

In both cases *a good mechanic* is indefinite, but there is a difference in specificness. In (1) we understand that there is a specific mechanic with whom John is acquainted, but not in (2). There is generally a close correlation between non-specificness and indefiniteness.

Pre-head modifiers may be adjectives (most commonly), nouns, participles or GPs:

*those **new** houses, all the **latest** gossip*	(adjective)
***brick** walls, our **Easter** vacation*	(noun)
*the **looming** crisis, **broken** promises*	(participle)
*my **second** accident*	(ordinal numeral)
*a **gentleman's** club*	(GP)

Theoretically there is no grammatical limit to the number of pre-head modifiers that may occur in an NP:

an exquisite doll
an exquisite old doll
an exquisite old Russian doll
an exquisite old Russian porcelain doll (and so on)

Furthermore there are restrictions on relative ordering:

*a porcelain old exquisite Russian doll

These restrictions are largely semantic rather than hard-and-fast grammatical rules: *an exquisite old porcelain Russian doll* sounds slightly odd, but it is hardly ungrammatical. It is in this spirit that the following table is to be interpreted (as a general principle, or set of tendencies, rather than a grammatical rule). Notice that the two 'class' slots are filled by different parts of speech, the first by verb participles, the second either by nouns or by adjectives formed from nouns.

Ordering principles for pre-head modifiers in the NP

'general'	size	age	colour	class I (Ven/Ving)	provenance	class II (N / N→Adj)	HEAD
strange nice	big small	old young	golden pallid	floating accomplished	Chinese American	seafood criminal	restaurant lawyer

Whereas determiners are characteristically members of a closed class which may mark such distinctions as definite/indefinite, singular/plural and count/mass, pre-head modifiers are characteristically from the open class of adjectives and have the semantic role of restricting the denotation of the head noun. So, for example, in *the ripe peach*, *ripe* restricts the denotation of *peach* to those members of the class of peaches which are ripe, whereas the *the* serves not to restrict the denotation, but rather to indicate that the description *ripe peach* is sufficient to enable us to identify the particular piece of fruit to which the speaker is referring.

3.6 Post-head dependents

Post-head dependents, as noted earlier, may be complements, modifiers or peripheral dependents.

Just as, in the case of clauses, **complements** are 'subcategorised' or 'controlled' by the verb, so complements in NPs are subcategorised by the noun functioning as the head. For example there is a small class of nouns, including *idea*, *suggestion*, and *hypothesis*, that subcategorise for a *that*-clause as their complement (as the following example shows, the nouns *notion*, *idea*, *suggestion* and *hypothesis* belong to this class, but not *girl*, *tree* and *concert*):

> the notion/idea/suggestion/hypothesis/*girl/*tree/*concert that certain races are genetically superior

Post-head complements may belong to a number of classes. In the example above the complement is a noun clause. Also possible as post-head complements within the NP are prepositional phrases and infinitival clauses:

$$\overset{H}{students} \quad \overset{C}{of\ philosophy}$$
$$\underset{N}{} \qquad \underset{PP}{}$$

$$\overset{Dr}{} \quad \overset{H}{} \qquad \overset{C}{}$$
$$his \quad decision \quad to\ surrender$$
$$\underset{Dv}{} \quad \underset{N}{} \qquad \underset{Cli}{}$$

Sometimes complements in NP structure have parallels in clause structure. Compare the examples above with the clauses *They study philosophy* and *He decided to surrender*, where *philosophy* and *to surrender* respectively function as object complements.

Post-head modifiers differ from complements in that they do not rely for their occurrence upon the presence of a particular type of noun. Compare:

$$students \quad \overset{C}{of\ philosophy} \qquad\qquad\qquad (complement)$$
$$\underset{PP}{}$$

$$students \quad \overset{M}{in\ taxis} \qquad\qquad\qquad\qquad (modifier)$$
$$\underset{PP}{}$$

Student belongs to a small class of nouns that subcategorise for an *of*-PP (compare *collector of Australian paintings*, *advocate of capital punishment*). By contrast, the modifier *in taxis* in *students in taxis* is less closely tied to the head noun; potentially, it contrasts with a range of PPs expressing location:

> *students* **on bicycles**
> *students* **under the bridge**
> *students* **at the basketball match**

The modifier function in NP structure can be served by a range of different classes, including PP, relative clause, infinitival clause, participial clause, and AdjP:

$$students \quad \overset{M}{in\ taxis} \qquad\qquad\qquad\qquad (PP)$$
$$\underset{PP}{}$$

$$the\ car \quad \overset{M}{which\ Sue\ used\ to\ drive} \qquad (relative\ clause)$$
$$\underset{RCl}{}$$

a dog food ^M*to tempt fussy eaters*   (infinitival clause)
_{Cli}

children ^M*throwing stones*   (participial clause)
_{Cling}

boys ^M*keen on cricket*   (AdjP)
_{AdjP}

Finally, **peripheral dependents** differ from both complements and modifiers in so far as they have a parenthetical character, being set off from the rest of the NP by a comma in writing or by a pause in speech. In the following example a relative clause functions as a peripheral dependent:

^{Dr} *the* ^H *car,* ^{PD} *which Sue used to drive*
_{Dv}   _N   _{RCl}

Sometimes the two constituents separated by the comma are said to be in 'apposition'; that is, literally placed alongside (or 'apposed to') each other:

> *the recommendation, that we should increase the joining fee*
>
> *Chelsea Roberts, the Vice-President*

Contrast the relationship of equivalence here between *the recommendation* and *that we should increase the joining fee* and the quite different relationship – of modification – in *the recommendation that he put forward*.

Exercises

3a.   In addition to the regular plural suffix in -(*e*)*s* many nouns have irregular plural forms of various types. Provide three examples of the following types of irregular plural.

1. Plurals involving a change of vowel (e.g. *mouse ~ mice*)
2. Plurals ending in -*a* (e.g. *phenomenon ~ phenomena*)
3. Plurals with the same form as the singular (e.g. *sheep ~ sheep*)

3b.   Do the underlined nouns in the following sentences have a count or mass interpretation?

1. *Would you prefer tea or coffee?*
2. *I'll have a coffee please; with just a drop of milk and two sugars*
3. *Would you care for a cake?*
4. *No thanks, I'm watching my weight*

3c.   Many nouns are able to act as both count nouns and mass nouns, each with a different meaning. For each of the following nouns, devise a pair of sentences which illustrate the difference between the count and mass meanings:

Example:
gold: *Gold is a precious metal* (Mass) ~ *She has won yet another gold* (Count)

hair, glass, lemonade, paper, weakness

3d.   Are the underlined NPs in the following sentences definite or indefinite?

1. *Sue was the best player in both tournaments*
2. *Many spectators were injured in the collapse*
3. *Could you give me some help with my assignment?*
4. *Every exit has been sealed to prevent their escape*

3e.   Select determiners, predeterminers, and postdeterminers from the sets presented on p. 55 in order to form the following:
1. Three NPs with a combination of predeterminer + determiner
2. Three NPs with a combination of determiner + postdeterminer
3. Three NPs with a combination of predeterminer + determiner + postdeterminer

3f.   The following NPs are ambiguous between a reading where:

A: The head noun is followed by two PPs;
B: The head noun is followed by one PP (with another PP embedded in it).

Using the following example as a guide provide two analyses for each phrase and explain the meaning associated with each analysis.

Example:
guardians of children with criminal records

A: *guardians (of children) (with criminal records)* – it is the guardians who have criminal records

B: *guardians (of children (with criminal records))* – it is the children who have criminal records

1. *a purveyor of smallgoods from Turkey*
2. *the report of the train disaster on Friday*
3. *some photographs of the girls on the sofa*

3g. Construct NPs which conform to the following patterns:

Example:

Dr:Dv	M:AdjP	H:N	M:RCl
that	*antique*	*clock*	*that I bought*

1. (Pre)Dr:Dv   Dr:Dv   M:AdjP   H:N
2. M:N   H:N
3. M:AdjP   H:N   M:RelCl
4. Dr:GP   (Post)Dr:Dv   H:N   M:PP

3h. Make a list of all the NPs in the following sentences and underline the head word in each one. Remember that NPs may have other NPs embedded within them:

1. *Please don't tell the family that pathetic joke about the Irish pilot*
2. *People shouldn't treat the rumours about Tom's lifestyle with such indifference*
3. *Every contestant in the quest will win a prize which will be treasured for years*

3i.   Analyse the following NPs using labelled bracketing with both function and class labels. Do not analyse embedded phrases or clauses.

Example:

$$(\ \overset{Dr}{\underset{Dv}{another}}\ \overset{M}{\underset{Adj}{fine}}\ \overset{H}{\underset{N}{example}}\ \overset{C}{\underset{PP}{(}}\ of\ his\ artistry)))$$

1. *all the members of the athletics club*
2. *Mary's older brother, who excels at chess*

4 | Verbs and verb phrases

4.1 Verbs

As is the case with nouns, so with verbs, we find that there are subclasses which cut across the open-closed dichotomy. In the case of verbs, a distinction may be drawn between 'main verbs' (sometimes called 'lexical verbs') and 'auxiliary verbs' (or simply 'auxiliaries'). Main verbs have the distinctive property of functioning as the head of VPs (which in turn function as the predicator within the clause) and auxiliaries have the distinctive property of functioning as their dependents.

As we have noted in Chapter 2, it is the inflectional morphology of verbs that is their most distinctive feature. The six different inflectional categories that are associated with verb lexemes are distinguished below and illustrated for the verbs *dance*, *cut* and *eat*:

				dance	*cut*	*eat*
TENSED	PRESENT	3rd pers sg	[Vs]	*dances*	*cuts*	*eats*
		General ('other')	[Vo]	*dance*	*cut*	*eat*
	PAST		[Ved]	*danced*	*cut*	*ate*

			dance	*cut*	*eat*
NON-TENSED	INFINITIVE	[Vi]	*dance*	*cut*	*eat*
	PRESENT PARTICIPLE	[Ving]	*dancing*	*cutting*	*eating*
	PAST PARTICIPLE	[Ven]	*danced*	*cut*	*eaten*

The tensed forms are the most typical verb forms; they are to be found in almost all main clauses (except for imperatives). The non-tensed forms have a number of different uses, but they can be most easily recognised when they follow a tensed auxiliary (e.g. *may* **dance**, *was* **dancing**, *has* **danced**). Many grammars use the terms 'finite' and 'non-finite' instead of 'tensed' and 'non-tensed'. However, in this grammar we shall contrast finiteness as a property of clauses, with tense as a property of verbs. It is certainly true that there is a close relationship between tense and finiteness, but it is not a one-for-one relationship. Thus, for example, the *that*-clause in *He demanded that the prisoners be released* is a finite clause even though it contains the non-tensed verb *be*. (**Finite** clauses include all main clauses and those subordinate clauses which may take a nominative pronoun as the subject.)

Regular verbs such as *enjoy*, *injure* and *nudge* have identical Ved and Ven forms ending in *-ed*. How then, in a given context, do we know if a given verb form is Ved or Ven? The answer is that we can use the following substitution test: substitute a verb which does have differing Ved and Ven forms. Compare, for example:

1. *They danced all night*
2. *They had danced all night*

In (1) we can confirm that *danced* is a Ved form and not a Ven form by comparing it with *They ate all night* (where *ate* could not be anything else but the Ved form of *eat*). By contrast, we can confirm that in (2) *danced* is a Ven form rather than a Ved by comparing it with *They had eaten all night* (where *eaten* could only be the Ven form). Some irregular verbs also have identical Ved and Ven forms, but these do not involve the *-ed* suffix (e.g. *cut* is the Ved form in *John cut the rope* and the Ven form in *John has cut the rope*).

All verbs in English have identical Vo and Vi forms except for *be* (which has *be* as its Vi form, and two Vo forms, *am* and *are*). It follows that *be* is the only verb that can be used as a substitute in cases where we may be in doubt as to whether a verb form is Vo or Vi. Consider *show* in:

1. *Show kindness to us*
2. *They show kindness to us*

We can provide some evidence that *show* is a Vi in (1) by

noting its comparability with *Be kind to us* and that *show* is Vo in (2) by comparing it with *They are kind to us*.

4.1.1 Tensed verb forms

Let us now explain the differences between the three tensed and the three non-tensed inflectional forms of the verb. There are two present tense forms, the **third person singular present** (Vs) and the **general present** (Vo). The Vs form is required to agree with NP subjects such as *he, she, it, the road* and *my old aunt* (i.e. those which are singular, with the exception of 1st person *I* and 2nd person *you*). By contrast, the Vo form is required to agree with all **other** NP subjects (1st person *I*, 2nd person *you* and plural NPs).

A distinctive feature of auxiliary verbs is that they either have an irregular Vs form (in the case of *be*, *have* and *do*: see Section 4.2 below) or they lack a Vs form altogether (in the case of the modal auxiliaries: *cans, *musts, etc.).

The **past tense form** (Ved) results from the addition of the -*ed* suffix to the verb stem in the case of regular verbs (e.g. *walked, rolled*). In the case of irregular verbs there may be simply a change in stem vowel (e.g. *hung, took*) or a vowel change accompanied by suffixation (e.g. *caught, told*), or various other types of irregularity too specific for us to pursue here.

4.1.2 Non-tensed verb forms

The second three inflectional verb categories are tenseless (in other words, their primary use is not to locate an event or state in time). Tenseless verb forms are used to accompany tensed verbs in most types of finite clause, or are used without an accompanying tensed form in non-finite clauses (see Section 7.4).

The **infinitive**, or 'base', form (Vi) is the same as the lexical stem. The infinitive has a number of uses.

- With auxiliary *do* or after a modal auxiliary in verb phrases:

  *Did you **finish** it?*

*You didn't **finish** it*
*We might **be** interrupted*

- In infinitival clauses, normally with the infinitival marker *to*:

   *He wants to **leave***
   *She helped us **finish** it*

- In imperative clauses:

   ***Leave** immediately!*
   ***Be** careful!*

- As the present subjunctive:

   *It's important that they **be** notified*

The **present participle** (Ving) is always constructed by adding *-ing* to the stem. It actually covers two traditional forms, the present participle and the gerund. The main role that the present participle has to play is in the formation of the progressive aspect (see Section 4.3 below), as in:

   *They were **crying** uncontrollably*

The present participle may also function as a modifier in NP structure, as in *He can't stand **crying** babies*, where *crying* modifies *babies* (compare *He can't stand noisy babies*).

   The **gerund**, or 'verbal noun', is like a verb in its form and like a noun in its function:

   ***Crying** won't help*

Crying is a Ving verbal form, but has affinities with a noun in so far as it functions as subject of the clause. In Section 7.4 we shall see that *crying* in this example represents a highly re-duced subordinate clause (consisting solely of the predicator).

   The **past participle** (Ven) is the same as the past tense for regu-lar verbs (and for most irregular verbs as well). The symbol 'Ven' reflects the fact that when a past participle is not iden-tical to a past form, it generally carries the *-(e)n* suffix (e.g. *forgotten, blown*). The past participle is used in the expression of the perfect aspect and the passive voice, as discussed further in Section 4.3 below:

> *We have **eaten** all the cakes*   (perfect aspect)
>
> *All the cakes have been **eaten***   (passive voice)

We finish this section by commenting on an apparent contradiction in our selection of terminology for the present and past participles. We have described the participles as 'non-tensed', and yet we have used the terms 'present' and 'past' to distinguish them. These terms in fact derive from the most characteristic uses of the participles, in constructions such as:

1. *Sue has made a sponge cake*
2. *Sue is making a sponge cake*

In (1) the making of the cake is located in past time and in (2) it is located in present time. Note however that it is not the participles themselves that suggest this difference, but rather the total constructions. Consider:

> *Sue was making a sponge cake*

Here the making of the cake is certainly not located in the present but rather, as *was* indicates, in the past. We thus wish to retain the traditional terms on the grounds that they relate to the characteristic uses of the two forms, but at the same time insist that the forms are tenseless: there is no tense contrast between them.

4.2 Auxiliary verbs

Auxiliary verbs are a closed class consisting of two subclasses: the 'primary' auxiliaries *be*, *have* and *do*, and the 'modal' auxiliaries – often simply referred to as 'modals' – *can*, *may*, *will*, *shall*, *must*, *ought*, *need* and *dare*. The auxiliaries are so called because they always function as dependents of main verbs and have a similar role to that of verbal inflections in many languages, expressing verbal distinctions relating to tense, aspect, mood and voice. Therefore auxiliaries cannot occur alone in a VP except in the special case of ellipsis. For example, *She will* is grammatically incomplete unless we understand it to be elliptical, as in:

> *She doesn't want to come with us, but I hope she will*

An inflectional difference between auxiliaries and main verbs is that auxiliaries have negative tensed forms ending in *n't*, unlike main verbs. Thus while forms such as **singn't* and **sailedn't* are impossible, we have negative auxiliaries such as *hadn't, can't, won't*.

The modal auxiliaries are further morphologically distinguished by their lack of tenseless forms (thus there is no **(to) may, *maying, *mayen*), and as noted above in Section 4.1.1 by their lack of a Vs form (thus there is no **mays*).

4.2.1 Auxiliaries and main verbs

Be, have and *do* belong not only to the class of primary auxiliaries, but also to that of main verbs. In the following three pairs they are respectively auxiliaries – in each case a dependent of the main verb – and main verbs:

AUXILIARY	MAIN VERB
John (**is** *watering*) *the garden*	*John* (**is**) *a keen gardener*
Sue (**has** *forgotten*) *her sunglasses*	*Sue* (**has**) *new sunglasses*
(**Do**) *they* (*enjoy*) *dancing?*	*They never* (**do**) *the dishes*

Ought, need and *dare* are borderline members of the class of modal auxiliaries: *ought* takes a *to*-infinitive (**We ought go*), while auxiliary *need* and *dare* are rarely used in contexts other than those which are interrogative or negative (e.g. *Need we go?/We need not go*, but not **We need go*).

There are also the main verbs *need* and *dare* which, unlike their auxiliary counterparts, have a full set of inflections and take a *to*-infinitive (e.g. *He needs to go*; *Does he need to go?*).

Be, *have* and *do* have exceptional Vs forms:

- The Vs form of *be* is not **bes*, but rather *is*.
- The Vs form of *have* is not **haves*, but rather *has*.
- The Vs form of *do*, namely *does*, has a pronunciation that is not reflected in the spelling – rhyming with *buzz* rather than *booze*. (The only other verb in English with an irregular Vs form is *say*: *says* rhymes, at least for most people, not with *phase*, as we might expect, but rather with *fez*.)

4.2.2 Operators

Another important property of auxiliary verbs is their capacity to function as **operators**. They share this property with the main verb *be*, and also, for some speakers, the main verb *have* in its possessive meaning (as in *Has she enough money?*). Operators have a role in certain 'operations' that result in various non-basic clause constructions. These are exemplified in:

1. *Mary **can't** sleep*
2. ***Can** Mary sleep?; Never **had** he seen such a sight!*
3. *Mary **CAN** swim*
4. *Tom cannot swim but Mary **can***

(a) **Negative contraction** Operators can be used to form negative clauses in which *not* is contracted and suffixed to the verb, as in (1) (compare **Mary sleepsn't*, whose ungrammaticality stems from the fact that the main verb *sleep* cannot function as an operator).

(b) **Inversion** Operators can be inverted with the subject in interrogative clauses and in some constructions which are largely retricted to formal literary use, as in (2) (compare the ungrammaticality of **Sleeps Mary?*; **Never saw he such a sight!*).

(c) **Emphatic polarity** Operators can be used to emphasise the positiveness or negativeness of an assertion, as in (3) (compare *Mary SWIMS*, which may be possible in some contexts, as in the contrastive statement *Mary SWIMS, but she doesn't JOG*, but which is not possible as an emphatic polarity statement (e.g. as a response to *Mary doesn't swim* made by a speaker who disagrees with the proposition).

(d) **Post-operator ellipsis** Operators can be used in constructions in which material is ellipsed directly following them, as in (4), where the main verb *swim* is ellipsed (compare *Tom doesn't like swimming but Mary likes*, where *swimming* cannot be ellipsed after *likes* because *like* cannot be an operator).

Do is sometimes called a 'dummy' operator because it is required if no other operator is present: it conveys no meaning, merely serving a syntactic requirement of English. For instance, since the verb *be* is always an operator, *do* is not required to form the interrogative of *John is unhappy*, namely *Is John unhappy?* However, *seem* is not an operator, so *do* is required to form the interrogative of *John seems unhappy*, namely *Does John seem unhappy?*

4.3 Verb phrase structure and meaning

The structure of the VP is similar to that of other phrases in that it comprises an obligatory head (a main verb) and optional dependents (auxiliaries). However, dependents in the VP are always pre-head and they occur in an absolutely fixed order. There are four linguistic categories – tense, modality, aspect and voice – which are expressed by the various components of the VP.

(a) **Tense** English has two tenses which are marked inflectionally in the verb. English does not have an inflectional future tense. Traditional grammarians treat VPs such as *will go* and *shall go* as representing the future tense. However, *will* and *shall* are not tense inflections, but rather modal auxiliaries. A VP allows one selection of tense, which is marked on the first (or only) verb; any subsequent verbs are non-tensed. Thus the VPs in the following clauses are all past tense VPs because *saw*, *had* and *would* are inflectionally marked as past:

*She **saw** an acupuncturist*
*She **had seen** an acupuncturist*
*She **would have seen** an acupuncturist*

By contrast the VPs in the following clauses are all present tense VPs because *sees*, *has* and *will* are all inflectionally marked as present:

*She **sees** an acupuncturist*
*She **has seen** an acupuncturist*
*She **will have seen** an acupuncturist*

The terms 'present tense' and 'past tense' derive from their primary uses; namely to locate the activity or state described in the clause respectively in present time in the case of the present tense, or in past time in the case of the past tense.

The **present tense** sometimes applies to activities that are largely simultaneous with the utterance (as in running commentaries), but more often it is applied to 'general' or 'habitual' situations that extend beyond the time of utterance, as in:

*Tom **owns** a mountain bike*
*She **walks** the dog every afternoon*

The present tense is not limited to referring solely to present time. It has secondary uses where it may refer to future time, as in:

The train leaves at 7 o'clock

The present tense may even refer to past events and situations (as in the 'historic present', used for narrative vividness):

Yesterday this big guy taps me on the shoulder and says ...

The **past tense** is not only used for past time situations, but it also has several secondary uses. In **indirect reported speech** the past tense may be used to report the content of the speaker's original words (as in the case of *owned* in (2) below), replacing the present tenses that would be associated with 'direct speech' (as in the case of *own* in (1) below).

1. *Tom said, 'I **own** a mountain bike'*

2. *Tom said he* **owned** *a mountain bike*

Secondly, in certain types of subordinate clause, the past tense expresses 'factual remoteness'; for instance, the time of the owning in the following pair is distinguishable not in terms of time reference, but in terms of remoteness in reality.

If Tom **owns** *a mountain bike, we are in luck*

If Tom **owned** *a mountain bike, we'd be in luck*

In the second sentence Tom's owning of the mountain bike is depicted as a more distant possibility than it is in the first sentence: the two sentences are not distinguishable in terms of present and past time.

(b)   **Modality**   The modal auxiliaries (or simply 'modals') are *can, may, will, shall, ought, need* and *dare*. The first four, *can, may, will* and *shall*, have past tense forms, namely *could, might, would* and *should*. Morphologically, these are past tense forms. However, it is only occasionally that they are used to locate events in past time (as in *He* **could** *bowl well when he was young*). More commonly, they are used to express factual remoteness (as in *I* **would** *come if I* **could**) and politeness (as in **Might** *I trouble you?*).

The modals express 'modality'; that is, they 'qualify' a proposition in various ways. For example the difference between the sentences in the following pair derives from the presence of modal *may* in (2), which suggests that the speaker is less certain about the injury than is the case in (1):

1. *Carol is injured*
2. *Carol may be injured*

In the next pair of sentences we may compare the factual nature of (3) with the modal qualification (involving an obligation on Tom to perform the activity) in (4):

3. *Tom starts early*
4. *Tom must start early*

There are three types of modal meaning:

- **Epistemic modality** relates to the speaker's knowledge

concerning a situation, as in (2) above and the following:

She could/must/will be in hospital

- **Deontic modality** is concerned with permission, obligation, undertaking and the like, as in (4) above and the following:

  You must/should/may try again

- **Subject-oriented modality** is a less frequent type of modal meaning which involves some attribute or characteristic of the subject-referent, as in:

  Liz can/won't endure extreme pain

If a modal auxiliary is selected in a VP, it must always be the first auxiliary (e.g. *Bill may have been lying*, but not **Bill has may been lying*) and the verb which follows it – whether it is an auxiliary or a main verb – must be in the Vi form (see further below).

(c) **Perfect aspect** English has two 'aspects' – perfect and progressive – which express contrasts that are in some ways similar to those expressed by the tense system. But, whereas tense is concerned with locating events and situations at particular points along a 'time line', aspect is concerned with certain other temporal aspects of an event or situation, such as whether it is 'in progress' and whether or not it has been completed.

The **perfect aspect** characteristically involves a situation which results from the completion of an earlier event or state (the term 'perfect' is derived from the Latin word meaning 'completed'). This meaning is clearest with the so-called **present perfect**, which involves the duration of a period of time that includes the present as well as the past, as in:

*They **have been** on a holiday*

Here we would normally expect that the holiday has extended up to and includes the time of utterance, and therefore that the past situation has some relevance to the present moment: witness their suntans and/or the long grass on their front lawn! By contrast with the present perfect, the simple past (as in *They **were** on a holiday*) is concerned with an event or situation whose occurrence is exclusively in the past.

The perfect aspect is expressed by the auxiliary *have* in conjunction with a following Ven form, as in:

> *They **had won** again*
>
> *She may **have forgotten** to turn off the stove*

The **past perfect**, expressed by a past form of *have* plus a past participle, involves two 'doses' of pastness: one earlier than the time of utterance, and another even earlier than that. For instance, in *Hearst had accumulated huge debts by the time of his death* the accumulation of Hearst's debts is understood to have begun before – and extended up to – the time of his death, which itself is prior to the time of utterance.

One final observation we must make is that the notion of 'completeness' cannot be applied to all instances of the perfect aspect. For example a speaker who asserts that *Mary has been in Prague for three days* certainly implies that Mary's stay in Prague is relevant to the time of utterance, but not necessarily that it is complete at the time of utterance. Thus there would not be any semantic anomaly if the speaker were to continue by saying *So she has two more days left there*.

(d) **Progressive aspect** As the name suggests the **progressive aspect** presents an event as being 'in progress': in other words, considered from a particular point in time, we would normally understand the event to have an earlier starting point and a later finishing point. Thus we are not attending to the complete time span of the event, merely a subinterval. With the **present progressive** this subinterval will be the time of utterance, as in:

> *John **is repairing** his fence*

In this case we would normally understand that the repair job began earlier than the time of utterance and will continue into the future. The use of the progressive aspect thus enables us to focus on a point or period within the temporal totality of the event. The progressive aspect is expressed by the auxiliary *be* in conjunction with a following Ving form, as in:

> *It **is snowing***

*They **were eating** breakfast*

The **past progressive** differs from the present progressive in that the point in time during which the activity is presented as being in progress is located in the past rather than the present. For example the past reference point in the following sentence is the speaker's Tuesday visit:

*John **was repairing** his fence when I visited him last Tuesday*

Notice the contrast between this sentence, where the past progressive presents the repair as in progress at the time of the visit, and *John **repaired** his fence last Tuesday*, where the simple past is used to represent the activity in its totality in past time.

The perfect and progressive aspects can of course be combined, as in:

*They **have been eating** breakfast*

Here the **present perfect progressive** combination suggests that over a period of time beginning before the time of utterance, and extending up to and including the time of utterance, the eating of breakfast has been in progress, and that in all likelihood it will extend beyond the moment of utterance.

(e) **Passive voice** We shall discuss the passive voice only in part here, because the passive is a separate type of clause construction and is treated more fully in Chapter 8. It is relevant to note here that one feature of this construction is a VP containing the auxiliary *be* (or, typically in more informal usage, the verb *get*) in association with a Ven form, as in :

*His bike **was/got stolen***

The four structures we have described in (b)–(e) occur in a fixed order as follows:

modal – perfect – progressive – passive

Tense is always marked on the first element. An example containing all four structures is:

He might have been being interviewed

Notice that there is an 'interlocking' pattern here:

- the modal *might* is followed by the Vi form of the following verb *have*
- in turn *have* is used to express the perfect aspect in conjunction with the following Ven form *been*
- in turn *been* is used to express the progressive aspect in conjunction with the following Ving form *being*
- in turn *being* is used to express the passive voice in conjunction with the Ven form of the following verb *interviewed*

Some further examples are:

has been defeated	(perfect aspect + passive voice)
will be leaving	(modality + progressive aspect)
must have been joking	(modality + perfect aspect + progressive aspect)
was being mauled	(progressive aspect + passive voice)

We will represent these structures as follows:

Aux *has* Aux *been* H *defeated*
Perf   Pass   Mv

Aux *will* Aux *be* H *leaving*
Mod   Prog   Mv

Aux *must* Aux *have* Aux *been* H *joking*
Mod   Perf   Prog   Mv

Aux *was* Aux *being* H *mauled*
Prog   Pass   Mv

Exercises

4a. Give the six inflectional forms of the following verbs.

> **Example:** *break*
>
> Vs *breaks* Vo *break* Ved *broke* Vi *break* Ven *broken* Ving *breaking*
>
> *come, sing, forbid, fight, lay, put, buy*

4b. Is the underlined verb in the following examples a past tense (Ved) form or a past participial (Ven) form?
Hint: Try substituting the forms of a verb which does not have identical Ved and Ven forms.

1. *If you underline{injured} him, he would be angry*
2. *If underline{injured}, he would be angry*
3. *Have you underline{injured} him again?*
4. *Have you been underline{injured} again?*
5. *Having underline{injured} him, you should apologise*

4c. Is the underlined verb in the following examples a base (Vi) form or a general present (Vo) form?
Hint: Try substituting the forms of a verb which does not have identical Vi and Vo forms.

1. *You should underline{leave}*
2. *When they underline{leave}, I will too*
3. *I demand that he underline{leave}*
4. *underline{Leave} straightaway!*
5. *I understand that you underline{leave} early on Mondays*

4d. Identify each verb in the following sentences and say which inflectional category it belongs to (Ved, Vs, Vo, Vi, Ven or Ving).

1. *I was hoping to hear if you expected an improvement*
2. *Get started before it's too late*

4e. There are several verbs in English which are sometimes used as operators, sometimes not. For example *have* (expressing 'possession') is an operator in *He hasn't any equipment* and *Has he any equipment?*, but not an operator in *He doesn't have any equipment* and *Does he have any equipment?* Provide negative and interrogative examples to illustrate the operator and non-operator uses of the following verbs:

need, used (to), dare

4f. Comment on the different meanings associated with the progressive and non-progressive in the following pairs:

1. a. *Bill plays chess*
    b. *Bill is playing chess*
2. a. *The crowd pushed forward*
    b. *The crowd was pushing forward*
3. a. *I visit Grandma this Saturday*
    b. *I am visiting Grandma this Saturday*

4g. Comment on the different meanings associated with the perfect and non-perfect in the following pairs:

1. a. *France won the World Cup*
    b. *France has won the World Cup*
2. a. *He ruins everything*
    b. *He has ruined everything*
3. a. *It was a great summer*
    b. *It has been a great summer*

4h. The following sentences contain a modal auxiliary which is ambiguous between an epistemic and a deontic interpretation. Explain the different meanings.

1. *Mary may visit him after lunch*
2. *He must have regular treatment*
3. *They should contact us soon*

5 | Adjectives, adverbs, prepositions and associated phrases

Having discussed the two most important word and phrase classes in the previous two chapters, we will turn our attention in this chapter to the major remaining word and phrase classes: adjectives and AdjPs, adverbs and AdvPs, prepositions and PPs. Determinatives were discussed in Chapter 3 and we shall discuss subordinators and coordinators in Chapter 7.

5.1 Adjectives

The two most distinctive properties of adjectives in English are their characteristic functions and their characteristic gradability.

Adjectives function as the head of AdjPs. Most adjectives in turn have the two main functions referred to in Section 2.3 above as 'attributive' and 'predicative'. Compare:

A *large* dog attacked me	(attributive)
The dog was *large*	(predicative)

Attributive AdjPs function as (pre-)modifiers within NPs, whereas **predicative** AdjPs function as predicative complements within clauses.

The majority of adjectives are **gradable**, denoting properties that can be present in varying degrees. This property is indicated by the adjective's capacity to take degree expressions as dependents. Compare in this regard the gradable adjective *beautiful*, which is compatible with *quite*, *extremely* and *rather*, with the non-gradable adjective *forensic*, which is not compatible with these degree adverbs:

GRADABLE	NON-GRADABLE
quite beautiful	**quite forensic*
extremely beautiful	**extremely forensic*
rather beautiful	**rather forensic*

Non-gradable adjectives (such as *Australian, musical, parallel, metallic*) denote absolute rather than relative properties. However, we need to enter a caveat here: adjectives which are non-gradable in their central meaning quite commonly develop additional, figurative senses in which they are gradable. For example *Australian*, in its primary sense, has the categorical meaning 'of Australian nationality', but in its metaphorically extended sense it means 'pertaining to the Australian stereotype', as in *He's very Australian*. The adjective *musical* is non-gradable in its primary meaning, as in *a musical instrument*, but gradable when applied to people, as in *She's very musical*.

A particular type of gradability is known as **comparison**. Comparison is a property associated with many adjectives, including the most commonly occurring ones, expressed by the three separate inflectional forms known as **absolute, comparative** and **superlative**. The three forms for the adjective *tall* are exemplified in the following sentences:

1. *Sally is **tall*** (absolute)
2. *Sally is **taller** than Bill* (comparative)
3. *Sally is the **tallest** in the class* (superlative)

In (1) Sally is understood to be tall in an absolute sense, whereas in (2) she is located higher on a scale of tallness relative to Bill. In (3) Sally is located at the maximum end of the scale covered by the members of the class.

Some further examples follow:

Absolute	*poor*	*strong*	*good*	*bad*
Comparative	*poorer*	*stronger*	*better*	*worse*
Superlative	*poorest*	*strongest*	*best*	*worst*

Poor and *strong* are inflectionally regular (their stems undergoing suffixation with -*er* and -*est* to form the comparative and superlative), whereas *good* and *bad* are irregular.

While the adjectives we have discussed thus far express the comparative and superlative degrees inflectionally, others do so 'analytically', that is, in conjunction with the degree adverbs *more* and *most* (e.g. *respectable*). With some adjectives there is a choice (e.g. *angry*):

INFLECTIONAL COMPARISON	ANALYTIC COMPARISON
respectable	*respectable*
*respectabler	*more respectable*
*respectablest	*most respectable*
angry	*angry*
angrier	*more angry*
angriest	*most angry*

As a postscript, we need to note that the boundary between adjectives and verbs is sometimes unclear. Many adjectives are formed from Ven and Ving forms. For instance, *disturbed* (below) is a past participle in both (1) and in (2), its passive counterpart. In both cases *disturbed* is the head verb in a VP:

1. *Our dog had **disturbed** the prowler*
2. *The prowler had been **disturbed** by our dog*

By contrast, *disturbed* is an adjective in (3) and (4):

3. *He has a very **disturbed** look on his face*
4. *He seems very **disturbed***

In both cases *disturbed* functions as the head of the AdjP *very disturbed*, in which its gradability is indicated by the modifier *very*. In turn, the AdjP functions attributively in (3), predicatively in (4). Similarly, *reassuring* functions as a present participle in *He tried reassuring us*, but as an adjective in *He gave us a very reassuring smile* and *His smile was very reassuring*.

5.2 Adjective phrase structure

AdjPs have a simpler structure than NPs and VPs. An AdjP consists of an adjective alone or an adjective accompanied by one or more dependents. There are two types of dependents, modifiers and complements. As we have already noted, modifiers are always optional, while complements are controlled by the headword and are normally not omissible.

AdjP modifiers express degree. The most common type are adverbs (AdvPs, to be more accurate) which – apart from *enough* – precede the head:

$$\underset{\text{Adv}}{\overset{\text{M}}{\textbf{\textit{very}}}} \quad \underset{}{\overset{\text{H}}{\textit{naughty}}}$$

$$\underset{\text{AdvP}}{\overset{\text{M}}{(\textit{quite } \textbf{\textit{unbelievably}})}} \quad \underset{\text{Adj}}{\overset{\text{H}}{\textit{crowded}}}$$

$$\underset{\text{Adv}}{\overset{\text{M}}{\textbf{\textit{quite}}}} \quad \underset{\text{Adj}}{\overset{\text{H}}{\textit{long}}} \quad \underset{\text{Adv}}{\overset{\text{M}}{\textit{enough}}}$$

Also found, though less commonly, are postmodifiers. These may be PPs:

$$\underset{\text{Adj}}{\overset{\text{H}}{\textit{large}}} \quad \underset{\text{PP}}{\overset{\text{M}}{\textbf{\textit{for a frog}}}}$$

$$\underset{\text{Adj}}{\overset{\text{H}}{\textit{taller}}} \quad \underset{\text{PP}}{\overset{\text{M}}{\textbf{\textit{than two metres}}}}$$

or clauses:

$$\underset{\text{Adj}}{\overset{\text{H}}{\textit{better}}} \quad \underset{\text{CCl}}{\overset{\text{M}}{\textbf{\textit{than he thought}}}}$$

$$\underset{\text{Adv}}{\overset{\text{M}}{\textit{so}}} \quad \underset{\text{Adj}}{\overset{\text{H}}{\textit{heavy}}} \quad \underset{\text{NCl}}{\overset{\text{M}}{\textbf{\textit{that it sank}}}}$$

$$\underset{\text{Adv}}{\overset{\text{M}}{\textit{too}}} \quad \underset{\text{Adj}}{\overset{\text{H}}{\textit{sick}}} \quad \underset{\text{Cli}}{\overset{\text{M}}{\textbf{\textit{to eat}}}}$$

If an attributive AdjP (i.e. one which functions within NP structure) has a post-head modifier, that postmodifier will be separated from the rest of the AdjP. For instance, the AdjP in the following example is *smaller ... than he expected*, consisting of the head *smaller* and the postmodifier *than he expected* (a structurally more straightforward, but less idiomatic version would be *a reward smaller than he expected*, where the AdjP is no longer discontinuous). As noted earlier, we use a superscript horizontal line to link discontinuous elements.

Dr   M   H –   H   – M
a   (**smaller**) *reward*   **[*than he expected*]**
Dv   AdjP Adj   N   CCl

Complements in AdjPs are controlled by the head adjective. As the following examples indicate, *angry* belongs to a class of adjectives that select a noun clause as complement, *keen* selects an *on*-PP, and *afraid* selects an *of*-PP.

H   C
angry **that his shirt was stained**
Adj   NCl

H   C
keen **on skiing**
Adj   PP

H   C
afraid **of the dark**
Adj   PP

5.3 Adverbs

Adverbs form a somewhat heterogeneous word class. They typically function as the head of AdvPs. In turn, AdvPs have several functions. They may serve as adjuncts, modifying a VP:

A
He was driving **carelessly**
AdvP

They may also function as modifiers, modifying an adjective within an AdjP or another adverb within an AdvP:

M   H
sufficiently *precise*
AdvP   Adj

M   H
extremely *carefully*
AdvP   Adv

Finally, they may also function as peripheral dependents (see Section 2.6) modifying an entire clause (either by connecting it with what has preceded or by commenting upon it):

PD
He smokes heavily; **nevertheless**, *he is in remarkably good health*
AdvP

PD
Amazingly, *no-one was hurt*
AdvP

Like adjectives, many adverbs are gradable. Comparison, however, is normally expressed analytically (e.g. *heavily, more heavily, most heavily*) rather than inflectionally (e.g. *slow, slower, slowest; hard, harder, hardest*).

Adverbs express various kinds of meaning, especially those adverbs which function as adjuncts. Amongst the most common types of meaning here are:

- manner (e.g. *carefully, leniently, well*)
- time (e.g. *now, afterwards*)
- place (e.g. *there, locally*)
- direction (e.g. *away, home*).

Adverbs which function as modifiers in AdjP or AdvP structure (e.g. *very, slightly, quite*) express degree. Adverbs which function as peripheral dependents either express a connection with what precedes or express an aspect of the speaker's attitude towards the content of the clause (as noted above).

5.4 Adverb phrase structure

AdvPs are headed by adverbs: apart from this, their structure is similar to that of AdjPs, with adverbs taking an even more limited range of dependents than adjectives. Both premodifiers and postmodifiers are possible:

M   H   M
very   *calmly*   *for someone in mortal danger*
Adv   Adv   PP

H   M
better   *than we had anticipated*
Adv   CCl

Not only are there very few adverbs which take complements, but the complements are always PPs, as in:

H   C
independently   *of the rest*
AdvP   PP

Connective adverbs (*moreover*, *nevertheless*) do not allow dependents at all.

5.5 Prepositions and prepositional phrases

As we noted in Chapter 2, prepositions function as relators in prepositional phrases. The axis slot in a PP is filled by a phrase, characteristically an NP, as in:

$$\underset{\text{Prep}}{\overset{\text{Rel}}{on}} \quad \underset{\text{NP}}{\overset{\text{Ax}}{(\textit{the table})}}$$

$$\underset{\text{Prep}}{\overset{\text{Rel}}{with}} \quad \underset{\text{NP}}{\overset{\text{Ax}}{(\textit{a smile})}}$$

Occasionally, however, the axis slot may be filled by an AdjP, or even another PP:

$$\underset{\text{Prep}}{\overset{\text{Rel}}{as}} \quad \underset{\text{AdjP}}{\overset{\text{Ax}}{(\textit{inferior})}} \qquad \text{(as in } \textit{He regarded us as inferior})$$

$$\underset{\text{Prep}}{\overset{\text{Rel}}{from}} \quad \underset{\text{PP}}{\overset{\text{Ax}}{(\textit{under the bridge})}}$$

Note: An alternative analysis of PPs quite commonly found in contemporary grammars is that they are head-dependent phrases, with the preposition as head. Thus, it would be argued, in a sentence such as *He lent it to his brother*, the justification for analysing *to* as head of the PP *to his brother*, would be that it (rather than the dependent *his brother*) determines the capacity of the PP to function as a complement of *lent*. However, if we were to accept this analysis of prepositions as the head of PPs, then they would be the only primary closed class to regularly have the head function.

PPs serve a wide range of functions. Within the structure of the clause they may serve the following functions:

$$\textit{We are playing tennis} \quad \underset{\text{PP}}{\overset{\text{A}}{\textit{after lunch}}} \qquad \text{(adjunct)}$$

He put the sauce $\overset{\text{Cx}}{\underset{\text{PP}}{\textbf{in the cupboard}}}$ (complement)

$\overset{\text{PD}}{\underset{\text{PP}}{\textbf{In all honesty}}}$ *I do not know*   (peripheral-dependent)

$\overset{\text{S}}{\underset{\text{PP}}{\textbf{Under the mat}}}$ *is the best spot*   (subject)

In NP structure PPs may serve the following functions:

a connoisseur $\overset{\text{C}}{\underset{\text{PP}}{\textbf{of fine wines}}}$ (complement)

the girl $\overset{\text{M}}{\underset{\text{PP}}{\textbf{in the blue dress}}}$ (modifier)

In AdjP structure they may serve as:

fond $\overset{\text{C}}{\underset{\text{PP}}{\textbf{of children}}}$ (complement)

faster $\overset{\text{M}}{\underset{\text{PP}}{\textbf{than Fiona}}}$ (modifier)

In AdvP structure they may serve as:

regardless $\overset{\text{C}}{\underset{\text{PP}}{\textbf{of his influence}}}$ (complement)

too slowly $\overset{\text{M}}{\underset{\text{PP}}{\textbf{for my liking}}}$ (modifier)

In PP structure they may serve as:

$\overset{\text{Rel}}{\underset{\text{Prep}}{\textit{from}}}$ $\overset{\text{Ax}}{\underset{\text{PP}}{\textbf{over the top}}}$ (axis)

The normal position for a preposition – as the etymological prefix 'pre-' suggests – is before the axis. However, this ordering is reversed in certain non-basic clause constructions. Consider:

1. *Where's the pen* $\overset{\text{Ax-}}{\underset{\text{NP}}{(\textbf{which})}}$ *I was writing* $\overset{\text{-Rel}}{\underset{\text{Prep}}{\textbf{with}}}$?

2. $\overbrace{\underset{\text{NP}}{\overset{\text{Ax-}}{(\textbf{\textit{Which shop}})}}\ \textit{are you going}\ \underset{\text{Prep}}{\overset{\text{-Rel}}{\textbf{\textit{to}}}}}$?

3. $\overbrace{\underset{\text{NP}}{\overset{\text{Ax-}}{(\textbf{\textit{The side-effects}})}}\ \textit{were referred}\ \underset{\text{Prep}}{\overset{\text{-Rel}}{\textbf{\textit{to}}}}\ \textit{by both authors}}$

The PP in question in the relative clause in (1) is *with which*. In the interrogative in (2) it is *to which shop*. In the 'prepositional passive' in (3) it is *to the side-effects*.

There is considerable overlap between the preposition, adverb and subordinator classes. For example *past* is a preposition when it is used with an axis phrase, as in (1) below, but an adverb when there is no axis and none is recoverable from the context, as in (2):

1. *He walked* $\underset{\text{PP}}{\overset{\text{A}}{(}}\ \underset{\text{Prep}}{\overset{\text{Rel}}{\textbf{\textit{past}}}}\ \underset{\text{NP}}{\overset{\text{Ax}}{(\textit{the bank})}})$ (preposition)

2. *Just then John walked* $\underset{\text{AdvP}}{\overset{\text{A}}{\textbf{\textit{past}}}}$ (adverb)

Similarly, *before* is a preposition when it combines with an NP-axis, as in (1) below, and a subordinator when it takes a clause-axis, as in (2):

1. *They left* $\underset{\text{PP}}{\overset{\text{A}}{(}}\ \underset{\text{Prep}}{\overset{\text{Rel}}{\textbf{\textit{before}}}}\ \underset{\text{NP}}{\overset{\text{Ax}}{(\textit{the speech})}})$ (preposition)

2. *They left* $\underset{\text{ACl}}{\overset{\text{A}}{[}}\ \underset{\text{Subord}}{\overset{\text{Rel}}{\textbf{\textit{before}}}}\ \underset{\text{Cl}}{\overset{\text{Ax}}{[\textit{the speech began}]}}]$ (subordinator)

Exercises

5a.   The following adjectives have uses where they are gradable and uses where they are non-gradable. Give an example to illustrate each use and comment on the difference in meaning in the two cases.

Example: *French*
She is a French woman (non-gradable: 'of French nationality')

She is very French (gradable: 'pertaining to the French stereotype')

musical, foreign, magnetic, abstract, odd, moral

5b. Which of the adjectives, as used in the following phrases, are gradable?

a total stranger   *a guilty verdict*   *an overweight boxer*
a sweet victory   *a mature attitude*   *a chemical reaction*
an African safari   *a positive attitude* *sulphuric acid*

5c. Are the underlined words adjectives or adverbs? Give one grammatical   reason for each answer.

  1. *He's not feeling well*
  2. *Did you sleep well?*
  3. *Have they been well behaved?*
  4. *You have made it hard*

5d. Many adverbs end in '*-ly*', but some do not. For each '*-ly* adverb' in the following sentences substitute a 'non *-ly* adverb' (there will inevitably be some change of meaning), and for each 'non *-ly* adverb' substitute an '*-ly* adverb'.

  1. *Soon he will be living locally*
  2. *They live apart*
  3. *She performed meritoriously*
  4. *Tom walks fast*

5e. Identify each relator in the following sentences and subclassify it as a preposition or subordinator.

  1. *It will be the end of civilisation as we know it*
  2. *Although he plays tennis, he doesn't watch it on the television*
  3. *She will be upset if he leaves early*
  4. *He claims that when he arrived the crowd was already restless*

5f. Replace each underlined AdvP by a PP, and each underlined PP by an AdvP. Inevitably there will be some change of meaning.

Example: *I have <u>never</u>   liked living <u>on my own</u>*
                        at no time   alone

1. *<u>Moreover,</u> he always drives <u>at great speed</u>*
2. *<u>Honestly,</u> you should do it <u>on a regular basis</u>*
3. *<u>Rarely</u> do they go <u>there</u>*

5g. Are the underlined words in the following sentences prepositions or verbs?

   1. a. *<u>Following</u> the track, we came to a beautiful lake*

       b. *<u>Following</u> the grand final, there will be a presentation*

   2. a. *<u>Considering</u> his age, it would be a great honour*

       b. *We are <u>considering</u> the best course of action*

6 | Clause structure and clause type

In this chapter we revisit the clause after our preliminary overview in Chapter 2. We shall complete our discussion of the structure of basic clauses, and then introduce the concept of 'clause type'. The chapter concludes with a brief examination of negation in the clause.

6.1 The structure of basic clauses

In Chapter 2 we introduced the functional categories of subject, object and predicative complement. There are actually two subtypes of object complement and of predicative complement.

The two kinds of object are the **direct object** (Od) – the type discussed above - and the **indirect object** (Oi). The names reflect a semantic difference:

- A direct object characteristically refers to a 'patient', someone or something directly affected by an event.
- An indirect object characteristically refers to a 'recipient' (one who receives something) or a 'beneficiary' (one on whose behalf an activity occurs). Recipients and beneficiaries participate less directly in events than do patients.

In both (1) and (2) below the coffee table is patient, while Tom's wife is recipient in (1) and beneficiary in (2).

1. *Tom gave   his wife   a coffee table*
       NP   NP

2. *Tom made   his wife   a coffee table*
       NP   NP

There are several syntactic differences between direct and indirect objects:

- The most obvious difference is positional: when a direct and an indirect object co-occur, the indirect object will, with very few exceptions (as in the British dialectal *He gave it me*) precede the direct object (as in (1) and (2) above).
- The indirect object can usually be replaced by a PP introduced by *to* or *for* (e.g. *He gave a coffee table **to his wife***; *He made a coffee table **for his wife***). Some grammars treat such PPs as (indirect) objects. However, they are not objects; they cannot, for example, become subject via passivisation. They are, nevertheless, a type of complement, rather than adjunct, in so far as their occurrence is licensed by the verb.

The two types of predicative complement are **subjective predicative** (PCs) and **objective predicative** (PCo), as in:

1. *Dave was* $\overset{\text{PCs}}{handsome}$ ~ $\overset{\text{PCs}}{a\ genius}$
   $\quad\quad\quad\quad\underset{\text{AdjP}}{}\quad\quad\quad\underset{\text{NP}}{}$

2. *They considered Dave* $\overset{\text{PCo}}{handsome}$ ~ $\overset{\text{PCo}}{a\ genius}$
   $\quad\quad\quad\quad\quad\quad\quad\quad\underset{\text{AdjP}}{}\quad\quad\quad\underset{\text{NP}}{}$

Predicative complements serve to predicate attributes or properties: in the examples above the attributes 'being handsome' and 'being a genius' are predicated of Dave. Thus a subjective predicative, as in (1), has the subject as its 'target', while an objective predicative, as in (2), has the object as its target. As these examples indicate, the relationship between a subject and corresponding subjective predicative is similar to that between an object and corresponding objective predicative (sentence (2) could be paraphrased as *They considered Dave was a genius*: notice that the subordinate clause here has the same form as the sentence in (1)).

In clauses with *be* as predicator there is a further distinction to be made between two kinds of PC, 'attributive' and 'identifying'. Compare:

> *Mrs Williams is elderly/a grandmother*   (attributive)
> *Mrs Williams is the culprit*   (identifying)

Attributive predicative complements ascribe an attribute, and typically have the form of an AdjP (such as *elderly*) or a descriptive (non-referring) NP (such as *a grandmother*). **Identifying** predicative complements do not attribute properties, but rather identify the referent as the one matching a particular description. A feature of the identifying type is that the order of the two NPs can be reversed (*The culprit is Mrs Williams*), so that either can be the subject (before *be*) and either can be the PC (following *be*). By contrast, reversibility is not possible with the attributive type: **Elderly/a grandmother is Mrs Williams*.

6.2 Five major complementation patterns

The syntactic functions we have examined allow us to identify five major patterns of complementation in the English clause involving combinations of object complements and predicative complements, as presented below:

STRUCTURAL PATTERN	NAME	EXAMPLE
S P	Intransitive	*Tom sneezed*
S P Od	Monotransitive	*Tom greeted his friend*
S P PCs	Copulative	*Tom was happy/ a dentist*
S P Oi Od	Ditransitive	*Tom gave his friend a surprise*
S P Od PCo	Complex-transitive	*Tom considered her brilliant/a genius*

The five names are used with reference not just to clauses, but also to verbs (for example the term 'ditransitive' may be applied both to the clause *Tom gave his friend a surprise* and to the way the verb *give* is used here as well). The term 'complex' in 'complex-transitive' refers to the presence of a PC: thus 'complex transitive' means 'taking an object' ('transitive') plus taking a PC ('complex'). An alternative term that some grammarians have suggested for 'copulative' is therefore 'complex-intransitive' (i.e. 'taking no object but taking a PC').

It is common for individual verbs to belong to more than one of the five classes. The verb *faint* is untypical in having only a single use (intransitive), as in:

> *They all fainted*   (intransitive)

More typical are verbs such as *grow* and *find*, whose range of uses is given below:

> *He found a job*   (monotransitive)
> *Please find me a job*   (ditransitive)
> *They found him bigoted*   (complex-transitive)

> *My assets are growing*   (intransitive)
> *They grow sugarcane*   (monotransitive)
> *She grew tired*   (copulative)
> *He grew her some daffodils*   (ditransitive)
> *He grew his pumpkins too large*   (complex-transitive)

6.3 Non-central types of complement

In addition to objects and predicatives there are a number of less central elements that are classified in a variety of different ways in English grammars, but which qualify as types of complements in terms of the criteria that we have used for identifying complements (subcategorisation and non-omissibility). We shall label these as 'Cx' (and not attempt any more delicate classification as we did with the central complements). They are as follows:

(a) **Locative and temporal complements** Locative and temporal expressions may function as complements (in addition to their more typical function as adjuncts). Compare:

> 1. *Grandpa* ^{S} *is sleeping* ^{P} *on the sofa* ^{A}

> 2. *Grandpa* ^{S} *is* ^{P} *on the sofa* ^{Cx}

In (1) the omissibility of the PP *on the sofa* (*Grandpa is sleeping* is an acceptable sentence) confirms that it is an adjunct, but in (2) *on the sofa* could not be omitted without producing ungrammaticality (**Grandpa is*), and thus can be classified as a complement.

Consider another example:

$$\overset{\text{A}}{Every} \quad \overset{}{year} \quad \overset{\text{S}}{the\ concert} \quad \overset{\text{P}}{starts} \quad \overset{\text{Cx}}{at\ 8\ p.m.}$$

Here the first temporal expression, *every year*, can be regarded as an adjunct because it is less closely tied to the predicator *starts* than the second, *at 8 p.m.*, which we, accordingly, regard as a complement. Notice also that the first can be more readily omitted than the second (*The concert starts at 8 p.m.* is acceptable, but *Every year the concert starts* is of marginal acceptability).

(b) **PP-complements of prepositional verbs** Verbs which have a use where they require a particular type of prepositional phrase as their complement are called 'prepositional verbs' (e.g. *apply for x, take on x, borrow x from y, force x on y*). For example:

$$\overset{\text{S}}{John} \quad \overset{\text{P}}{approves} \quad \overset{\text{Cx}}{of\ our\ plan}$$

It may be noted that in our analysis of this sentence, the preposition *of* does not form a syntactic constituent with the verb *approves*. We thus disagree with those grammarians who would analyse a sentence such as this as having an SPO structure, with the verb being *approves of* rather than simply *approves* (i.e. *John* + *approves of* + *our plan*). Certainly, there is a close lexical bond between the verb and the preposition (together they mean something like 'endorses' or 'likes'), and the lexical entry for *approve* must certainly specify that this verb can take an *of*-phrase complement. However, from a syntactic point of view the *of* does not belong with the verb, but rather with the following NP. Support for this claim comes from the fact that it is possible to insert an adjunct such as *wholeheartedly* between the two syntactic constituents *approves* and *of our plan*, yielding *John approves wholeheartedly of our plan*. However, we cannot insert *wholeheartedly* between *of* and *our plan*: the ungrammaticality of *John approves of wholeheartedly our plan presumably results from the fact that of our plan is a unitary constituent which has been split by the insertion of the adjunct.

Prepositional verbs may be intransitive or transitive:

$$\overset{S}{\text{1. }John}\ \overset{P}{insisted}\ \overset{Cx}{on\ his\ first\ choice}\qquad(\text{intransitive})$$

$$\overset{S}{\text{2. }John}\ \overset{P}{separated}\ \overset{Od}{the\ nails}\ \overset{Cx}{from\ the\ screws}\quad(\text{transitive})$$

In (1) there is a PP-complement but no object, while in (2) there is both an object-complement and a PP-complement.

(c) Particle-complements of phrasal verbs Consider:

$$\overset{S}{Colin}\ \overset{P}{strode}\ \overset{Cx}{in}$$

$$\overset{S}{Everything}\ \overset{P}{will\ turn}\ \overset{Cx}{out}\ \overset{PCs}{fine}$$

In and out, as used in such sentences, are traditionally re-garded as adverbs (adverbs which have derived historically from prepositions). However, the fact that they function as complements – entering into a close grammatical relation-ship with the verb – indicates that they are at best peripheral members of the adverb class. In modern grammars they are more commonly referred to as 'particles' and the verbs which take particles as complements are known as **phrasal verbs**.

Like prepositional verbs, phrasal verbs may be either transitive or intransitive. Examples follow:

INTRANSITIVE	TRANSITIVE
$\overset{S}{He}\ \overset{P}{gave}\ \overset{Cx}{in}$	$\overset{S}{He}\ \overset{P}{turned}\ \overset{Cx}{down}\ \overset{Od}{the\ offer}$
$\overset{S}{They}\ \overset{P}{pulled}\ \overset{Cx}{through}$	$\overset{S}{She}\ \overset{P}{switched}\ \overset{Od}{the\ light}\ \overset{Cx}{off}$

The majority of particles form part of idioms (an idiom is an expression whose meaning is not directly inferable from the meanings of its parts – such as give in, turn out and pull through).

We noted above that with prepositional verbs the preposition does not form a syntactic constituent with the verb. Similarly, with phrasal verbs the particle does not belong syntactically with the verb. Thus *turn out* and *give in* are not verbs as such, but they can be described as idioms – or more precisely as 'phrasal verb idioms' – because an idiom does not have to be a syntactic constituent.

Sometimes there will be an apparent resemblance between a sentence with a transitive phrasal verb (i.e. with a particle as complement plus an object complement, as in *Mary turned down the volume*) and a sentence with an intransitive prepositional verb (i.e. with just a PP-complement, as in *Mary turned down the lane*). Compare:

	S	P	Cx	Od
1.	*Mary*	*turned*	*down*	*the volume*
	NP	VP	Pcle	NP

	S	P	Cx
2.	*Mary*	*turned*	*down the lane*
	NP	VP	PP

The analyses here reflect the syntactic differences between the two sentences. In (1) there are two complements following the verb, the particle *down* and the object *the volume*, and, accordingly, their order can be reversed (*Mary turned the volume down*), but in (2) following the prepositional verb there is only one complement, whose constituents cannot be rearranged (**Mary turned the lane down*). Furthermore, because it is a single constituent, the PP *down the lane* in (2) can be moved (as in *Down the lane Mary turned*), but since *down the volume* in (1) is not a single constituent, it is not possible to move it (**Down the volume Mary turned*).

Finally, we may note the existence of **phrasal-prepositional verbs**, verbs that amalgamate the properties of both phrasal and prepositional verbs. For instance, *look down on*, as in *He looks down on ethnic minorities*, has the phrasal verb property of taking a particle-complement (i.e., *down*), and the prepositional verb property of taking a PP-complement (i.e. *on ethnic minorities*).

	S	P	Cx	Cx
	He	*looks*	*down*	*on ethnic minorities*
	NP	VP	Pcle	PP

(d) **Non-finite complements of 'catenative' verbs** Non-finite clause complements often do not correspond neatly to any of the central complement types (object or predicative). Consider:

$$\underset{\substack{\text{S} \\ \text{NP}}}{Our\ plan}\ \underset{\substack{\text{P} \\ \text{VP}}}{is}\ \underset{\substack{\text{PCs} \\ \text{Cli}}}{to\ go\ soon}$$

$$\underset{\substack{\text{S} \\ \text{NP}}}{My\ watch}\ \underset{\substack{\text{P} \\ \text{VP}}}{has\ stopped}\ \underset{\substack{\text{Cx} \\ \text{Cli}}}{working}$$

$$\underset{\substack{\text{S} \\ \text{NP}}}{Julia}\ \underset{\substack{\text{P} \\ \text{VP}}}{got}\ \underset{\substack{\text{Od} \\ \text{NP}}}{herself}\ \underset{\substack{\text{Cx} \\ \text{Clen}}}{injured}$$

While the construction in (1) is clearly copulative, with *to go soon* functioning as a predicative complement, the non-finites *working* in (2) and *injured* in (3) cannot be convincingly analysed as objects or predicatives. The latter are better treated as a special type of complement, **catenative complements**. They occur with so-called 'catenative' verbs, those such as *stop* and *want*, which have the capacity to 'chain' together, as in the following (rather cumbersome, but not ungrammatical) example:

> *Paul plans to try to stop getting me to keep helping him do his assignments*

Within the chain, each catenative verb will be analysed as being followed by its own non-finite complement (plus, in some cases, an object complement). Thus *helping* has two complements, *him* + *do his assignments*; *keep* has one complement, *helping him do his assignments*; *getting* has two complements, *me* + *to keep helping him do his assignments*; *stop* has one complement, *getting me to keep helping him do his assignments*; *try* has one complement, *to stop getting me to keep helping him do his assignments*; and *plans* has one complement, *to try to stop getting me to keep helping him do his assignments*.

Catenative complements may occur either alone or – as we have just seen – in combination with other complements. Here there are several possibilities:

- object (as in *We instructed **Chris** to follow*; *I found **him** shoplifting*; *She had **it** repaired*)

- PP-complement (as in *She prevailed **upon him** to offer assistance*; *He yelled **at her** to leave*)
- particle complement (as in *They kept **on** annoying us*; *She succeeded **in** convincing us*)

For further discussion of the internal structure of the non-finite clauses whose function we are examining here, see Section 7.4 below.

Note: Some grammarians treat sequences such as *stop getting* as single VPs. This analysis is problematical for several reasons. One is that such VPs have a structure that is quite different in kind from the head-dependent VP structures that we have described in Chapter 4. A second problem is that, as noted above, some catenatives occur in combination with various complements, which 'break the chain', as it were, making a single-VP analysis implausible.

6.4 Clause type ('mood')

It is now time to discuss the classification of clauses in terms of what is traditionally called **mood**. There are four moods, or main clause types, in English:

You are thoughtful	Declarative
Are you thoughtful?	Interrogative
Be thoughtful	Imperative
How thoughtful you are!	Exclamative

Declarative clauses are characteristically used to make statements, interrogative clauses to ask questions, imperative clauses to give orders and make requests, and exclamative clauses to make exclamations. Many grammarians group the declarative, interrogative and the exclamative as subcategories of the **indicative** mood. The indicative versus imperative contrast is then relatable to the main uses of human language: respectively to communicate information (by stating, asking, exclaiming, and the like) and to act upon others (by ordering them, requesting them, and the like).

6.4.1 Declarative clauses

There is little that we need to say about the **declarative** mood. The declarative is the 'unmarked' clause type (as noted earlier in Section 2.5, it is a requirement of basic clauses that they be declarative) and we can analyse the other three clause types in terms of how they differ from it.

6.4.2 Interrogative clauses

There are two subclasses of **interrogative** clauses, closed and open.

Closed interrogatives are so named because the set of possible answers is closed. In fact, the answers are usually restricted to positive or negative, as in:

Q: *Have you found it?*
A: *Yes I have/No I haven't*

Hence the term 'yes/no question' is commonly used. We have avoided this term here for two reasons:

1. Firstly, *yes* and *no* are not always relevant answers (e.g. neither *yes* nor *no* would be an appropriate answer to the closed interrogative *Is she happy or sad?*).
2. Secondly, it is desirable to have two separate terms, one grammatical ('interrogative') and one semantic ('question'), since grammar and semantics quite frequently do not correspond where mood is concerned. For example, although, as noted above, closed interrogatives are characteristically used to ask questions, they may also be used to issue requests or to make exclamations:

Can you please help me?   (request)
Haven't we had fun!   (exclamation)

A closed interrogative is formed by placing the operator verb before the subject. As noted in Section 4.2 above, *do* is used in the absence of any other operator:

1. *Sue will find it difficult*   ⟶   *Will Sue find it difficult?*
2. *Sue found it difficult*   ⟶   *Did Sue find it difficult?*

Open interrogatives are so-named because the set of answers is, in principle, open. If I ask *Who found it difficult?*, the set of individuals who might represent 'values' for the 'variable' *who* is theoretically without limit (*Tom, Viv, your sister, Dr Smith*, etc.). Open interrogatives contain one of the interrogative words *who, whom, which, whose, what, where, when, why* or *how*. Open interrogatives are sometimes called '*wh*-questions' in recognition of the fact that they always include one of these '*wh*-words' (but again we wish to be careful in distinguishing 'interrogative' as a syntactic term from 'question' as a semantic term). *Wh*-words may belong to a number of different parts of speech, such as:

- determinatives (*which, whose, what*, as in *Which racquet can I borrow?*)
- pronouns (*who, whom, which, whose, what*, as in *What did you see?*)
- adverbs (*where, when, why, how*, as in *Why are you leaving?*)

✗ Open interrogatives have two distinctive structural features:

- the appearance of a *wh*-interrogative phrase in initial position
- subject-operator inversion

Compare the following with their declarative counterparts:

They will leave sometime   ⟶   *When will they leave?*
She gave him someone's coat   ⟶   *Whose coat did she give him?*
You did something   ⟶   *What did you do?*

One special type of closed interrogative is the **interrogative tag**, which has the structure of a closed interrogative clause with everything omitted except for the operator verb and the subject (always in the form of a personal pronoun). Normally, the tag will have the opposite polarity to that of the preceding clause, as in:

> *John found it in the garden, **didn't he**?*
> *John didn't find it in the garden, **did he**?*

If the tag has the same polarity as the preceding clause, it will have an emotive meaning (typically indicating disapproval):

> *John found it in the garden, **did he**?*

6.4.3 Imperative clauses

The **imperative** has three main distinguishing features.

1. Firstly, it normally lacks a subject (understood to be *you*), as in:

> *Give me your hand*
> *Have a good time*

We say 'normally' here, because of the occasional occurrence of examples such as the following (which have *you* and *something* respectively as subjects):

> *You stand in front*
> *Somebody stand in front*

Notice that *You stand in front* is grammatically ambiguous (though one would expect the ambiguity to be resolved via intonation) between an imperative, used as a command, and a declarative, used as a statement about where the addressee habitually stands. The ambiguity resides in the verb, which is a base Vi form in the imperative, but a tensed Vo form in the declarative. A third possible interpretation is as a standard subject-less imperative, with *you* functioning as a vocative.

2. This brings us to the second distinctive feature of imperatives: the verb is always Vi. Thus if the verb *be* is used in an imperative it takes the Vi form *be*, and not the Vo form *are*.

Compare:

>   *Be good*
>   **Are good*

Further proof that it is not the Vo form that occurs in imperatives is the fact that the verb does not contrast with the other tensed forms. Thus, if *have* were the present Vo form in *Have a rest*, then it should contrast with Vs *has* and Ved *had* (but it doesn't, as we see from the ungrammaticality of **Has a rest* and **Had a rest*).

3. The third distinguishing feature of imperatives is that they normally form their negatives with *don't* (e.g. *Don't leave them there*), or *do not* in more formal usage (e.g. *Do not be late*).

For first person inclusive ('you and I') imperatives a special type of subject form, *let's*, is used, as in:

>   *Let's go for a walk*
>   *Let's have lunch*

This *let* is different from the *let* (meaning 'permit') that is used in ordinary second person imperatives (e.g. *Let them go*). Notice that *Let us go* is ambiguous between a first person interpretation (where *let us* can be reduced to *let's*), and a second person interpretation (where *let us* cannot be reduced to *let's*: *Let's have lunch* can only mean 'I suggest we have lunch', and not 'Permit us to have lunch').

6.4.4 Exclamative clauses

Exclamative clauses are introduced by the determinative *what* or the degree adverb *how* (the latter normally only in formal style), as in:

>   *What a fantastic time we had!*
>   *How peaceful it is in this town!*

Usually, the subject stays in its normal position before the predicator, but occasionally – normally only in formal literary style – subject-operator inversion occurs, as in:

How often have I yearned for a better life!

Occasionally in such cases ambiguity between an exclamative and an interrogative interpretation can occur (though in spoken language they will be differentiated intonationally). For example:

What rich people live there

This clause could be exclamative ('How rich the people are who live there!') or interrogative ('Who are the rich people who live there?').

6.5 Negation in the clause

It is important at the outset to draw a distinction between clausal negation (where the clause is syntactically negative, rather than positive), and subclausal negation (where the clause itself is syntactically positive, and yet contains a negative element within its structure).

Note: *Not* is assigned to a variety of word classes by traditional grammarians; this being so, we shall simply treat it as a particle.

6.5.1 Clausal and subclausal negation

The most common and straightforward type of **clausal negation** is that involving 'verb negation' with *not* or *n't*. Compare:

1. *George has left*
2. *George has not/hasn't left*

3. *George left*
4. *George did not/didn't leave*

The positive clause in (1) is negated by inserting *not* after the operator *has*. The *not* may be contracted and attached to the operator, yielding the inflectional negative form *hasn't*. If the positive clause has no operator, as in (3), then dummy *do* is introduced as operator: again there is a choice between analytic negation (*did not*) and inflectional negation (*didn't*).

The two main tests for determining whether a clause is positive or negative are as follows:

- **'Extending' clauses** Positive clauses can be followed by elliptical 'extending' clauses with *so* or *too*:

  George has left and so has Martha

  George has left, and Martha has too

  By contrast, negative clauses can be followed by elliptical extending clauses with *neither* or *nor*:

  George hasn't left, and neither has Martha

  George hasn't left, and nor has Martha

- **Interrogative tags** Positive clauses take negative tags:

  George has left, hasn't he?

  Negative clauses take positive tags:

  George hasn't left, has he?

  Here we are speaking only of 'neutral' tags: it is of course possible to say *George has left, has he?*, but here the tag, which carries the same polarity as the preceding clause, is emotively charged rather than neutral.

Clausal negation may result from the presence of a morphologically negative word, such as *nothing*, *no one* or *never*, in the clause. For example:

We saw nothing

I will never go there again

These sentences pass the tests for clausal negation just as readily as their verb-negation counterparts with *not/n't* (namely *We didn't see anything* and *I won't ever go there again*):

We saw nothing, did we?   (positive tag)

We saw nothing, and neither did they   (*and neither* extension)

I will never go there again, will I?   (positive tag)

I will never go there again, and neither will they (*and neither* extension)

Whereas words such as *nothing* and *never* are negative in both form and meaning, there are several words that are negative in meaning but not in form, including *few*, *little*; *rarely*, *seldom*; *barely*, *hardly*, *scarcely*. The fact that sentences such as *Bill hardly tries* and *They seldom attend* are negative is shown by the results of applying the negation tests:

> *Bill hardly tries, does he?* (positive tag)
>
> *Bill hardly tries, and neither does his sister* (*and neither* extension)
>
> *They seldom attend, do they?* (positive tag)
>
> *They seldom attend, and neither does she* (*and neither* extension)

Subclausal negation occurs when only a word or phrase, and not the entire clause, is negated, as in:

> *We had a not very successful workshop*
>
> *She had a major operation not long ago*

The fact that the negation here is subclausal – and that the clause itself is positive – is indicated by the results of applying the negation tests:

> *We had a not very successful workshop, didn't we?* (negative tag)
>
> *We had a not very successful workshop, and so did they* (*and so* extension)
>
> *She had a major operation not long ago, didn't she?* (negative tag)
>
> *She had a major operation not long ago, and so did he* (*and so* extension)

6.5.2   The scope of negation

An important consideration in interpreting clausal negation is the 'scope of negation'. Compare:

> 1. *Helga deliberately didn't make herself a nuisance*
> 2. *Helga didn't deliberately make herself a nuisance*

These differ with respect to which parts of the meaning the negative has influence over. In (1) *deliberately* falls outside the scope of the negation ('In a deliberate fashion, Helga didn't make herself a nuisance'), but in (2) *deliberately* falls within the scope of the negation ('It is not the case that Helga deliberately made herself a nuisance').

Scope interacts closely with 'focus' (the prominence that is indicated by the position of main stress). Compare the following, where focus is indicated by capital letters:

1. *I didn't WRITE it, because I was depressed*

2. *I didn't write it because I was DEPRESSED*

In (1) the *because*-clause is outside the scope of the negation ('Because I was depressed, I didn't write it'), but in (2) the *because*-clause is within the scope of the negation ('I wrote it, but not because I was depressed').

Modal auxiliaries may or may not fall within the scope of negation. Compare:

1. *You may not smoke in here*

2. *You may not feel comfortable in here*

In (1) *may*, expressing permission, falls within the scope of the negative ('It is not the case that you are permitted to smoke in here'), but in (2) *may*, expressing possibility, falls outside the scope of the negation ('It is possible that you will not feel comfortable in here').

Exercises

6a. The following sentences are ambiguous. Each one can be analysed as either ditransitive or complex transitive. Explain the ambiguity, indicating which meaning is associated with which structural pattern.

1. *She found him a reliable guide*

2. *They will call her a doctor*

3. *They made him a model soldier*

6b. For each of the following verbs say which of the five major complementation patterns it can enter into: intransitive, copulative, monotransitive, complex-transitive or ditransitive. Provide an example of each one.

Example: *ask*

He keeps asking (intransitive); *He asks many questions* (monotransitive)
bring, elect, seem, tell, drink, die

6c. The following sentences are analysed into their constituents. Classify each one according to its function, as: S, P, PCs, PCo, Oi, Od, Cx or A.

1. *We | treated | them | as friends*
2. *They | sold | him | a house | yesterday | for one million dollars*
3. *He | makes | me | angry*
4. *She | accused | them | of neglect*
5. *Henry | seemed | quite depressed | last week*
6. *I | told | my friends | that it was unfair*
7. *You | should take | on | some more work*

6d. The following pairs of sentences would normally be used with the same pragmatic or semantic force, but they belong to different clause types. Indicate the clause type in each case (declarative, interrogative, imperative or exclamative).
Note: Punctuation is deliberately omitted.

1. a. *What a mess you've made*
    b. *Haven't you made a mess*
2. a. *Will you help me*
    b. *Help me please*
3. a. *I would like to have a turn*
    b. *Let me have a turn*

6e. Is the underlined verb in the following sentences being used as a prepositional verb (i.e. taking a PP as complement) or as a phrasal verb (i.e. taking a particle as a complement)?

1. *He <u>threw</u> out the rule book*
2. *We <u>applied</u> for a loan*
3. *Did he <u>take</u> off the discount?*
4. *Make sure you <u>follow</u> up every lead*
5. *She <u>referred</u> to our heroic efforts*

6. He *called* out our names
7. They finally *gave* up all hope
8. They *blamed* us for the inconvenience

6f. Convert the following declaratives into open interrogatives. In each case the indefinite *some* phrase will be converted into a *wh*-phrase and will be moved into initial position (unless it is already in initial position).

Example: *Mary has seen something→ What has Mary seen?*

1. *Someone can help us*
2. *Phillip went to college somewhere*
3. *He said something was worrying him*
4. *The train leaves sometime*
5. *He is waiting for some bus*

6g. Following sentences are ambiguous between an interrogative and exclamative interpretation. Explain the different meanings of each sentence.
Note: Punctuation is deliberately omitted.

1. *What terrible music is played there*
2. *How often have I told you to behave yourself*

6h. Is the negation in the following examples clausal or subclausal?

1. *Nothing lasts forever*
2. *She went to a lot of trouble for nothing*
3. *Clive knows no one in the neighbourhood*
4. *We tried not to look directly at the sun*
5. *They are not to leave your sight*

7 | Subordination and coordination

7.1 Sentences and clauses

In modern grammars there tends to be more attention paid to the clause than to the sentence. This is mainly because it is very difficult to devise stringent principles for analysing spoken language into sentences (by contrast with written language, where the beginning and ending of sentences is clearly marked by punctuation). Traditional grammars commonly define a sentence as the expression of a complete thought, but such a meaning-based definition suffers from the same type of circularity as the other meaning-based definitions that we criticised in Section 1.2 above: if a grammatical unit is a sentence, then it must express a complete thought, but we cannot know if a grammatical unit is expressing a complete thought unless we know in advance that it is a sentence. How could the traditional definition assist us, for example, in deciding how many sentences are involved in the following examples?

1. *I opened the jar. It contained my favourite type of marmalade.*
2. *I opened the jar, which contained my favourite type of marmalade.*

The distinction here between (1) as containing two sentences, and (2) as containing only one, is surely not made on the basis of how many 'thoughts' they express. Both (1) and (2) presumably express the same number of thoughts: how many sentences they contain is determined by considerations of grammar and punctuation.

7.2 Subordination and coordination

Our focus in this chapter will be on the relationships of subordination and coordination within the sentence. So far, our focus has bccn on **main clauses**, those which can stand alone as a simple sentence and are not embedded within any larger clause. Main clauses are to be differentiated from **subordinate clauses**, which are embedded within a larger clause. Thus *John reads widely* in (1) below is a main clause as it stands, but not in a sentence such as (2), where the clause *John reads widely* is embedded as the object of *believe*. A sentence of the type in (2) is sometimes referred to as a **complex sentence**; that is, one containing a subordinate clause. A complex sentence is to be differentiated from a **compound sentence** (one containing two or more main clauses in a relationship of coordination, as in (3). A **simple sentence**, as in (1), is then one which is neither complex nor compound.

1. *John reads widely*   (simple)
2. *I believe (that) John reads widely*   (complex)
3. *John reads widely, but his wife prefers TV*   (compound)

Note: In a rigorous theoretical description it would probably be difficult to maintain the simple-complex distinction. Both simple sentences and complex sentences share the property of having a single main clause (in the case of complex sentences, a main clause with a subordinate clause embedded within its structure), by contrast with compound sentences, which have more than one main clause. From this perspective we have a two-way distinction rather than a three-way distinction: between 'clausal sentences' (with a single main clause) and 'compound sentences' (with more than one main clause).

The essential difference between the relationship of clausal subordination as found in a complex sentence, and that of clausal coordination as found in a compound sentence, is as follows:

• In subordination the clauses are of unequal status, with the lower status clause being embedded within the structure of the other.
• In coordination the clauses are of equal syntactic status, with neither being contained within the other.

This difference can be seen more clearly in tree-diagram representations. (Triangles are used in these and subsequent diagrams to indicate that details which are not pertinent to the discussion have been omitted. Note also that we are using 'SCl' as a very general category: from Section 7.3 onwards we shall use more specific labels for different classes of subordinate clause.)

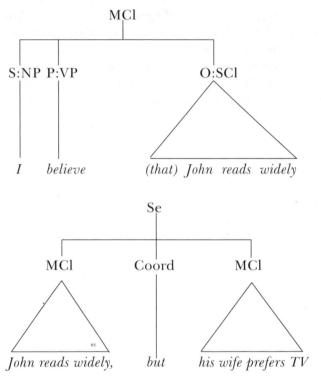

The clause within which a subordinate clause is embedded is said to be **superordinate**. A superordinate clause may be a main clause (as in *I believe that John reads widely*), but it does not have to be. Consider:

I believe that everyone knows that John reads widely

Here the subordinate clause, *that John reads widely* is an immediate constituent of the superordinate clause *that everyone knows that John reads widely*, and this clause in turn is an immediate constituent of the superordinate (and main) clause *I believe that everyone knows that John reads widely*. Again, the relationships may be seen more clearly in a tree diagram:

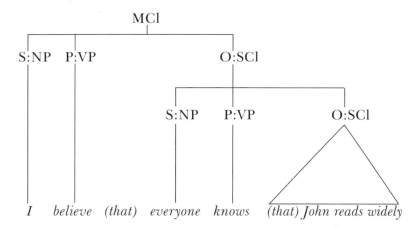

Notice that some subordinate clauses are not embedded directly as an element in the structure of a superordinate clause, but rather they are embedded indirectly (within one of the phrases of the superordinate clause). In the sentence *John helps those people who have reading disabilities, who have reading disabilities* is a subordinate clause because it is embedded within a larger structure. In this case the larger structure is the NP *those people who have reading disabilities*, which in turn functions as an element in the main clause. A tree diagram analysis is presented below:

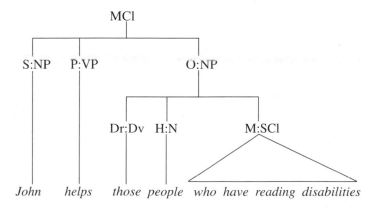

Finally, it may be noted that while compound sentences usually have a coordination of clauses (with the clauses linked by *and*, *but*, *or*, etc.), other kinds – with 'unlinked' coordination – may occur as well. For example:

> *The poorer they became, the more desperate they grew*
> *She was favoured to win, wasn't she?*

7.3 Subordinate clauses

The reason why subordinate clauses typically cannot stand alone as sentences, in the way that main clauses can, is that they usually have some structural marking of their subordinate status. This may be:

- the presence of a subordinator (e.g. *that*, *although*, *if*, *because*)
- the presence of a relative word (e.g. *that*, *which*, *who*)
- non-finiteness (e.g. **To stop now** *would be premature*)

   Not all subordinate clauses have such markers. The subordinate status of *John reads widely* in *I believe John reads widely* is a by-product of its function as object of *believe*: it is not structurally any different from the main clause *John reads widely*, and thus obviously could stand alone as a sentence.

   We shall begin by examining four major classes of finite subordinate clauses (**noun clauses, adverbial clauses, relative clauses** and **comparative clauses**) before looking at non-finite subordinate clauses and the less important category of verbless clauses.

   The four classes of finite subordinate clauses derive their names from their characteristic functions. Prototypical noun clauses are similar to NPs in their capacity to function as subject, object and complement; adverbial clauses function mainly, like AdvPs, as adjuncts; relative clauses characteristically function, like AdjPs, as modifiers in NP structure; comparative clauses are similar to AdvPs and AdjPs which function as degree modifiers.

7.3.1 Noun clauses

Noun clauses are similar in many ways to main clauses. Like main clauses they may be classified according to clause type:

*I believe **(that) John is involved***	(declarative)
*I doubt **whether/if John is involved***	(interrogative)
*I realise **how involved John is***	(exclamative)

Declarative noun clauses are introduced by the subordinator *that*, which can sometimes be omitted, sometimes not, as can be seen from the further examples below (which illustrate – but by no means exhaust – the range of functions that noun clauses may serve):

My belief is $\overset{\text{PCs}}{\underset{\text{NCl}}{[}}$ [***that John is involved***] (predicative complement)

I am $\overset{\text{PCs}}{\underset{\text{AdjP}}{(}}$ $\overset{\text{H}}{\underset{\text{Adj}}{upset}}$ $\overset{\text{Cx}}{\underset{\text{NCl}}{[\textit{that John is involved}]}})$ (complement in AdjP)

I am $\overset{\text{PCs}}{\underset{\text{AdjP}}{(}}$ $\overset{\text{M}}{\underset{\text{Adv}}{so}}$ $\overset{\text{H}}{\underset{\text{Adj}}{upset}}$ $\overset{\text{M}}{\underset{\text{NCl}}{[\textit{ that I will resign}]}})$ (modifier in AdjP)

$\overset{\text{S}}{\underset{\text{NCl}}{[\textit{That John is involved}]}}$ *surprises me* (subject)

$\underset{\text{NP}}{(}$ $\overset{\text{Dr}}{\underset{\text{Dv}}{our}}$ $\overset{\text{H}}{\underset{\text{N}}{belief,}}$ $\overset{\text{PD}}{\underset{\text{NCl}}{[\textit{that John is involved}]}})$ (peripheral dependent in NP)

$\underset{\text{NP}}{(}$ $\overset{\text{Dr}}{\underset{\text{Dv}}{our}}$ $\overset{\text{H}}{\underset{\text{N}}{belief}}$ $\overset{\text{Cx}}{\underset{\text{NCl}}{[\textit{that John is involved}]}})$ (complement in NP)

Interrogative noun clauses differ from their main clause counterparts in two ways.

1. Subject-operator inversion normally only applies in the case of main clauses. Compare:

   1. *Why are my friends involved?*

2. *I'd like to know **why my friends are involved***

The interrogative main clause in (1) requires inversion of the subject *my friends* and the operator *are*, but not the subordinate interrogative clause in (2).

2. Closed interrogatives are introduced by *whether* or *if* when subordinate, but not when they are main clauses. Compare:

1. *Is she unwell?*
2. *I asked **whether she was unwell***

With exclamatives there is normally no difference between main and subordinate clauses. Compare:

1. *What a genius she is!*
2. *I know **what a genius she is***

Note that there are no subordinate imperative clauses. Witness, for example, the ungrammaticality that results if we attempt to subordinate the imperative main clause *Be there!*, as in:

*He demands that be there

The closest thing to a subordinate imperative construction is a clause with the so-called **mandative subjunctive** use of *be*, as in:

He demands that you be there

It may be more plausible, however, to treat these merely as a type of declarative, for the subject is not necessarily *you*:

$$He\ demands\ that \begin{Bmatrix} they \\ she \\ John \end{Bmatrix} be\ there$$

7.3.2 Adverbial clauses

A characteristic feature of finite adverbial clauses is that they are introduced by subordinators such as *because, although, until* and *when*, whose function is that of relator (see Section 2.2 above for discussion of relator-axis constructions). Examples follow:

$$\textit{Carol hasn't visited the zoo} \ \ {}^{A}_{ACl}[\ {}^{Rel}_{Subord}\textit{since} \ {}^{Ax}_{Cl}[\textit{she was a child}]]$$

$$\ {}^{A}_{ACl}[\ {}^{Rel}_{Subord}\textit{If} \ {}^{Ax}_{Cl}[\textit{you are willing,}]] \ \ \textit{I am able}$$

Finite adverbial clauses function as adjuncts, so we find that the meanings they express are similar to those listed for adjuncts in general (see Section 2.6 above). The major semantic categories are listed below, along with an example of each:

MEANING	EXAMPLE
Time	**When the snow melts** *the water level will rise*
Place	*He travels* **wherever he wants**
Reason	*They have applied to foster an orphan* **because they cannot have children of their own**
Purpose	*They agreed to set out earlier* **so that they would arrive home before dark**
Condition	**If the rules prohibit smoking,** *then you must obey them*
Concession	**Although John studied hard,** *he still failed the exam*

7.3.3 Relative clauses

Relative clauses are typically introduced by a relative pronoun with anaphoric reference:

$$\textit{There's} \ {}^{Cx}_{NP}(\ {}^{Dr}_{Dv}\textit{the} \ {}^{H}_{N}\textit{car} \ {}^{M}_{RCl}[\textbf{\textit{which I saw yesterday}}])$$

Here the interpretation of *which* derives from the antecedent *car*. It is this anaphoric relationship that lies behind the use of the term 'relative' (the relative pronoun 'relates' the relative clause to the antecedent expression).

The various relative pronouns differ with respect to the types of antecedents they allow. While the antecedents of *that* and *whose* are largely unrestricted, the antecedents of *who(m)* are normally human or human-like, and those of *which* are usually non-human. Finally, the antecedents of *when*, *where* and *why*, which are relative/interrogative adverbs, denote times, places and reasons respectively. Compare:

> *There's the girl **who** I met yesterday*
> *There's the girl **that** I met yesterday*
> **There's the girl **which** I met yesterday*

> *There's the car **that** I saw yesterday*
> *There's the car **which** I saw yesterday*
> **There's the car **who** I saw yesterday*

> *There's the girl **whose** brother I met yesterday*
> *There's the car **whose** owner I met yesterday*

> *That's the season **when** you should plant seedlings*
> *That's the part of your property **where** you should plant seedlings*
> *That's the reason **why** you should plant seedlings*

Unlike subordinators, relative pronouns function as one of the functional elements of the clause:

```
         Dr    H      M    S      P       Od
    (   the   bank   [   that   has    the best interest rates ])
         Dv    N      RCl NP     VP      NP
```

```
         Dr    H      M  Od     S     P
    (   the   key    [  which   I   borrowed ])
         Dv    N      RCl NP     NP   VP
```

```
         Dr    H      M  Od Dr        H      S    P
    (   the   girl   [  (  whose   father)  I   met ])
         Dv    N      RCl NP Pn        N      NP   VP
```

```
         Dr    H      M    A       S      P
    (   the   year   [   when   she   graduated ])
         Dv    N      RCl AdvP     NP    VP
```

It is often grammatically allowable to omit the relative pronoun from a relative clause, the main exception being cases where the relative phrase functions as the subject. Thus, in the examples above, *which*, *who* and *when* could be omitted, but not *that* (if *that* were able to be omitted in the first example, there would be considerable scope for confusion between the NP, *the bank has the best interest rates*, and the clause of the same structure).

Relative pronouns may fill the axis slot in a prepositional phrase, and here there are several structural possibilities. Either the preposition may occur together with the axis-NP, as in (1) below, or it may be 'stranded' (left behind at the end of the clause), as in (2). If a preposition is stranded, then it is possible to omit the relative pronoun serving as axis, as in (3):

```
        Dr    H           M   A              S     P
1. ( the woman [ with whom he was dancing])
        Dv    N          RCl PP             NP   VP
```

```
        Dr    H           M   A         S    P
2. ( the woman [ whom he was dancing with])
        Dv    N          RCl PP        NP   VP
```

```
        Dr    H           M  A  S    P
3. ( the woman [ ( ) he was dancing with])
        Dv    N          RCl PP NP  VP
```

There are two main types of relative clause, **restrictive** and **non-restrictive**, as exemplified respectively in:

```
       S   H              M
1.  ( Children [who are often naughty]) need discipline
      NP  N              RCl
```

```
       S   H              PD
2.  ( Children, [who are often naughty,] need discipline
      NP  N              RCl
```

In speech, non-restrictive relative clauses are set off from the larger construction by means of a separate intonation contour, while in writing they are marked off by commas or a comparable form of punctuation. The information they express is presented as separate and secondary to that in the larger construction. By contrast, the information in a restrictive relative clause is an integral part of the message conveyed by the larger construction. Thus the restrictive relative clause exemplified in (1) above forms part of the description of the set of children being referred to; by contrast, the non-restrictive relative clause exemplified in (2) above simply gives extra information about the full set of children rather than defining a subset of children.

Non-restrictive relative clauses normally don't allow *that* as relative pronoun nor the omission of the relative pronoun.

Compare:

> *The tree,* **which I planted only two years ago**, *is now taller than the house*

> ?*The tree,* **that I planted only two years ago**, *is now taller than the house*

> *_The tree,_ **I planted only two years ago**, *is now taller than the house*

Another difference between restrictive and non-restrictive clauses is that if an antecedent is non-specific (e.g. *anything, no one, any animals*), then only a restrictive relative clause is possible:

> *Anyone who swears will have to pay a fine*   (resrictive)

> ?*Anyone, who swears, will have to pay a fine*   (non-restrictive)

Conversely non-restrictive relative clauses, but not restrictive relative clauses, may take a proper noun or an entire clause as antecedent. Compare:

> *Ray,* **who had just joined the project**, *felt that the pressure was too great*   (non-restrictive)

> *_Ray_ **who had just joined the project** *felt that the pressure was too great*   (restrictive)

> *United lost to Arsenal,* **which surprised us all**   (non-restrictive)

> *_United lost to Arsenal_ **which surprised us all**   (restrictive)

One further type of relative clause needs to be mentioned, that which is commonly referred to as a **free relative clause** (sometimes also called a 'nominal' or 'fused' relative clause):

> *I know* **what you need**

> **Whoever thinks that** *must be crazy*

> *Put it* **wherever you can find a spot**

Here the relative clause occurs 'freely' rather than being integrated into the structure of an NP. In the first example *what* has, as it were, a dual function, which we can see more clearly by comparing this example with a sentence such as *I know* **the thing that** *you need. What* represents a 'fusion' of the NP *the thing* and the relative pronoun *that*. The major relative words occurring in free relative clauses are *what*, *where* and *when*, along with the *-ever* compounds *whatever*, *whoever*, *whichever*, *wherever* and *whenever*.

7.3.4 Comparative clauses

Comparative clauses are classified by many traditional grammars as a subclass of adverbial clause, but they are quite distinctive structurally in that they always have material missing, and are introduced by either of the subordinators *than* or *as*. Comparative clauses with *than* function as (post)modifiers of comparative adverbs, adjectives or determinatives. Some examples follow:

She ran (*faster* [***than we did***])   (modifier of the adverb *faster*)

They had ((*bigger*) *slices* [***than we were given***])   (modifier of the adjective *bigger*)

He now has ((*less*) *money* [***than he had as a teenager***])   (modifier of the determinative *less*)

Comparative clauses with *as* typically postmodify an adjective or adverb:

Sue is not (*as inept* [***as you may think***])   (modifier of the adjective *inept*)

In understanding what it is that is missing in comparative clauses it is helpful to bear in mind that they express the standard of comparison in a relationship between two terms. Let us consider the four examples analysed above, using parentheses to indicate missing material: *She ran faster than we {ran fast to that degree}* (ellipsis of predicate); *They had bigger slices than we were given {slices that big}* (ellipsis of object); *He now has less money than he had {that much money} as a teenager* (ellipsis of object); *Sue is not as inept as you may think {that she is that inept}* (ellipsis of object of *think*).

Note that we need to use a makeshift expression such as 'x to some degree' or 'that x' in order to target the nature of the comparison. For example, in (2) the comparison is between the size or 'bigness' of the slices that they had and the size or 'bigness' of the slices that we were given. We would be overlooking something if we were to suggest that the comparative clause here is simply *than we were given slices*.

7.4 Non-finite clauses

Until now we have been focusing on finite subordinate clauses. Non-finite clauses may be infinitival ('Cli') – sometimes with the particle *to* and sometimes without, present-participial ('Cling') or past-participial ('Clen'). Infinitival clauses have a Vi as the first verb in their VP, present-participial clauses have a Ving, and past-participial clauses have a Ven.

$$\text{Bill didn't dare } \underset{\text{Cli}}{[} \underset{\text{VP}}{(} \underset{\text{Vi}}{\overset{P}{}} \overset{H}{place}) \underset{\text{NP}}{(\overset{O}{another \ bet})}] \quad \begin{array}{l}\text{(infinitival:}\\ place = \text{Vi)}\end{array}$$

$$\text{Bill wanted } \underset{\text{Cli}}{[} \underset{\text{VP}}{(} \overset{O}{to} \underset{\text{Vi}}{\overset{P}{place}}) \underset{\text{NP}}{(\overset{O}{another \ bet})}] \quad \begin{array}{l}\text{(infinitival:}\\ place = \text{Vi)}\end{array}$$

$$\text{Cleo enjoys } \underset{\text{Cling}}{[} \underset{\text{VP}}{(} \underset{\text{Aux}}{\overset{O}{being}} \underset{\text{Mv}}{\overset{M \quad H}{pampered})}] \quad \begin{array}{l}\text{(pres-participial:}\\ being = \text{Ving)}\end{array}$$

$$\text{She had her toenails } \underset{\text{Clen}}{[} \underset{\text{VP}}{(} \underset{\text{Mv}}{\overset{Cx \quad P \quad H}{manicured})}] \quad \begin{array}{l}\text{(past-participial:}\\ manicured = \text{Ven)}\end{array}$$

In many cases there is a close relationship with a finite subordinate clause, which has tempted some grammarians to apply to non-finite clauses the same classification as is used with finite subordinate clauses. Consider:

1.　(　*The*　*man*　[**selling tickets**])　*is my cousin*

       S Dr   H   M

     NP Dv   N   Cling

2.　*We planned*　[**to take a detour**]

               O

               Cli

The present-participial clause *selling tickets* in (1) would be treated as a relative clause functioning as postmodifier of *man* (compare the finite relative clause *who is selling tickets*). Here there are certainly parallels between the finite and non-finite clauses, but in other cases they are less persuasive. For instance, in (2) the infinitival clause *to take a detour* would be treated as a noun clause functioning as object of *planned* (compare the finite clause *that we would take a detour*). Here there may be a functional similarity between the finite and non-finite clauses, but structurally the non-finite clause is not simply an elliptical version of the finite clause (it is closer to something like *that we would take a detour* than to *that we were to take a detour*).

Even more problematical are cases such as those in *Bill didn't dare (to) place another bet* and *Cleo enjoys being pampered* above, where the infinitival and present-participial clauses appear not to have any finite clause counterparts (**Bill didn't dare that he should place another bet* and **Cleo enjoys that she is pampered* are of questionable grammaticality).

In view of these problems we will not attempt to force non-finite clauses into the same classificatory mould (i.e. NCl, RCl, ACl and CCl) as finite clauses, but simply classify them along two dimensions:

• formal: infinitival, present-participial or past participial
• functional: subject, object, predicative complement, catenative complement, modifier, adjunct or peripheral-dependent

Examples follow, with abbreviations representing the functional and formal classification of the non-finite clause:

   S

  [**Painting this room**] *has exhausted all my energy*

Cling

S Dr   M   H   M
(*The* *first* *person* [***to climb Mt Everest***]) *was Hilary*
NP Dv   Adj   N   Cli

A
[***If called upon,***] *you must work overtime*
Clen

O
He wants   [***to do it by himself***]
Cli

A H   M
There's nothing he likes (*more* [***than winning***])
AdvP Adv   Cling

Od Dr   H   M
I have found (*some* *funds* [***with which to purchase it***])
NP Dv   N   Cli

We turn finally in this section to a problematical issue. There
has been much debate in linguistic circles about the status of
NPs that may occur between catenative verbs and their non-
finite clausal complements. Compare:

> *Tom instructed* **Sue** *to prepare the submission*
> *Tom intended* **Sue** *to prepare the submission*

The issue here is: what is the status of *Sue*? Is *Sue* the object
of *instructed/intended* in the superordinate clause, or the subject of *prepare* in the non-finite subordinate clause? It may
appear from a semantic point of view that we need to give
different answers for the two sentences. With *instruct* there is
a direct semantic relationship between the verb and the object (Sue is the one to whom the instruction is given), whereas
with *intend* there is no such semantic relationship (it is not
that Sue is the one to whom an intention is addressed, but
rather that Tom has a certain attitude towards the event of
Sue's preparing a submission). But is this difference supported by grammatical evidence? At first sight it would seem so.
The two sentences respond differently to passivisation. Compare the results if we apply passivisation to the main clause
(*Sue* can become the subject of the main clause via passivisation with *instruct* but not *intend*):

> *Sue was instructed by Tom to prepare the submission*

Sue was intended by Tom to prepare the submission

Compare the results if passivisation is applied to the non-finite clause (*the submission* can become the subject of the non-finite clause via passivisation with *intend* but not *instruct*):

Tom instructed the submission to be prepared by Sue
Tom intended the submission to be prepared by Sue

However, when we look more closely at the behaviour of other catenative verbs, we find that the facts are less clear. Consider, for example, *expect*, as in:

Tom expected Sue to prepare the submission

Expect is semantically similar to *intend* in so far as it denotes an attitude that a person has towards an event. Like *intend*, *expect* allows passivisation to be applied to the non-finite clause:

Tom expected the submission to be prepared by Sue

However, *expect* behaves differently from *intend*, and similarly to *instruct* in so far as it also allows passivisation to be applied to the main clause:

Sue was expected by Tom to prepare the submission

Another verb which, like *expect*, allows both types of passivisation is *consider*. Compare:

Tom considered Sue to have prepared the submission
Tom considered the submission to have been prepared by Sue
Sue was considered by Tom to have prepared the submission

There are clearly semantic differences between these verbs, but in light of the conflicting syntactic evidence it seems unwise to assume that these semantic differences are reflected in syntactic differences. We shall therefore assume that the sentences we have examined containing such catenative verbs as *instruct*, *intend*, *expect* and *consider* have a similar syntactic structure, with the catenative verb in the main clause taking two complements, an object complement and a catenative complement, as in:

$$\text{Tom instructed} \underset{\substack{\text{O}\\\text{NP}}}{(Sue)} \underset{\text{Cli}}{\overset{\text{Cx}}{[to \; prepare \; a \; submission]}}$$

$$\text{Tom intended} \underset{\substack{\text{O}\\\text{NP}}}{(Sue)} \underset{\text{Cli}}{\overset{\text{Cx}}{[to \; prepare \; a \; submission]}}$$

7.5 Verbless clauses

Even further removed from finite subordinate clauses than non-finite clauses, are verbless clauses, as illustrated in:

$$He \; was \; running \; \underset{\substack{\text{ACl}}}{[} \; \underset{\text{Subord}}{\overset{\text{Rel}}{with}} \; \underset{\text{Cl}}{\overset{\text{Ax}}{[\textbf{his hands on his head}]}} \;]$$

$$\underset{\substack{\text{ACl Subord}}}{[} \; \overset{\text{Rel}}{\textbf{When}} \; \underset{\text{Cl}}{\overset{\text{Ax}}{[\textbf{angry}]}} \;] \; he \; becomes \; a \; formidable \; opponent$$

In both cases the verb *be* is 'understood': thus the verbless clauses here can be related to the finite clauses *his hands were on his head* and *when he is angry*. The verbless clause in the first example is introduced by the subordinator *with* (not the more familiar preposition *with*): like the subordinator *for*, as in *It would be better for you to leave*, the subordinator *with* cannot introduce a finite clause.

7.6 Coordination

Whereas subordination is a relationship between elements that do not have the same syntactic status, coordination – as the name implies – is a relationship between elements that are of equivalent rank. Accordingly, we cannot specify individual functions for the coordinated elements; rather, it is only the coordination itself whose function we shall specify.

Coordination (typically indicated by the coordinators *and*, *or* and *but*) is a relationship that obtains not only between clauses, but also between phrases and words. Let us nevertheless begin with the coordination of clauses. We have defined a compound sentence as one containing two or more main clauses, as in:

> *John is an accountant and his girlfriend is studying philosophy at university*

We can represent the constituent structure in the following way (again using triangles to indicate that irrelevant details have been omitted). The sequence comprising the coordinated elements will be referred to as a 'coordination'. This may be the entire sentence (as in the example below) or, as we shall see, less than a sentence:

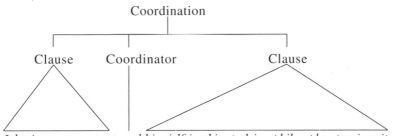

John is an accountant and his girlfriend is studying philosophy at university

The coordinator has a closer affinity with the following constituent than with the one preceding, but in order to keep the structure of our trees as simple as possible, we have analysed the coordinator as an immediate constituent of the coordination (if *and* were analysed as being in construction with *his girlfriend is studying philosophy at university* there would have to be a further layer in the constituent analysis).

Consider some further examples involving phrase and word coordinations:

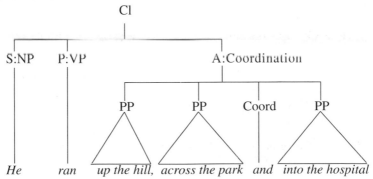

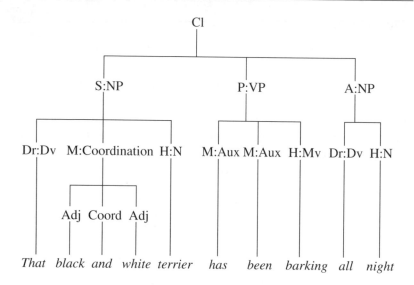

The relationship of coordination is not always marked by the presence of a coordinator. When no marker is present, we talk of 'unlinked', or **asyndetic,** coordination (as between the first two coordinated elements in *He ran up the hill, across the park and into the hospital* above).

Ambiguities may sometimes occur, as in *He likes German beer and wine*. As the two tree diagrams below indicate, the ambiguity here derives from whether we have a coordination of NPs functioning as object (as in (1): 'He likes German beer and any type of wine'), or a coordination of NP heads (as in (2): 'He likes German beer and German wine'):

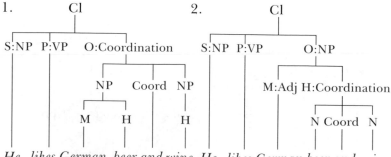

7.7 'Flattened tree' analysis

Tree diagrams can become very complex, which is why we
have often used triangles to indicate the omission of details
not considered pertinent to our discussion. In this section we
will present a method of notation that systematically uses 'flattened' triangles in order to reduce tree diagrams to the bare
essentials – to remove unnecessary 'flesh', thereby revealing
the structural 'skeleton'.

In this method class labels may be dispensed with: only
function labels are used. Flattened trees are used to indicate
constructions: the symbol at the apex of the triangle indicates the type of construction, while everything below the base
of the triangle represents the constituents of the construction. The type of brackets placed below the endpoints of the
base indicate whether the construction is a phrase (round
brackets), a clause (square brackets) or a coordination (angle
brackets). Within a coordination a plus sign represents any
coordinator and a comma represents unlinked coordination).
Consider some examples:

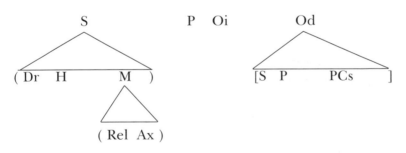

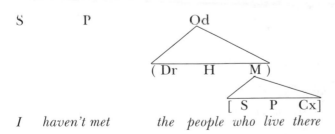

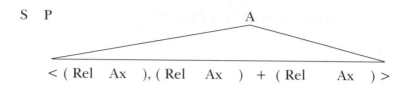

S   P   A

< (Rel   Ax   ), (Rel   Ax   ) + (Rel   Ax   ) >

We climbed   up   the ladder,   over the railing   and   through   the window

Exercises

7a. Each of the following sentences contains one finite sub-
     ordinate clause. For each sentence:

     (i) Identify the subordinate clause
     (ii) Say whether it is NCl, RCl, ACl or CCl
     (iii) Describe the function of the subordinate clause
           within the construction containing it in terms of
           the elements S, P, O, PC, A, PD or M

     Example: *That he left so early was a major disappointment*
     (i) *That he left so early* (ii) NCl (iii) S

     1. *He claims that he's a doctor*
     2. *I'll leave you everything that I own*
     3. *Department stores do not offer as much friendly service as
        they used to*
     4. *She arranged an excursion, which pleased the class
        immensely*
     5. *I wonder if they will offer her the job*

7b. The underlined relative clauses in the following exam-
     ples can be interpreted as either restrictive or non-
     restrictive. Comment on the difference in meaning be-
     tween the two interpretations.
     Note: Punctuation is deliberately omitted.

     1. *You should ask the neighbours <u>who saw the incident</u>*
     2. *He was driving a car <u>which I hadn't seen before</u>*

7c. Each of the following sentences contains a non-finite clause (as underlined). For each one:

   (i) Classify the clause as a Cli, Cling or Clen

   (ii) Indicate the type of construction containing it

   (iii) State its function within that construction

Example: *Children born in hospital are more likely to survive*
   (i) Clen   (ii) NP   (iii) M
   He was lucky to survive the ordeal
   (i) Cli   (ii) AdjP   (iii) C

1. *He regrets dividing their assets equally*
2. *She intends to make us another offer*
3. *Delilah entered gracefully, attired in a seductive gown*
4. *Try to keep your back straight when lifting heavy objects*
5. *The time to do it is now*
6. *Anyone caught cheating will be punished severely*
7. *It was difficult for him to maintain his concentration*
8. *They persisted in whispering all through the lecture*

7d. Using primarily functional terms, explain the different interpretations of the following ambiguous sentences. **Note**: Punctuation is deliberately omitted.

1. *He forgot the time when he was in prison*
2. *I revealed that I had written the note before they suspected me*
3. *He admits defaming them openly*
4. *He was unwise to speak honestly*
5. *He said that he saw them last week*

7e. For each of the following verbs say whether it can take a noun clause that is:
(i) declarative   (ii) interrogative   (iii) exclamative

Give an example of each.

Example: *realise*
declarative: *John realised that he had been foolhardy*
interrogative: *John realised why he had been foolhardy*
exclamative: *John realised how foolhardy he had been*

enquire
declarative: –
interrogative: *John enquired whether tickets were still available*
exclamative: –

wonder, promise, ask, assume, doubt, forget

7f. Elements which are coordinated do not always belong to the same class (e.g. in *Please come next Tuesday or sooner*, an NP and AdvP are coordinated). Construct sentences containing coordinations of the following elements:

1. PP + AdvP
2. NP + AdjP
3. NP + non-finite clause
4. PP + AdjP

7g. Coordination may occur at a variety of positions in constituent structure (e.g. in PPs there may be a coordination in the relator position, as in *up and over the wall*, as well as in the axis position, as in *over the wall and the hedge*). Construct sentences containing coordinations in the positions indicated below:

1. (Clause) (a) subject (b) predicator (c) indirect object (d) predicative complement (objective)
2. (NP) (a) determiner (b) pre-head modifier (c) head (d) post-head modifier
3. (AdjP) (a) pre-head modifier (b) head (c) post-head modifier (d) complement

7h. The following sentences are ambiguous. Use angle brackets
      < > to enclose coordinations and explain the difference
      in meaning.

1. *Women and men over thirty are welcome*
2. *Alsations can be extremely aggressive and temperamental*
3. *Mary and Bill or Peter made this mess*
4. *Tom plays indoor cricket and football*

8 | Information structure in the clause

8.1 Information structure

In this chapter we shall consider various types of alternation between clauses which differ not in the basic meaning expressed, but in the way it is structured as a message. Within a particular context, the types of factors which will determine whether one clause variant is selected over another will involve considerations of 'topic', 'information' and 'weight'.

The **topic** of a clause is what it is about and tends to be expressed as the first element in the clause. Consider the active-passive pair:

1. *Monet is the best known of the French Impressionists*

2. *The best known of the French Impressionists is Monet*

The sentence in (1) is likely to be construed as being about the painter Monet, used in a context where the speaker/writer has already made mention of him, whereas the sentence in (2) is likely to be construed as being about the French Impressionist school, used in a context where the speaker/writer has previously referred to it.

Another factor that may influence the selection of one variant over another is **end-focus**, the tendency for 'focal' constituents to appear towards the end of the clause. Focal, or **new**, information is signalled by the placement of stress. Prototypically, this falls on the last open-class word in the information unit. Consider the sentence:

Algernon drove the bus

Here *bus* is most likely to be nuclear, and as a consequence the new information may be expressed by:

- *the bus* (e.g. as a response to *What did Algernon drive?*, where it is assumed, or **given**, that Algernon drove something)
- *drove the bus* (e.g. as a response to *What did Algernon do?*, where it is assumed that Algernon did something)
- *Algernon drove the bus* (e.g. as a response to *What happened?*, where nothing is given)

In the light of what we have just said about end-focus, consider the alternation between sentences such as:

1. *Sam sent the largest parcel to Marcia*
2. *Sam sent Marcia the largest parcel*

Other things being equal, (1) is likely to be preferred over (2) in a context where it is given that Sam sent the largest parcel and the new information is that Marcia was the recipient ('Who did Sam send the largest parcel to?'). Conversely, (2) is likely to be favoured in a context where it is given that Sam sent Marcia something, and the news is that that something was the largest parcel.

Finally, there is a tendency – called **end-weight** – for long and complex constituents of the clause to occur at or towards the end of the sentence. For example, (1) below is likely to be preferred over (2) because the latter is 'front-heavy' (it has a long subordinate clause in initial position).

1. *It is a pity that all efforts to revive the study of Latin in secondary schools have been in vain*
2. *That all efforts to revive the study of Latin in secondary schools have been in vain is a pity*

8.2 Active and passive clauses

The names 'active' and 'passive' are motivated by the different semantic roles associated with the subject in typical clauses expressing an activity: namely, in active clauses that of 'actor', (*the inspector* in (1) below), and in passive clauses that of 'patient', (*Jim* in (2) below):

1. *The inspector confronted Jim*   (active)

2. *Jim was confronted by the inspector*   (passive)

If we compare the active and passive clauses in (1) and (2), it can be seen that, taking the active clause as basic, the passive can be derived by:

* Converting the object of the active (*Jim*) into the subject of the passive
* Making the subject of the active (*the inspector*) into the axis of a *by*-phrase
* Making the VP passive (by adding auxiliary *be* to the VP before the main verb and converting the main verb into the Ven form)

The 'agent' *by*-phrase is optional, and, in fact, passives without it (such as *Fred was injured*) are far more common in English than those with it (such as *Fred was injured by a falling rock*).

The passive of ditransitive clauses normally has the indirect object as subject of the passive, as in (2) below, with passives such as that in (3) – with the subject corresponding to the passive direct object – being restricted to certain dialects (note that *A rebate was given us by the Taxation Department* is the passive counterpart of *The Taxation Department gave us a rebate*, not of *The Taxation Department gave a rebate to us*).

1.   S   P   Oi   Od
    The Taxation Department   gave   us   a rebate
    NP   VP   NP   NP   (active)

2.   S   P   Od   Cx
    We   were given   a rebate   by the Taxation Department
    NP   VP   NP   PP   (passive)

3.   S   P   Oi Cx
    A rebate   was given   us   by the Taxation Department
    NP   VP   NP PP   (passive)

The element that becomes passive subject may be the axis-NP of a PP, rather than the object of the verb, as in:

                        Cx
Many scientists have referred   (to this effect)
                        PP

$$\underset{\text{NP}}{\overset{\text{S}}{(This\ effect)}}\ has\ been\ referred\quad\underset{\text{prep}}{\overset{\text{Cx}}{(to)}}\ by\ many\ scientists$$

In typical cases the informational factors involved in the choice between active and passive sentences are those which we have discussed in the previous section. In so far as passivisation reverses the sequential arrangement of the two NPs, the choice will be influenced by the tendency for the topic expression to appear early, and for focal and complex constituents to appear late. An additional factor relates to the fact that the agent phrase in the passive is syntactically optional and can be omitted if the speaker/writer wishes to omit information that would have to be expressed in the corresponding active. Consider:

1. *The cathedral was built in 1458*

2. *The river broke its bank and half the town was flooded*

3. *Twenty milligrams of sodium chloride were added to the solution*

4. *Payment by cheque or bankcard is required within 20 days*

In (1) the identity of the builders may not be known, and even if it is, it is likely to be of less significance than the age of the cathedral. In (2) the understood agent (*by the water*) can be readily inferred. In (3) and (4) the passive enables the writer to avoid self-reference: such agentless passives are a typical feature of scientific and bureaucratic writing.

8.3 Subject-complement switch

Subject-complement switch bears some similarities to passivisation. It applies to clauses containing the main verb *be* in its identifying use, with a predicative complement that is identifying rather than attributive (see section 6.1 above), as in:

1. $\underset{\text{NP}}{\overset{\text{S}}{George}}\ \underset{\text{VP}}{\overset{\text{P}}{is}}\ \underset{\text{NP}}{\overset{\text{PCs}}{the\ tallest\ one}}$

2. $\underset{\text{NP}}{\overset{\text{S}}{The\ tallest\ one}}\ \underset{\text{VP}}{\overset{\text{P}}{is}}\ \underset{\text{NP}}{\overset{\text{PCs}}{George}}$

As in passivisation, the two NPs here switch places and their functions change (*George* is the subject in (1), and *the tallest one* in (2)). However, unlike passivisation, there is no change in the verb and the preposition *by* is not added.

Identifying *be* does not permit passivisation proper (we can't say **The tallest one is been by George*), but subject-complement switch allows a similar type of rearrangement of clausal elements to that occuring in transitive clauses with passivisation.

One special kind of construction that belongs here is the one often referred to as the **pseudo-cleft**, as illustrated by:

1. $\overset{\text{S}}{\underset{\text{RCl}}{\textit{What he said}}}$ $\overset{\text{P}}{\underset{\text{VP}}{\textit{was}}}$ $\overset{\text{PCs}}{\underset{\text{NCl}}{\textit{that he approved wholeheartedly}}}$

2. $\overset{\text{S}}{\underset{\text{NCl}}{\textit{That he approved wholeheartedly}}}$ $\overset{\text{P}}{\underset{\text{VP}}{\textit{was}}}$ $\overset{\text{PC}}{\underset{\text{RCl}}{\textit{what he said}}}$

Here the subject in the basic sentence (and thus the predicative complement in the switched version) is a free relative clause. The name 'pseudo-cleft' reflects the affinities that the construction has with the cleft sentence (see further Section 8.6 below).

8.4 Extraposition

Extraposition involves the movement of a subordinate clause from subject position, as in (1) – or occasionally from object position, as in (2) to the right of the predicate and insertion of the dummy pronoun *it* in the position vacated by the clause:

1. $\overset{\text{S}}{\underset{\text{NCl}}{\textit{That he escaped without injury}}}$ $\overset{\text{P}}{\underset{\text{VP}}{\textit{is}}}$ $\overset{\text{PCs}}{\underset{\text{AdjP}}{\textit{amazing}}}\longrightarrow$

    $\overset{\text{S}}{\underset{\text{NP}}{\textit{It}}}$ $\overset{\text{P}}{\underset{\text{VP}}{\textit{is}}}$ $\overset{\text{PCs}}{\underset{\text{AdjP}}{\textit{amazing}}}$ $\overset{\text{Cx}}{\underset{\text{NCl}}{\textit{that he escaped without injury}}}$

2. $\overset{\text{S}}{\underset{\text{NP}}{\textit{I}}}$ $\overset{\text{P}}{\underset{\text{VP}}{\textit{find}}}$ $\overset{\text{Od}}{\underset{\text{NCl}}{\textit{that he escaped without injury}}}$ $\overset{\text{PCo}}{\underset{\text{AdjP}}{\textit{amazing}}}\longrightarrow$

    $\overset{\text{S}}{\underset{\text{NP}}{\textit{I}}}$ $\overset{\text{P}}{\underset{\text{VP}}{\textit{find}}}$ $\overset{\text{Od}}{\underset{\text{NP}}{\textit{it}}}$ $\overset{\text{PCo}}{\underset{\text{AdjP}}{\textit{amazing}}}$ $\overset{\text{Cx}}{\underset{\text{NCl}}{\textit{that he escaped without injury}}}$

Occasionally, non-finite clauses may be extraposed over short predicates, as in:

> *It's been fun talking to you*
> *It's been fun to talk to you*

The only exception to the generalisation that extraposition applies to clauses involves NPs that are semantically equivalent to subordinate interrogatives (as in *It's extraordinary the amount of energy our leader has*, where the extraposed NP, *the amount of energy our leader has*, may be compared with *how much energy our leader has*).

The informational motivation for extraposition is endweight: the location of a longer and more complex constituent in final position makes the sentence easier to process.

8.5 Existential sentences

Another type of construction which has a dummy pronoun as subject (in this case *there*), and in which material is moved to a later position, is called an 'existential sentence', as exemplified in:

$$
\begin{array}{cccc}
\text{S} & \text{P} & \text{Cx} \\
\textit{Someone} & \textit{is} & \textit{at the door} & \longrightarrow \\
\text{NP} & \text{VP} & \text{PP}
\end{array}
$$

$$
\begin{array}{cccc}
\text{S} & \text{P} & \text{Cx} & \text{Cx} \\
\textit{There} & \textit{is} & \textit{someone} & \textit{at the door} \\
\text{NP} & \text{VP} & \text{NP} & \text{PP}
\end{array}
$$

The name 'existential' derives from the use of such sentences to express propositions of existence:

> *There are many species of pine tree*

It is important to note, however, that this is not their only use. Existential sentences may, for example, express the occurrence of events rather than the existence of entities, as in:

> *There was a robbery at the bank yesterday*

The unstressed dummy pronoun *there* is to be distinguished from the locative adverb *there* (from which it derives historically). Compare the two *there*s in:

```
    S        P   Cx        A
  There    's   a leak    there
 NP        VP   NP        AdvP
```

The second *there* is a place-indicating adverb (which is in contrast with other locative expressions such as *here* and *in the pipe*). The first *there* does not indicate place; rather it is a dummy pronoun, as seen by its capacity to:

* invert with the operator in interrogatives (e.g. *Is there a leak there?*)
* enter into agreement with the verb (e.g. *There's three people away today*) – at least in informal usage

In the vast majority of cases the 'displaced subject' NP is indefinite (as one would expect, given that the primary informational motivation of existential sentences is to introduce a referent newly into the discourse). However, definite NPs are not entirely excluded. A speaker may use a definite NP in an existential sentence to refer to an entity which, though familiar to the addressee, does not happen to be salient in a particular context, as with *the football* in:

A: *What do you suggest that we should do this weekend?*

B: *Well, there's always the football*

In addition to *be*, existential sentences allow a small set of intransitive verbs such as *follow*, *remain* and *appear*, as in:

There appeared a large ship on the horizon

What follows the 'displaced subject' is sometimes called the 'extension'. A number of different types of extension are possible:

* locative complement:

```
    S        P   Cx        Cx
  There    's   a toad   in the pool
 NP        VP   NP        PP
```

Here we have to understand 'locative' complement in a broad sense in order to include expressions such as *yesterday* in *There was no hearing yesterday*.

- predicative complement:

S	P	Cx		PC
There	*were*	*some non-members*		*present*
NP	VP	NP		AdjP

The predicative complement must normally denote a state (*absent, open, sick*, etc.) rather than a property (*short, green, American*, etc.). Compare:

There were several people sick

*There were several people American

- 'zero' complement:

S	P	Cx
There	*'s been*	*an accident*
NP	VP	NP

This type is sometimes called 'bare existential' since there is no extension. Bare existentials have no non-existential counterpart (**An accident has been*).

- Relative clause:

S	P	Cx	Cx
There	*are*	*three things*	*I'd like to say*
NP	VP	NP	RCl

This is the existential counterpart of *I'd like to say three things*. This type excludes cases with an NP containing a relative clause as modifier (e.g. *There are machines that can think like humans*), which can be straightforwardly handled as bare existentials.

- Non-finite clause:

S	P	Cx	Cx
There	*'s*	*someone*	*knocking at the door*
NP	VP	NP	Cling

S	P	Cx	Cx
There	*were*	*lots of people*	*arrested*
NP	VP	NP	Clen

These are the existential counterparts of *Someone's knocking at the door* and *Lots of people were arrested* respectively. The extension is either a present participial clause or a past participial clause.

From an informational point of view, existential sentences allow a non-topical NP – one which in many cases serves to introduce a new entity into the discourse – to be moved out of the subject position to a later position in the sentence.

8.6 Cleft sentences

The cleft sentences below are all informational variants of the basic sentence *Lois rang Ben at lunchtime*:

S	P	PC	Cx		
It	*was*	*Lois*	*who rang Ben at lunchtime*		
NP	VP	NP	RCL		

S	P	PC	Cx		
It	*was*	*Ben*	*that Lois rang at lunchtime*		
NP	VP	NP	RCL		

S	P	Cx	Cx		
It	*was*	*at lunchtime*	*that Lois rang Ben*		
NP	VP	PP	RCL		

In each case the basic clause has been divided – 'cleaved' – into two parts, one of which is highlighted as complement to *be* in a main clause with *it* as subject, while the other is subordinated in the form of a relative clause which has the highlighted element as its antecedent. The subordinate clause is not a typical relative clause. Structurally, it is similar to a restrictive relative, in being introduced by a relative phrase (*who, that,* etc.) which may often be omitted (e.g. *It was Ben Lois rang at lunchtime*; *It was at lunchtime Lois rang Ben*). However, there are some notable differences: it differs in the strong preference for *that* as the relative item, and in the range of elements that occur as antecedent. These include:

- PPs   (e.g. *It was **in Paris** that they met*)
- finite clauses (e.g. *It was **because Lois had a technical problem** that she rang Ben at lunchtime*)

The highlighted element is so called because it is typically focal (and very often contrastive: *It was Lois who rang Ben at lunchtime* is likely to imply a contrast between Lois and other people who might have rung Ben). By contrast, the relative clause is usually non-focal; in fact, the information in the relative clause is often so readily recoverable from the context that the relative clause is omitted, as in:

A: *Who was it who saw the accident?*
B: *It was my brother.*

However the relative clause is not necessarily non-focal. Examples of the following type, where the information in the relative clause is unlikely to have been previously mentioned, are not uncommon in journalistic writing:

> *It was at 8.30 last night that the Prime Minister received the first of two telephone calls from the White House*

The constructions discussed in Sections 8.2–8.5 all involve differences in the sequential arrangement of elements. In a cleft sentence the order of elements in the corresponding basic clause may be altered, but is not necessarily so (e.g. *It was Kim who fainted*; compare *Kim fainted*).

Another type of construction in which the sequential arrangement of elements may or may not be changed is the so-called 'pseudo-cleft' (which we introduced in Section 8.3 above). The following example corresponds to the basic clause *The bathroom requires a fresh coat of paint*:

> *What the bathroom requires is a fresh coat of paint*

The term 'pseudo-cleft' suggests that despite the apparent resemblances to cleft sentences, they should not necessarily be described in the same way. Thus whereas we shall regard cleft sentences as 'deriving from' their more basic non-cleft counterparts, we shall not regard pseudo-clefts as being derived in this way. The reason is that there are pseudo-cleft sentences which could not be derived from a more basic sentence, such as the following (compare **I like about him his sense of humour*):

> *What I like about him is his sense of humour*

8.7 'Reordering'

We shall treat together in this section a number of constructions in which elements of the clause are moved from their basic position in response to informational factors.

8.7.1 Topicalisation

Topicalisation is the term that is generally applied to the reordering process that puts an element in front position in the clause in order to make it the topic:

Od   S   P
Cheeky children *he* *can't stand*
NP   NP VP

A   S   P   A
The following Sunday *we*   *went* *to the Gold Coast*
NP   NP VP   PP

These two examples are plausibly interpreted as being about 'cheeky children' and 'the following Sunday' respectively; that is, as having these as their topics. However, the term 'topicalisation' is slightly misleading because the motivation for moving an element into front position is not necessarily to make it the topic:

PCs   S   P
Humble *he* *is* *not*
AdjP   NP VP

                   P H-   S   -M
{I promised to pay and} (***pay***) *I*   *will*)
                     VP Mv   NP   Aux

Here the motivation for the fronting is more plausibly interpreted as being connective: *humble* most likely contrasts with something earlier, while *pay* repeats an earlier mention (in the previous clause).

8.7.2 Locative inversion

Locative inversion is the name often used in grammatical descriptions of English for another, similar process which moves a locative expression to the front of the clause, but at the same time moves the subject to post-verbal position, as in:

Cx   P   S
On top of the wardrobe *was* *a battered old trunk*
PP   VP   NP

A   P   S
Over the hill *appeared* *the cavalry*
PP   VP   NP

Here the reordering enables the displaced subject to receive prominence as the focal information. The use of the adjective 'locative' in 'locative inversion' is arguably too restrictive given that the same process occurs with a sentence such as the following, where the expression moved into initial position does not express a locative meaning:

PCs   P   S
More important *are* *the moral objections*
AdjP   VP   NP

8.7.3 Dislocation

Dislocation is a process that may move an element of the clause to the left, with a personal pronoun being put in its place (called **left dislocation**), or it may move an element to the right (called **right dislocation**). These processes, which are largely confined to informal speech, are illustrated respectively below:

Cx   S   P   Od
Racial prejudice, *I don't like it*   (left dislocation)
NP   NP VP   NP

S   P   Od Cx
I don't like it, **racial prejudice**   (right dislocation)
NP VP   NP NP

Left dislocation serves to explicitly announce the topical status of the dislocated element, while right dislocation generally serves to clarify or reinforce the identity of a referent by giving it the focal prominence associated with final position. The dislocated element may represent a variety of functions within the 'governing' clause. Consider:

S
My brother, (he) had a nasty accident   (subject)

S
(He) had a nasty accident, my brother   (subject)

Od
My brother, someone has attacked (him)   (object)

Od
Someone has attacked (him), my brother   (object)

Cx Rel   Ax

The attack on your brother, I heard (*about* (*it*)) (axis of PP)

Cx Rel   Ax

I heard (*about* (*it*)), *the attack on your brother* (axis of PP)

8.7.4 Complex NP shift

A relatively minor process involving movement into final position that is sometimes called **complex NP shift** is illustrated in:

S   P   Od   PCo

*They pronounced **each of the accused** guilty* ⟶

NP   VP   NP   AdjP

S   P   PCo   Od

*They pronounced guilty **each of the accused***

NP   VP   AdjP   NP

This process involves the movement of a long and complex object NP to a later position in the sentence.

8.7.5 Extraposition from NP

Another minor process involving movement into final position (of a dependent element from an NP) is sometimes called **extraposition from NP**. This process differs from ordinary extraposition in that it does not involve insertion of a dummy *it*. An example follows:

S   Dr   H   M   P

(*The time* [**to paint the house**]) *has come* ⟶

NP Dv   N   Cli   VP

S   Dr   H-   P   -M

(*The time*) *has come* [**to paint the house**]

NP Dv   N   VP   Cli

8.7.6 Dative movement

Finally, consider a process referred to by many grammarians as **dative movement**, which converts a PP-axis into an indirect object, as in:

S   P   Od   Cx

*Penny sold the refrigerator **to him*** ⟶

NP   VP   NP   PP

$$\underset{\text{NP}}{\underset{\text{S}}{Penny}} \quad \underset{\text{VP}}{\underset{\text{P}}{sold}} \quad \underset{\text{NP}}{\underset{\text{Oi}}{\textbf{\textit{him}}}} \quad \underset{\text{NP}}{\underset{\text{Od}}{the \; refrigerator}}$$

While it is undoubtedly the case that the alternation between such sentences is motivated by informational factors, it is not clear that we can legitimately regard one of the sentences as being more 'basic', with the other being derived from it. It makes more sense to treat both clauses as basic because there are many verbs which exhibit one pattern of complementation, but not the other. Compare:

They reported the result to Tom
**They reported Tom the result*

The judge fined him 2000 dollars
**The judge fined 2000 dollars to him*

Exercises

8a. Some of the following active sentences can be trans-formed into a passive, but others cannot. For those that have a passive counterpart, say what it is. For those that do not, suggest a reason why not.

1. *Eliot became a major literary figure*
2. *Colonel Carruthers ordered the troops to advance*
3. *Uncle Ted called last week*
4. *Saussure established that language is a sign system*
5. *Our supervisor instructed us to begin working*
6. *He died a pauper*
7. *We know John to be a fraud*

8b. The agent may be omitted in passive sentences for a variety of reasons. Suggest a reason for its omission in each of the following cases.

1. *The President has been assassinated*
2. *The crowd pushed forward and <u>we were pressed against the fence</u>*
3. *Your gum tree was blown over last night*

4. *Trespassing is forbidden*

8c. Pick out from the following sentences those which have an existential counterpart and say what it is:

Example: *A large spider was under the bricks*
There was a large spider under the bricks

1. *Someone is absent*
2. *Mrs Murphy is at the door*
3. *Three competitors are disabled*
4. *No one was hurt in the accident*
5. *Jan is approaching*
6. *A mysterious figure appeared*

8d. Convert each of the following sentences into three different cleft sentences, by selecting different clause elements to be highlighted in each case.

Example: *The professor spoke to Jane on Friday;*
It was to the professor that Jane spoke on Friday;
It was Jane to whom the professor spoke on Friday;
It was on Friday that the professor spoke to Jane.

1. *The swimmers were attacked by a large shark near the pier*
2. *He gave a detailed report to the police after the accident*

8e. Each of the following sentences is an example of one of the following:

i. extraposition
ii. cleft
iii. right dislocation
iv. none of these

Say which of these four classifications applies to each sentence and, in the case of those that are (i)–(iii), provide the corresponding unmarked (i.e. non-extraposed, non-cleft or non-dislocated) version.

1. *It was Margaret who did it*

2. *It was surprising how cold it was*
3. *It was very strange, the way he behaved*
4. *It was very cold yesterday*
5. *It was undecided who was to peel the potatoes*
6. *It was a clever ploy to gain a further extension*
7. *It was on a cold morning in June that we set out*
8. *It was a cold winter's morning*
9. *It was a Honda, the car she was driving*

Part B

Looking at Language in Context

9 | From separate sentences to connected text

9.1 Some preliminary considerations

In the preceding chapters, we have dealt with grammatical possibilities involving elements 'below' sentence level, such as words, phrases and clauses. In particular, we were concerned with the inflectional forms of words (singular/plural, present tense/past tense, etc.), and with the ways individual words can be combined into phrases, phrases into clauses and clauses into sentences. These issues, known as morphology and syntax respectively, are what are usually considered to be the domain of grammar proper. Furthermore, it is important to note that in those chapters we have always used as our examples artificially constructed sentences, specifically designed to illustrate a particular point.

The main concerns of this part of the book (text analysis), on the other hand, are categories operating 'above' sentence level and our illustrations are mostly taken from 'real life' texts. We will be using several extended texts as our resource material throughout Part B, and these texts appear in full in the appendix. In addition, short illustrations: jokes, proverbs, snippets of overheard conversation are quoted here and there throughout.

Not only have the examples used in Part A been specifically constructed to illustrate certain grammatical points, but they have generally been restricted to a special type of sentence, the informationally unmarked basic sentence (see Section 2.5). Not until the very last chapter of Part A did we acknowledge that the elements of a sentence can be combined in a number of different ways. The different combinations that we select as speakers/writers in the communication process are motivated by considerations of style rather than grammaticality. Sentences that show variation between active and passive, cleft and non-cleft, and the like, are all equally grammatically acceptable, in contrast to the un-English ordering of, for example, N Dv Adj in the NP *dog the black*. Our choices here are motivated rather by such matters as **register**[1] appropriateness and the need to create a good flow of information between the separate sentences. It will be primarily such choices that will concern us in Part B.

Before turning our attention to how texts are created, we must introduce an important digression. In 'real life' texts, both spoken and written, we often encounter 'fuzzy' areas: structures which contemporary grammarians label variously **non-sentences, irregular sentences** or **minor sentences**. Such structures are extremely common; in fact they dominate some of the registers which are most familiar to the average person, notably informal conversations and newspaper headlines, which we will be examining in Chapters 10 and 11.

9.2 Reconsidering sentences

At school, from the time when students begin to write factual texts, they are urged not to produce so-called **sentence fragments** – in other words incomplete sentences, usually subordinate clauses or prepositional phrases, which are punctuated as separate sentences:

> He'll be in hospital for quite a bit longer. **At least another week.**

Such 'sentence fragments' are usually easy to 'correct' by altering the punctuation or supplying a missing main clause. In certain registers, for example advertisements, such sentence fragments may be used deliberately to reflect the intonation of casual speech:

> ... *soon the time came to pack the day away.* **Until next weekend, anyway.**   (Appendix C)
> **Just when you thought it was safe to go back into the water.**
>   (Advertisement for film, *Jaws*)

In Section 7.1 we raised the problem that the notion of sentence poses for the analysis of spoken language as, in recent years, it has been shown that spoken language is not readily analysable

---

[1] Register is a term used in sociolinguistics and stylistics to refer to situational varieties of language, e.g. scientific or religious English (see Chapter 10).

into the structures and constituents normally expected of a sentence. To the general public a sentence has reality either as 'the expression of a complete thought' or in terms of punctuation; that is, 'a sentence begins with a capital letter and ends with a full stop'. Nevertheless, it is obvious that especially in informal written language we often find units – minor sentences – which are punctuated as sentences, but which are even more severely defective than the examples above. The following sections will examine the forms of and the motivation for minor sentences.

9.2.1 Form of minor sentences

In their form, all minor sentences are characterised by reduction. There are three basic subtypes:

1. Ellipsis Constructions characterised by ellipsis involve the omission of various obligatory clause or phrase elements, which must be recoverable in their precise form from either the immediate context or the surrounding text (**co-text**) or on the basis of our knowledge of the grammar of English. Ellipsis may involve the omission of a main clause, as in the above example from *Jaws*. It may also involve the omission of clause elements. Thus in addition to the ellipsis found in co-ordinated and comparative constructions (see Sections 7.2, 7.3.4), and to the usual omission of subject *you* in imperative clauses, other normally obligatory constituents may be omitted. For example, in informal speech dialogue responses are often drastically minimal.

1. *Are you ready?* ***In a minute.***
   Well, where are you? ***Coming.***

In the following examples, the common response *Because* and the comment *Stupid buses* are so cryptic that interpretation can be achieved only on the basis of shared knowledge.

2. *Why are you so grumpy?* ***Because.***
3. (Mother and son meeting at the front door of their house)

   A: *Hi! Off again? Where to now?*

B. *Rehearsal ... Gotta rush ... Stupid buses ...*

In some written genres – postcards, diaries, telegrams and personal letters – NPs in subject function, auxiliary verbs and other closed class items such as determinatives and prepositions are typically omitted. In instructional writing, for instance recipes, NPs in object function may also be omitted if predictable from the preceding text. Headlines tend to omit the copula *be* as well as the closed class elements.

4. (Note on fridge)
   Gone fishing. Back Monday.

5. (Newspaper headlines)
   Girl happy to help homeless.
   Noah way ark exists: scientist.
   Theory on health not watertight.

6. (From a recipe)
   Beat whites with half the sugar till stiff and set aside.

Following are some possible 'restored' versions, with the recovered constituents in boldface and with relevant labels.

1a. $\overset{S}{(\textbf{\textit{I}})}$ $\overset{P}{(\textbf{\textit{will be}})}$ $\overset{PC}{(\textbf{\textit{ready}})}$ *in a minute*
     NP   VP   AdjP

     $\overset{S}{(\textbf{\textit{I}})}$ $\overset{P\ M}{(\ \textbf{\textit{am}}\ coming)}$
     NP   VP Aux

2a. $\overset{S}{(\textbf{\textit{I}})}$ $\overset{P}{(\textbf{\textit{am}})}$ $\overset{PC}{(\textbf{\textit{so grumpy}})}$ *because ...*
     NP   VP   AdjP

3a. *Hi!* [$\overset{P}{(\textbf{\textit{Are}})}$ $\overset{S}{(\textbf{\textit{you}})}$ *off again?*] [*Where* $\overset{P}{(\textbf{\textit{are}})}$ $\overset{S}{(\textbf{\textit{you}})}$
           VP   NP   VP   NP

     $\overset{Cx}{(\textbf{\textit{off}})}$ *to now?*]
     AdvP

[(*I*) (*'m going*) (*to a rehearsal*)] [(*I*) (*'ve got to rush*)]
NP   VP   PP   NP   VP Aux

(*These* stupid buses) (*are*) (*so unpredictable*)]
NP Dv   VP   AdjP

4a. [(*I*) (*'ve* gone) fishing] [(*I*) (*will be*) back
    NP   VP Aux   NP   VP

(*on* (Monday))]
PP Prep   NP

5a. (*A girl*) (*is*) happy to help (*the* homeless)
   NP Dv   VP   NP Dv

[(*There*) (*is*) Noah {i.e., no way} (*the* ark)
   NP   VP   NP Dv

exists: (*according to*) (*a scientist*)
      Prep   NP Dv

(*The theory on health*) (*is*) not watertight
NP Dv   VP

6a. Beat (*the* egg whites) with half (*of* (the
      NP Dv   N   Prep   NP

sugar)) till (*the egg whites*) (*are*)
         NP   VP

stiff and set (*them*) aside
       NP

Note: Block language, a special form of language found in public notices, product labels, dictionary and glossary entries as well as some headlines, often involves reduction to a single NP. The shorter items are often printed entirely in capital letters and lack neutral punctuation such as full stops. (However, marked and emotive punctuation, such as exclamation and question marks, may be used, e.g. *Warning!*.)

2. Formulaic non-sentences The items in this category are extremely reduced in form, very often consisting of one word only and commonly using forms not in general use in present-day English. All of them, however, are frequently used in everyday conversation. The two main sub-categories here are **phatic** and **poetic** (see Chapter 10 for discussion of these terms).

Phatic communion is the term used for stereotyped uses of language, often accompanied by physical actions, in everyday social activities. Phatic uses of language include:

(a) Greetings, exclamations, apologies, congratulations and expletives:
   Hi! Great movie! Appalling! Sorry. Shit!
(b) Conversational 'continuatives':
   Absolutely! Indeed! Sure! Try me! Will do. Not at all. Well ... Now ...
(c) Commands, offers, inquiries:
   Hands on heads! Back to bed! Taxi! My turn? Another coffee, please!
(d) Totally idiomatic expressions, such as: *How come? Guess what!*

Many of the items in the poetic category are reduced in form. However, their main distinguishing feature is the deliberate use of 'poetic devices' such as parallelism, rhyme and alliteration. Examples are:

(a) Proverbs: *Better late than never. More haste, less speed. No pain, no gain.*
(b) Slogans: *The more you spread, the more you spread.*
(c) Road safety signs: *Drowsy drivers die. Don't drive with .05. Stop Revive Survive. Ease up, don't smash up.*

3. Irregular sentences These are constructions which appear to be regular in their surface form, but which are not subject to the grammatical processes typical for normal sentences. Miscellaneous expressions, usually informal in nature and well-established historically, appear to be normal well-formed sentences, such as *Go to hell*. This item, in keeping with the normal construction of imperatives, does not contain the subject element, but is not reduced in any other way. It is, however, irregular; we are not able to vary it in any of the ways available to normal sentences in English: it cannot reverse its polarity (e.g. *Don't go to hell*); nor can we substitute any other verb in the structural paradigm (e.g. *Come to hell*), although there are parallel expressions which involve a change in the NP, such as *Go to the devil* and *Go to blazes*.

An additional category includes expressions which have become 'ossified', (i.e. preserved in the language for a long period of time and enshrining linguistic usages which have since become obsolete). Many of these involve the **subjunctive mood**, a mood additional to those descrtibed in Section 6.4 (the declarative, the imperative, the interrogative and the exclamative) used in older forms of English to express actions with uncertain outcomes, as in wishes and hypothetical statements. Modern English preserves a few relics of the subjunctive mood in expressions such as *Bless you! God forbid! So be it!*

9.2.2 Functions of minor sentences

There are a number of reasons why minor sentences should be regarded as pragmatically preferable to their expanded counterparts. Most minor sentences are produced in informal situations, where the immediate presence of the participating parties presupposes shared knowledge of the context. We could therefore invoke the 'principle of least effort': informal situations encourage us to 'take it easy'. Thus we readily use and accept phonetic processes resulting in, for example, the blend *gotta* and morphological processes resulting in, for example, the clipping *flu* (from *influenza*).

Newspaper headlines, road signs, labels and public notices are usually restricted in space and, importantly, often need to be read and understood at a glance. It makes sense therefore to omit any easily predictable and consequently redundant words. Moreover, the abbreviated versions are an effective way of presenting material which needs to attract immediate attention or to be memorised with relative precision.

They come directly to the point, may be more intriguing than their expanded counterparts and often exploit other linguistic resources which promote easy memorisation: balance, parallelism, word play and sound effects such as alliteration and rhyme. Consider the expanded versions of labels such as *Poisonous drug – do not ingest (This is a poisonous drug – do not ingest it)* or road signs such as *Wrong way, go back* or *No Entry*; *(You are going the wrong way, go back)* and *(This is not the entry)*. In all such cases the expanded version is less effective than its minor sentence counterpart. The omission of predictable items enables the 'new information' (see Section 8.1) to be foregrounded.

9.3 What is a text?

We have already encountered a number of texts in Section 9.2.1. Examples (1–6) were texts, as well as the various proverbs, slogans, road signs and other examples cited. Texts consisting of one sentence or an even smaller unit are unusual: we are more likely to cite as examples of texts units such as this book, a poem discussed in this book, a journal review of this book, or a radio interview with one of the authors of this book. However, a text may be as long as a 12-part television series or as short as the one-word notice *Danger*. It may be spoken or written, spontaneous or prepared, produced by one person or many. Unlike inflections, words, phrases and sentences, a text is not a unit of grammar. It is defined as a product of communication, a piece of language whose shape is motivated by its semantic purposes and pragmatic roles.

What gives a random collection of sentences, or even a single isolated word, the property of textuality is a combination of text-internal links and text-external relevance. Linguists commonly refer to these two factors respectively as **cohesion** and **coherence**. Cohesion is the type of organisation in a text that is created by the presence (or absence) in each sentence of distinctive, recognisable linguistic items which relate it to preceding and following sentences. These items, which include pronouns, coordinators, subordinators and repeated lexical items, will be discussed in detail in Section 9.4. It is important to note, however, that the absence of formal cohesion may not in itself prevent a stretch of language from being identified as a text. Take the example:

7. A: *The phone's ringing*
   B: *I'm washing my hair*

Most readers will assume that the sequence of sentences in (7) constitutes a text; that is that speaker B's utterance is not a *non sequitur*, even though its relationship to speaker A's utterance is indirect and relies heavily on inferences being drawn by the two speakers.

Nor does the presence of formal cohesion guarantee a collection of sentences the status of a text. The following examples may be cohesive, but they lack coherence:

8. I bought an old Ford. The car which President Ford used was black. Black English has been recently in the news. The latest news is that the drought will break next week. A week has seven days. Yesterday I found a cat. The fat cat sat on the mat. The word *mat* has three letters. I have just received a letter from my Mum ...

9. Fire engines sit 6 in the front and 6 in the back
   6 and 6 makes 12
   12 inches is a ruler
   Queen Elizabeth ruled the seven seas
   Seas have fish
   Fish have fins
   The Finns fought the Soviets
   The Soviet flag is red

However, consider example (9) again, this time prefaced by the question *Hey, do you know why fire engines are red?* and concluded by the clincher *And that's why fire engines are red.* It will now be recognised by most people as an example of a riddle, specifically of the 'shaggy-dog' joke variety, where the humour is derived precisely from the apparent mismatch between its cohesiveness and its apparent lack of coherence.

Whilst cohesion is an internal property of texts – an objective matter, capable of automatic recognition – coherence recognises the fact that linguistic communication takes place in an extra-linguistic environment. What is felt to be a text must be so because it has a recognised function and form in some 'real life' situation. Given a little imagination, we must be able to provide or invent some plausible potential extra-linguistic context for the stretch of language in question. As speakers, we tend to assume that any sequence must 'make sense' and will draw on a number of possible resources to make it so. We will use the immediate context in which we find ourselves, our socially and culturally 'shared' knowledge, and any inferences which seem viable. Our implicit knowledge of what H. P. Grice called the 'co-operative principle',[2] will predispose us to thinking that *I'm washing my hair* in (7) above is intended as a sensible response under the circumstances.

Another area where we must take into consideration the apparent inconsistencies between grammatical structure and language use is that of so-called indirect speech acts. For instance, it is generally considered more polite in English to express requests and commands in the form of interrogatives, or even declaratives with embedded interrogatives, rather than as imperatives. Thus *Close the door!* is less polite than *would you please close the door* or *I was wondering if you'd mind closing the door.*

And what teenager has not been tempted to respond to the indirect request *Do you have the time?* by merely answering *Yes?* As a final example of the situational considerations pertinent to the notion of coherence (which is more fully discussed in Chapter 10 below) consider the *because-* clause in *What's the time, because I've got to go out at eight?* The function of this clause is difficult to explain unless we take into account the

---

[2] The 'co-operative principle', first proposed by H. P. Grice, an American philosopher, in 1975, is characterised by the following maxims: in any conversation the speaker will typically be truthful and relevant, contribute to the conversation as much material as is necessary and appropriate to the purposes of the conversation, and avoid the expression of this information in an obscure or ambiguous manner.

speaker's intentions: more specifically, the speaker's explanation for the asking of the question.

9.4 Cohesion

It is possible to identify a number of connective 'devices' which interact closely and simultaneously to provide 'texture'. On the 'macro' level these include deictic, generic and logical 'signposts' which contribute to the overall shaping of a text. On the 'micro' level, cohesion is achieved by **co-reference**, **substitution** and **ellipsis**, the use of connective words and phrases, and the various patternings of lexis, sound and visual effects. This section will present in some detail the various categories of cohesion; while Section 9.5 will present analyses of the cohesive patterns in several extended texts.

9.4.1 Text orientation

Most sequences of language-in-use will contain *deictic* items which enable readers/hearers to find their bearings by situating the sequence in both its context and its co-text, indicating who is doing what and to whom and under what circumstances and at what given point in time. So a lecture is likely to begin with, for example:

> **Today I** would like to **begin** the detailed analysis of ...
>
> *In **this** lecture **we** are going to **continue**/ **complete** ...*
>
> ***You** will remember that **last** week **we**/ **you** began ...*

English contains a number of such deictic items:

- **Participant identification** The first and second person pronouns are commonly used deictically to establish the speech participants' identities. The third person pronouns may be used deictically to refer to entities outside the text. This deictic use of personal pronouns is to be distinguished from their anaphoric or text-internal use (i.e. as 'co-referential proforms', see Sections 3.3 and 9.4.3). In formal writing participant identification is often avoided (e.g. *The management regrets any inconvenience during repairs to the premises*.) On the other hand, in registers such as telephone conversations and legal writing, participant identification tends to be very precise *(e.g. Hi, Mary? It's Sue; I, the undersigned, declare ...)*

- **Place and time indicators** The meanings of adverbs such as *here, there, now, then* and *today* are entirely dependent on one's knowledge of the context in which they are found. The *here* and the *now*, with reference to the present time and the place where this book is being written, will be totally different for me, the writer in this very instance, and you, each unknown reader and your particular situation when you read it.

- **Temporal ordering expressions** Certain adjectives, adverbs, ordinal numerals, PPs and NPs provide temporal ordering, previous to or subsequent to or concurrent with a given time reference. Examples include:

  Adjectives: *former, previous, following, earlier, later*
  Adverbs: *already, then, meanwhile, lastly, finally, initially*
  Ordinals: *first, second, one-hundredth, next*
  PPs: *before this, until now, by now*
  NPs: *this week, next year, last Tuesday*

- **Tense and aspect** As we have seen in Section 4.3, the various tenses and aspects of English are used to relate events and situations to particular points in time and to express a range of further temporal meanings. For instance, the present tense is used not solely for activities that are simultaneous with the moment of utterance but also for events that happen 'habitually' (e.g. *I had forgotten that they **get** up very early*) or are recalled in a particularly vivid way, 'the historic present' (as in *There I was, minding my own business and they **rush** out and **start** shouting abuse at me*).

Generic signposts In addition to situating one's text with respect to the participants and the setting, we organise the material in it in such a way that the meaning of 'generic signposts' is made clear, and present it in set patterned ways. This involves the use of various signposts relevant to the genre to which the text belongs. (Further material on this topic is to be found in Chapter 10.)

- Written language is broken up into manageable 'chunks': chapters, subsections, paragraphs. Verse is arranged in lines and often stanzas. Other visual aids may be the use of bullets, different kinds of font and inset boxes. Compensating for the absence of intonation, we may resort to such tricks as 'shouting' in capitals and the use of 'smiley' faces (:-)), as found on the Internet.

- Spoken language may be organised dialogically, for instance in 'adjacency pairs', and signposted with various conversational continuatives or 'discourse particles' such as *well, now* and *oh*, and other interactive elements such as *you know, I mean* and *you see*. These items may indicate the speaker's intention to continue as well as involving the hearer in the communicative process. Typically, for example, *well* is used in dialogue as a sign of thinking or a show of reluctance, *now* is used to indicate a new incident or argument and is often common in extended monologues, such as university lectures. Note that these items, when used cohesively, are phonologically reduced, in contrast to their full lexical status.

- We often use institutionalised generic openings to alert the addressee to what is to come:

Knock knock
Did you hear the one about ...
Once upon a time ...
Unaccustomed as I am to ...

Logical progression

Different genres will tend to feature distinctive types of logical progression:

- Instructional texts as well as typical narratives and descriptions tend to introduce new material in a logical, often chronological, sequence (as in a recipe: *First take ... then add ... and then ...*)

- Information or expository texts tend to introduce one main point at a time and discuss various factors associated with it in a balanced manner. So a formal discussion may use phrases like *On the one hand ... on the other hand ...* A paragraph from a linguistics textbook is likely to introduce the topic in a topic sentence or subheading, and discuss each ensuing point in separate 'bullets' or subsections. Another technique is to create a chainlike effect between the focal, or 'new', information from one clause and the topic of the following clause. For example, *I read **a most interesting book** last week. **It** was about ...*

- Some texts may choose to meander exploratively from one point to another, often admitting to their digressiveness with the explicit *By the way ...*
- Other patterns of text development include moving from the general to the particular or vice versa, backtracking to make one's intention clear, or summarising the points made up to that stage. Special adjuncts employed for these purposes include *in effect, in particular, generally speaking, let's recap ...*

Most large texts will employ a number of different strategies, at any given point selecting those that seem most appropriate to the matter at hand.

9.4.2 Information 'packaging'

As well as using explicit orientation devices to guide the hearer/reader through a text, we can also make this easier by varying the way in which we package the information within the sentence. All language, whether spoken or written, is linear in time and space: we must begin somewhere and proceed one item at a time. In Chapter 8 we stated that there is a strong tendency in English for topic expressions to appear early, while focal and complex, lengthy items tend to appear later within the structure of a sentence. In speech this tendency to begin with the known, 'given' information and lead towards the unknown, 'new' items is supported by stress, rhythm and intonation. Informationally marked (unusual, less expected) structures, such as topicalisation, cleft and passive voice, may indicate prosodic features not present in writing.

Marked information structures may also strengthen a text's cohesive force by bringing compared or contrasted items closer together and by deliberately drawing attention to items obviously not in their regular syntactic order. Examples:

- **Topicalisation**
  I don't mind large dogs, **but tiny lap dogs I can't stand.**
  You'll need a warm coat for Europe. **In London it would be most unusual to need one.**

- **Cleft**
  Paul is my older son. **It was he who ...**
  It was Dave, the other one, who ...

- **Passive**
  John hit Paul with all the strength he could muster. **Paul had been hit many times before,** *but he was caught off guard.*

Active and passive structures allow us to change our perspective on the 'actor' and the 'patient' by alternating them in the topic position. Such alternation may produce the chain-like effect mentioned in the preceding section; that is, the 'new' (Paul) is immediately picked up as the 'given' in the following sentence and the pattern may be repeated a number of times in the text.

9.4.3 Grammatical cohesion

The cohesive devices described in this section are referred to as 'grammatical', in so far as they involve either closed-class words or grammatical categories such as definiteness and comparison.

Cohesion may be achieved through the use of **proforms** (the grammatical items which may be either co-referential or substitute). If the reference is to the same item as in the co-text, the link is said to be **co-reference**; in **substitution** the proform refers to a similar but different entity, that is, a different token of the same type. If the linkage is by **ellipsis**, all mention of the original item is omitted the second time. To illustrate:

10. A: ***That book*** [original reference] *you lent me over Easter – where did you buy **it** [co-ref = that book]? 'Coz I'd like to get **one** [substitution = another copy of that one] for myself.*

   B: ***It** wasn't mine, but you can get **one** at the Co-op. Would you mind getting me **one** too?*

   A: (i) *Sure, I'd love to [ellipsis = get you a copy].*
      (ii) *OK, will do [ellipsis = I; substitution do = get you a copy too].*
      (iii) *Of course not [substitution not = I wouldn't mind...]*

In **anaphoric** reference the proforms point back, referring to items already mentioned (see (12) below). Forward, or **cataphoric** reference (see (11) below) is much rarer. Examples of *this*, used in the two different manners below, are found in 'Mysteries' (see Appendix G):

   11. *In a version from the Austrian Tyrol, it runs like **this** ...*

   12. *Fairy stories like **this** ...*

Note that the original referent item must be found in the co-text, not the context. Many of the proforms, especially personal and demonstrative pronouns, are also commonly used deictically (see Section 9.4.1) and as such are not cohesive.

Grammatical cohesion is characterised by reduction, the maximally reduced option, ellipsis, generally being chosen whenever it is possible, especially in informal speech. The purpose of such reduction is in part to avoid repetition and redundancy and in part to force us to seek out for ourselves, in the adjacent text, the precise referent for the missing or vague items. Topics are often pronominalised: in fiction protagonists are usually referred to by personal pronouns; in non-fiction, pronoun reference is often made to sections of discourse rather than to concrete entities (as in (11) and (12) above).

Note: Not all abbreviation is cohesive, for instance see the categories other than ellipsis discussed in Section 9.2. Nor is all repetition to be avoided. Many 'poetic' cohesive devices (see Section 9.4.6) are based on repetition of phonological and syntactic patterns, and lexical repetition (see Section 9.4.5) is also a strongly cohesive strategy.

Co-reference proforms
Personal and reflexive pronouns: *I, you, he, she, myself, yourself, himself, herself*
Possessive pronouns and determiners: *mine, yours, his, hers, my, your, his, her*
Demonstrative pronouns: *this, that, these, those*
Definite pronoun/ determiner: *such*
Definite adverbs: *here, there, then*

Substitute proforms
Indefinite pronouns: *one(s), some, any, none, another, other(s), either, neither, several, enough, each, all, half, both, few, (a) little, many, much*, and the comparative and superlative forms of the last four items
Demonstrative pronouns: *that, this, these, those*
Pro-verb: *do*
Clausal proform: *so, thus*
Comparison items: *the same, likewise, similarly*
Complex proforms, combining several categories: *do so, do likewise* ...

There are a number of important differences between co-reference and substitution:

* As stated above, co-reference proforms must refer to an identical item in the co-text, whilst substitution proforms refer to another item of the same type. Comparison and contrast provide textual cohesion by substitution.
* Co-reference proforms are always pronouns or pronoun-related adverbs; that is, they always refer to NPs. Substitution proforms do not have to be pronouns. Substitution can, in principle, replace any kind of constituent, verbal or clausal as well as pronominal. The verbal substitute *do* can only be a main verb. Compare the following:

(i)   *John has **done** an excellent job.*
(ii) ***Did** John work hard?*
(iii) *John worked harder than he'd ever **done** before.*

In (i) *do* is a main verb, head of a VP, but it is not a pro-form as it does not substitute for any other verb. In (ii) *do* is an operator, used to satisfy the requirements of an interrogative construction. Only in (iii) is *do* a proform, a substitute serving to avoid the repetition of *worked*.

The predicative proform *so* and its negative equivalent *not* can substitute for an AdjP or an NP functioning as a complement, as well as for a *that*-clause in direct object function (e.g. *He was tall and **so** is his brother*; *I was told **so/ that** ...*; *I believe **not/that** ...*).

- Co-reference proforms are always definite. Similarly, one of the main functions of the definite determiner *the* is to provide cohesion. By contrast, many substitute proforms are indefinite quantitative pronouns, that is, pronouns used to express an indefinite amount or quantity, such as *same*, and *several*.
- While co-reference proforms must allow the original item to be restored in its exact form, substitution allows for such variation as contrastive polarity or difference in number.

Note: There are two substitute proforms *one*, one taking *some* as its plural and the other taking *ones*. *One/some* is a substitute for an indefinite NP, as in:

13. A: Can you buy me a few apples? I feel like **one**.
     B: I'll get you **some** this afternoon.

One/ones is a substitute for a sub-part of the referents of an NP. *One/ones* functions as the head of the NP and must be accompanied by at least one determiner or modifier, as in:

14. *I must get us **a good knife**? We don't have **any sharp ones** ...*

Little needs to be added here regarding ellipsis, as we have already fully discussed it in Section 9.2. Its distribution parallels substitution: ellipsis can be pronominal, verbal or clausal. In the following examples, the caret (^) is used to indicate the site of the ellipsis. Medial ellipsis usually omits verbs; for instance *Usually Paul drives the Saab and I ^ the Toyota*. In some cases the main verb and some of its complements may be omitted; for instance *We haven't seen it yet, but we will ^ by the end of the month*. In finite clauses ellipsis is usually final, leaving out as much of the predicate as possible. Typically, only the subject and the predicator remain. Elliptical NPs, especially if contrastive, also commonly result from final ellipsis, with heads and post-modifiers tending to be omitted. For example:

15. *My own camera, like Peter's ^, is Japanese.*

It may be difficult to distinguish between substitution and ellipsis with items such as *that, those, some, none*, etc. For example:

16. *When the children came, **each** was given a toy.*

Do we analyse this as involving substitution (of the NP *each child* by the proform *each*) or as ellipsis (either with omission of the head *child*, or alternatively with ellipsis of the partitive PP *of the children* and *each* as pronoun head)?

In the next example, *those* may involve either substitution for *the ones*, for *the quartets* or alternatively ellipsis of the head *quartet*:

17. *Beethoven's late string quartets are better than those that he wrote earlier.*

9.4.4 Logical connectors

The 'logical' items discussed in this section (coordinators, subordinators and connective adjuncts) are usually treated as markers of grammatical cohesion. There are, however, important differences between these and the grammatical items discussed in the last section. Unlike proform and ellipsis, where a previously mentioned entity or predication is linked to a later mention of the same, and where this later reference is at best vague or else altogether missing from the surface structure of the text, relationships brought out by logical connectors are both precise and explicit. Thus this category is somewhat like lexical cohesion (see Section 9.4.5).

Four different types of logical connections may be recognised: additive, adversative, causal and temporal. All the types of logical connectors may be used in each category. As already discussed in Chapters 5 and 7, coordinators and subordinators generally operate within a sentence. The adjuncts may be adverbs or closely related PPs and typically operate to link together separate sentences. These are much less strongly incorporated into the structure of the sentence of which they are a constituent and are therefore known as peripheral dependents. They are typically initial in the sentence, foregrounded to stress their cohesive function, and are usually separated by a comma from the rest of the clause. A selective list follows:

Additive: *and; besides, furthermore, in addition*
Adversative: *but; however, nevertheless, despite this*
Causal: *for; consequently, as a result*
Temporal: *while; previously, subsequently, after that*

9.4.5 Lexical cohesion

Lexical cohesion, which reinforces the unity of a text by repetition of its key words and concepts, is a very strong form of cohesion. Whereas in the case of proforms, the reader/hearer must seek out in the adjacent text the original item on which the proform is dependent, with lexical cohesion the topic of discussion is established and maintained by overt reference to items associated with it. For instance, items related to cooking are used in a recipe, linguistics-specific terminology in this book.

A word may be repeated in its exact form or a derivative

(for instance *friend, friendship, friendly*) may be used. Alternatively, the concept may be reiterated by the use of a synonym or another sense-related word. Linkage by the repetition of forms is obtrusive and tends to be avoided. Instead, handbooks on style recommend 'elegant variation'; that is, the use of synonyms as in *start, begin, commence*. However, in legal language, where misinterpretation is of greater concern than elegance of style, exact repetition is tolerated and even encouraged.

One basic sense-relation which develops **lexical sets** is inclusion (**hyponymy**). A **hypernym** is a superordinate word or phrase with a general meaning, for instance *flower*, and can be said to include a number of more specific terms, **hyponyms** (e.g. *rose, iris, lupin*). *Bed, table, chair* are said to be **co-hyponyms** of *furniture*. Often serving as hypernyms are 'general nouns' (basic categorisers such as *person, child, people, creature, thing, place* and 'summary words' which refer to whole slabs of text or context material, for instance, *situation, matter, question*, as well as the vague and whimsical *thingamajigs* and *gismos* we rely on in times of conversational pressure).

Other important sense-relations which need to be specified here are **synonymy** and **antonymy**, **synecdoche** and **metonymy**, and **collocation**. Like hyponymy, all these are based on particular kinds of association: synonymy and antonymy on similarity and contrast, synecdoche and metonymy on part/whole relationships, and collocation on the habitual association of various structural and lexical forms. Words that are synonymous share only a basic denotative core of meaning, but typically differ in their connotations, as in the case of the connotations of *climb* (a mountain), *ascend* (to heaven) and *mount* (a horse). Antonyms are words belonging to mutually exclusive categories. Three different forms of contrast are distinguishable. **Gradable** antonyms operate on a continuum, for example *hot, (warm), cold*. **Complementary** antonyms share an either/or relationship: a person is either *dead* or *alive, pregnant* or *non-pregnant*. Finally, **converse**, or relational, antonyms exist by virtue of each other, for instance *give* and *take, buy* and *sell, parent* and *child*. Synecdoche is a figurative device involving the use of a part of something to represent the whole, the whole for a part, or any subcategory to stand for the whole category, for instance *Lend me a hand, a head of cattle*, or the so-called gender neutral use of *man* to represent all human beings, male and female alike. Metonymy represents a similar but more general association, where the name of one thing is used figuratively for another, as in *The Crown = monarchy, Canberra = the Government of Australia*. Consider some of the metonyms for police officers: *cops* (from the copper buttons on police uniforms), *bobbies* (from Sir Robert Peel), *the law*. Collocations present a particular problem in that they must be learnt in their exact form: it rains *cats and dogs* not *dogs and cats*, we say *to and fro* not *to and from*, and butter may be *rancid* but not *rotten*.

As in the case of other cohesive relationships, different types of lexical cohesion tend to be associated with different registers. Science textbooks and technical journals in particular favour the use of hyponymy. Persuasive material often depends on antonymy in order to create and emphasise a sense of both contrast and inclusion, for example:

> *Men and women of Australia, …*
> *Whatever the weather, hot or cold, …*

9.4.6 'Poetic' features contributing to cohesion

The 'poetic' function of language, as described by Roman Jakobson, will be more fully discussed in the next chapter. However, a number of those features of language which are used for the sake of the pure enjoyment of form – repetition of sounds, parallelism of structures, novel uses of words – provide an additional level of textual connectivity. Many such devices had been designed by ancient preliterate societies to aid accurate retention and effective communication of important historical and ritual material, such as genealogies and legal details, prayers and expressions of collective wisdom.

Poetic devices exist at every level of language. Phonological repetition, such as alliteration and rhyme, is used to draw attention to linked meanings, and to make these associations easier to remember. Alliteration, especially, is used extensively in advertisements, political speeches, newspaper headlines, proverbs, and product and shop names. More overtly playful material, such as tongue-twisters and nicknames, is another fruitful area for these devices. Some examples are: *Tiny Tim, Big Ben, Dead as a dodo/doorknob, Look before you leap, Pasta Pantry,* as well as various informal reduplicative words such as *mishmash, zigzag* and *walkie talkie.* The same cohesive force can be created by word play and by structural parallelism. *Cancer is a word, not a sentence* illustrates both. Other examples are *Out of sight, out of mind* and *Garbage in, garbage out,* as well as shop names such as *A cut above* and *The Head Quarters* (both for hairdressers). Triadic parallelism is common, as it creates an impression of order and regularity and effectively leads us to a sense of accomplishment and climax. Some well-known triads are *thesis/antithesis/synthesis, Liberty, Equality, Fraternity* and *government of the people, by the people and for the people.*

9.5 Analysis of cohesion in sample texts

To illustrate how the various cohesive patterns outlined in Section 9.4 operate over a considerable stretch of 'real language', let us turn to two very different texts.

Our first example, the first section of this chapter (Section 9.1), has been deliberately constructed as a transitional passage between the two separate parts of this book, forming a bridge between Part A, with its primarily sentence-internal grammatical orientation, and Part B, dealing with problems and strategies associated with developing and structuring texts. The contrasts between Parts A and B are evident at every level of Section 9.1 – word, phrase, sentence and paragraph. These contrasts are brought out by the explicit grammatical parallelism of the opening words of the first paragraph, *In the preceding chapters,* and those of the second paragraph, *The main concerns of this part of the book* and are followed by further juxtapositions of:

> *grammatical possibilities* with *(text analysis)*
> *'below' sentence level* with *'above' sentence level*
> *artificially constructed sentences* with *'real-life' texts*

Note that the inverted commas and structural parallelism emphasising the semantic opposition of the complementary antonyms *below* and *above* show that several cohesive devices may be exploited concurrently.

The tense and aspect of the verbs further reinforce the contrast between parts A and B: in the first paragraph *have dealt*, *were concerned*, *have ... used*, in the second paragraph *are*, *will be using*. The temporal adverbs *usually* and *always* comment on the practice followed up to this point and are paralleled by *on the other hand* in the second paragraph.

Whilst the first and second paragraphs have led us through the macro-issues of grammaticality and stylistic variation, the third paragraph needs to point us to the business of the next section (Section 9.2). The contrasts explicitly set up in the third and fourth paragraphs therefore centre on the word *sentence*, firstly, juxtaposing the informationally unmarked sentences with those that are informationally marked, and secondly, introducing the digression to be dealt with in Section 9.2 (i.e. the contrast between sentences and non-sentences).

Throughout Section 9.1, specific devices are used to establish text orientation. The sub-heading 'Some preliminary considerations' identifies the section's content and is generic to an academic or pedagogic text. Participant identification is via the exclusive *we*, that is, *we, the authors*, again in keeping with texts such as this. A number of specific items identify the contrast: demonstratives *in these chapters*, *those chapters*, *this part of the book*, the adjective *preceding*, proforms *such* and *this*, the PPs *throughout Part B*, *in Part A* and *in the Appendix*. A number of adjuncts suggest logical progression: *on the other hand*, *furthermore*, *in particular*, *in fact*.

Several marked clause constructions contribute cohesive effect:

> Extraposition: *it is important to note that*
> Cleft: *it will be primarily such choices...*
> Passive: *our choices...*
> Object to subject repetition: *structures*

As well, Section 9.1 exhibits a considerable degree of lexical cohesion.

- The topics of grammar and style are established by a number of hyponymic sets. For example:

  grammar: morphology, syntax

  inflectional forms: singular/plural, present tense/past tense

  elements below sentence level: words, phrases, clauses

  There is one instance of a general word, *issues.* Another set of words: *jokes, proverbs, conversation, headlines,* points to the fact that this part of the book will deal with 'real life' texts.
- Contrasts are developed through the antonyms *same/different, extended/short, spoken/written, active/passive.*
- There is full repetition of important items *different, choices, structures.*

In contrast to the highly explicit and obviously cohesive text just examined, our second text, e. e. cummings's poem, 'anyone lived in a pretty how town' (see Appendix A for full text). presents a somewhat disconcerting collage of disconnected images, deviant syntax and minimal punctuation. There are only two full stops (and consequently only two capital letters), but an unexpectedly high degree of parenthesis. In the first stanza alone we find the following irregularities: the adverb *how* in a typically adjectival position, misplaced preposition *up* and present participle *floating* in line 2 (compare 'with so many bells floating up [and] down') and ungrammatical collocations *sang his didn't* and *danced his did.* Collocative possibilities for *sang his x* and *danced his y* are very limited in English, only *sang his song/aria* ... is allowed. Tensed verbs such as *didn't/did* are certainly not acceptable as NP heads.

Moreover, the poem opens with the indefinite pronoun *anyone.* Most pronouns are inherently definite: they stand for particular individuals, who are identifiable from the context. Only a small group of pronouns are indefinite, that is, they cannot be specifically identified, and these include *anyone, someone, no one.* Beginning a clause with the indefinite pronoun *anyone* suggests two possibilities:

1. A conversational elliptical question: *Anyone know where the cat is?*
2. *Anyone* followed by a restrictive relative clause: *Anyone who'd lived there would know.*

Both expectations are frustrated by our text. However, following through the whole set of indefinite pronouns, *anyone* (stanza 1), *no one* (3), *someones and everyones* (5), we can see that, together with the more expected items *women and men* (2 and 9) and *children* (3 and 6), they form a set of the poem's protagonists. Note that *anyone* is established as a specific individual by *women and men ... cared for anyone not at all.* The indefinite pronoun reading would have been given by 'they didn't care for anyone at all'. Furthermore, *anyone* and *no one* are revealed to be male and female respectively by the coreferential relationship established with the possessive pronouns *his* (1) and *her* (4). This is confirmed by the relationship set up in (3): *no one loved him more by more*, which suggests 'x loved y' rather than 'he was not loved by any other person'.

Other lexical sets helping to key us into the world of the poem concern the cycles of nature: the four seasons *spring, summer, autumn, winter* (1, 3 and 9) and the cycles of time and weather: *sun, moon, stars, rain* (2, 6 and 9). Notice the mimetic rotation of each set of four items in the different instances of their repetition. The cyclical nature of life is brought out also by the image of the bells (1, 6; and also *dong and ding* in 9), bells being associated with the ringing in of the seasons, and the rituals of marriages and burials. The cycle of life is likewise hinted at in the repeated image of children, forgetting as they grow up something they had known intuitively when young (3 and 6). This is emphasised by the complementary antonyms *up* and *down* (3) and by the figurative meaning of *snow* (6), associated with old age, knowledge and experience. In stanza 7, *busy folk* are at yet another stage in the cycle of life.

As expected of the compression of images associated with poetry, a number of lexical items in this poem have multiple associations:

- *Snow* collocates on the literal level with *rain* and seasons, winter stillness *(stir by still)* and the coming of spring *(bird by snow, earth by april)*. On the figurative level, its evocation of white hair and therefore age associates it with wisdom and experience (whilst children are associated with innocence). Note in stanza 6 that it is *only the snow* [that] *can begin to explain how children are apt to forget to remember* – paradoxically, since we typically associate old age with forgetfulness, as well as with wisdom.

- *Sowing* and *reaping* relate to the cycles of nature and social activities central to the poem's meaning, but also have connotations of getting one's just desserts ('you reap as you sow').

- When *anyone* dies (7), the *no one* [who] *stooped to kiss his face* is simultaneously the female protagonist, his wife, and also, in its more typical indefinite use, no other person, that is 'no one bothered to kiss him'. This image reinforces the isolation of the lovers from the rest of their community, as suggested by *women and men ... cared for anyone not at all, children guessed ...* as well as by the indifference of the image *busy folk*.

Once the cycle of life has been proposed as the central motif, other less transparent images can be fitted into this pattern. *Tree by leaf* may imply the autumnal shedding of foliage in parallel with the spring of *bird by snow*, *earth by april* and *stir by still*. Hope, future and rebirth, which are so deeply associated with spring in countries exposed to snowbound winters, may underlie the somewhat perplexing structures *wish by spirit* and *if by yes*. Hopes and dreams, as natural as sleeping and waking, a part of the cycle of life and the meaning of being human, are suggested by *sleep*, *wake*, *hope* and *slept their dream* (5).

The pattern of repeated but rearranged lines of either *spring summer autumn winter* or *sun moon snow rain* appears like a refrain in five of the nine stanzas. The poem employs relatively few rhymes; its principal cohesive device is the repetition of rhythmic patterns. Two other patterns are also constantly encountered and contribute importantly to the poem's unity. The patterns are:

1. Monotransitive (S-P-O) clauses with a personal pronoun as subject and the object NP containing a possessive pronoun which is often co-referential with the subject.

2. '*x by y*', with *x* and *y* representing various parts of speech.

A high proportion of both patterns are foregrounded by violating some co-occurrence restriction of standard English. Instances of the first construction are:

> *he sang his didn't he danced his did* (1)
>
> *they sowed their isn't they reaped their same* (2)
>
> *she laughed his joy she cried his grief* (4)
>
> *someones married their everyones* (5)
>
> *[they] laughed their cryings and did their dance* (5)
>
> *[they] said their nevers and slept their dream* (5)
>
> *they dream their sleep* (8)
>
> *[women and men] reaped their sowing and went their came* (9)

Instances of the second pattern are:

> *more by more* (3)
>
> *when by now and tree by leaf* (4)
>
> *bird by snow and stir by still* (4)
>
> *side by side* (7)
>
> *little by little and was by was* (7)
>
> *all by all and deep by deep* (8)
>
> *and more by more* (8)
>
> *earth by april* (8)
>
> *wish by spirit and if by yes* (8)

It is these two patterns which, together with the lexical set of indefinite pronouns, make this poem both coherent and cohesive. The second set builds on the standard English pattern of *side by side* and *little by little* and some of the other variants could be rendered standard with little alteration, for instance *more **and** more* and *tree **by** tree* or *leaf **by** leaf*, as well as *deeper **and** deeper*. Others, such as *was by was* and *if by yes*, gain their lyrical force from the strangeness of the construction (note that we can treat *if* as a noun in some constructions, such as *no ifs and buts*). The motif seems to suggest that life cycles change incrementally and cumulatively, little by little from the past to the future, from possibility to accomplishment. Hopes and possibilities are also picked up by the SPO pattern outlined above, some of these patterns as well being less 'alien' than others. For example, *someones married their everyones* would be acceptable if nouns or definite pronouns were substituted; *she laughed **with** joy and cried **with** grief* would be standard constructions. Some involve ungrammaticality, for instance *said their nevers, went their came* and *they sowed their isn't*, but in others it is collocational restrictions which are subverted, for example *they laughed their cryings*. Overall, the pattern suggests homely truths about life, its hopes, responsibilities and contradictions. Paradoxically, and essentially through the mechanisms of cohesion, the poem about 'anyone' develops into a vivid impressionistic picture of Everyman's (and Everywoman's) journey through life.

Exercises

Note: It is neither feasible nor advisable to supply answers for the exercises set in this part of the book. Guidelines and hints are provided for each question. The final answers are expected to show a great deal of variety and should be thought of as open-ended 'work in progress'.

1. Headlines may be characterised by structural irregularities such as ellipsis of the verb *be* and of function words such as determiners. Alternatively, an entire headline may consist of only one clause constituent, typically a noun phrase. Collect (i) a number of headlines all taken from the same newspaper and/or (ii) a number of headlines selected from different print media (newspapers, magazines, billboards). Analyse these examples in terms of form and function. (Keep your materials for further use in Chapters 10 and 11.)

2. Advertisements often contain sentence fragments. You have two advertisements included (Appendixes C and D). Use your local free newspaper or any other print media to collect a number of different advertisements (e.g. real estate,

personal, employment, luxury goods and services) and analyse these for features of irregularity and cohesion as outlined in Chapter 9 (ellipsis, lexical repetition, etc.). (Keep your data for further use in Chapter 10.)

3. Analyse the following items for features of cohesion (e.g., text orientation, proforms, lexical sets and poetic devices such as parallelism of sound and syntax).

   a. 'Fantastic caramel creamy rice' recipe (Appendix B). Look for ellipsis of function words and of objects.

   b. Army recruitment advertisement (Appendix D). Text orientation, conjunctions and lexical features are important here.

   c. 'Creature Features' (Appendix E). This is an excerpt, so there may not be many devices of text orientation. Lexical cohesion and proforms abound.

   d. FourPlay interview (Appendix F). It is particularly interesting to see how cohesive devices are passed from one speaker to another.

   e. 'Mysteries' (Appendix G). Three separate parts here, the first two being very short. Types of cohesive devices differ from part to part. Attempt to describe and compare cohesion devices typically used in Part A (Mapooram), Part B (the Austrian myth) and the first paragraph of Part C. (Note: Two introductory lines of Part C (i.e. the body of Koch's essay) are inserted between Parts A and B.)

10 | Text and context

10.1 Variation in language

In Chapter 9 we defined a text as 'a product of communication', a piece of language which exhibits not only systematic text-internal links (cohesion), but must also make sense within itself and be appropriate in its context (coherence). This chapter will describe those factors of the text-external context which are relevant to the production of texts.

As humans, we use language to accompany and facilitate virtually all our interactions with each other. We use language to inform and to deceive, to cajole and to insult, to express our deepest feelings and to amuse ourselves and others. We do not have to have training in linguistics to recognise the various ways in which the pronunciation of words and choice of words and constructions differ from day to day, from person to person, from activity to activity. Australians are amused by the New Zealanders' pronunciation of 'six' as 'sux', children are often disturbed by 'mummy's telephone voice' and know intuitively that certain 'naughty' words are best not said in front of their grandmother. We can usually recognise whether we are listening to a casual conversation or a prepared after-dinner speech, and to some extent can tell from the language alone whether it has been produced by a man or a woman, a young person or an older one, someone with a great deal of education or someone with very little. We shall discuss these aspects of language variation in greater detail in Section 10.2. But first, let us see how language use may vary in the life of an imaginary person, Jane Smith.

Jane Smith is a tall, 38-year-old redhead. Born in a small country town, she has lived half her life in a capital city, having gone to university there and married a student boyfriend who now teaches linguistics at a major university. They have two young children. Jane is a consultant cardiologist with a private practice. She is involved in research and is on the board of a large local hospital. In what spare time she has she loves to read and play games with her children, sings with the university choir and shares with her children their love of horses. During their holidays she loves to 'muck around' on a friend's farm. Jane leads a very busy life and although she is not particularly vain, she has an extensive wardrobe of clothes. She needs a white coat for hospital ward rounds, formal suits for board meetings, a long black skirt for choir performances and a range of other clothes suitable for work and relaxation.

What place has all the above in a book on English grammar, you ask? The metaphor of clothes is not uncommonly used by linguists to account for our use of different linguistic patterns to suit different social situations. Jane does not normally wear a night-gown to go horse riding or a hospital gown to a dinner party; in similar fashion she modifies her language, both deliberately and intuitively, to fit the circumstances of its use. It is not that some of her clothes are wrong, unacceptable or improper in themselves, any more than slurring or abbreviating words, using slang or conducting a conversation in disjointed, incomplete sentences are wrong, unacceptable or improper in their place. It is just that there are times when you wear your track suit and others when only your 'Sunday best' will do, and so it is with your use of language. In her private life Jane loves puns, jokes and all sorts of linguistic play; she restrains herself at the public Board meetings, though not always with her patients. The terminology she uses to discuss medical issues with her colleagues needs to be made less technical and more everyday when she explains these issues to her patients. As a doctor, she needs to be particularly aware of the special sensibilities of some of her patients, to adjust her language according to their age, sex and regional background, and to be on the alert for various verbal cues to hidden problems and delicate matters. In her professional communication with other doctors Jane can make a quick phone call or send a fax or an e-mail. Occasionally, she will write a long, formal letter and have it typed by her secretary. She must, however, always remember to send handwritten thank-you letters to her great-aunt; the old lady is rather old-fashioned and does not consider a telephone call to be appropriate.

The variety of names to which Jane answers are a good indication of her relationship with different people. Most of her patients address her as Dr Smith, but she is not a particularly formal person and many patients, as well as her secretary, call her by her first name. To her family she is 'Mum', 'Sweetie', 'Janey', 'Jennikins'; her siblings call her 'E. J'., 'Jano' or 'pud'(for pudding face); the school secretary often addresses her by her married name as 'Mrs Jones', Smith being her maiden and professional name.

The only aspects of our description of Jane that are not relevant to the issue of language variation are those involving her physical characteristics (her height and the colour of her hair). In the next section we shall explore the impact of age, sex and regional background on language variation.

10.2 Dialect and register

Every individual speaker of a language can be said to have a separate **idiolect**, a way of using language which, like our other mannerisms, reflects both the linguistic features we share with many other speakers of the language and also our own personal favourite expressions. Being able to create a character with a credible distinctive idiolect is a valuable skill for writers of fiction. For a broader, descriptive analysis of language, the common core background features that contribute to our idiolect can be separated into two categories. The term **dialect** is used to describe language varieties determined by fairly permanent characteristics of the language 'user': the region they come from, their age, sex and social class. **Register** is a term many modern linguists use to describe what is also known as 'style', that is, the variations in language which reflect such factors of 'use' as whether the language used is spoken or written, formal or informal, everyday or belonging to a particular occupation. Whilst most speakers habitually use only one dialect, they will typically control a considerable **repertoire** of registers.

10.2.1 Dialect

The original nineteenth-century work on dialectology concentrated on providing detailed descriptions of regional dialects, for example the distinctive features of the English used in different rural and urban communities, such as West Yorkshire or New York, and extending to broader distinctions such as American, Australian, Indian or Irish Englishes. The association of **dialect** with regional spoken language only has led to some confusion with the term **accent**. The difference is that while accents are based on phonological features, dialects show distinctive patterns in all areas of language: phonology, grammar and lexis.

In the second half of the twentieth century sociolinguists turned to study the effects of social variables on language use. For example, young people tend to use language less conservatively and their innovativeness influences the direction of the rest of the language. A number of differences in the language use of men and women have also been proposed, suggesting that men and women may employ some different communicative strategies, that women show a preference for the use of more prestigious forms and that there are some predictable differences in vocabulary choice.

While all dialects in principle serve the common needs of their community, none being less correct, proper or pleasant-sounding than any other, in all language communities one dialect is singled out for further development, standardisation and prestige status. This dialect, known as the **standard**, begins life as an ordinary regional variety, but comes to be accepted (often as an accident of fate, such as its use in the capital city and in centres of education and government) as the appropriate variety for written communication, education, official use and in the mass media, evolving to suit the changing needs of the whole country, and cutting across regional and register differences. Sometimes standardisation is undertaken deliberately, for example as part of a country's process of attaining nationhood, and one dialect becomes standardised in dictionaries and grammar books. Through its association with the dominant groups in society, this dialect often comes to be considered as representing an absolute standard of correctness for that language. The standard variety is often spoken with an associated accent (e.g. 'RP', or Received Pronunciation, in England), although it is now more common for users of the standard dialect to retain their local way of speaking.

The standard, prestige, dialect is typically used by the wealthier and better educated members of the community, irrespective of their regional roots. On the other hand, some regional and social dialects, especially where their speakers belong to the lower socioeconomic classes, become stigmatised (e.g. dialects like Black English in the USA). Children from socially disadvantaged backgrounds often have considerable problems at school, where Standard English is promoted and their use of stigmatised dialects may be identified with low intelligence and potential ineducability. Such children will often find it difficult to forsake the language of their normal home environment for a dialect with which they do not identify and which appears to devalue their background and group identity. The children who come to school speaking the standard prestige variety do not experience this discontinuity and are advantaged by this. Relevant in this area is the work of the British sociologist Basil Bernstein, who has suggested the terms **restricted** and **elaborated** code to account for two different orientations towards language. According to Bernstein, users of the restricted code see their society as closed, with strongly defined social positions and roles and a predominant sense of common values and group solidarity. Their language is oriented towards assumptions of 'shared' knowledge and so favours implicit, context-dependent expression of meaning. Users of the elaborated code see society as open-ended, with less strongly defined social roles and more opportunity for expression of individual identity. They make no presumption of shared knowledge and express themselves with greater explicitness and less reliance on the immediate context.

Bernstein originally proposed a strong correlation between the codes and social-class background, and this correlation was thought to explain why certain children experience a strong sense of discontinuity between their home and school environments, and the consequent lack of success experienced by these children in an education based predominantly on middle-class values. It is now thought that these are communicative 'fashions', related less to the social class of their users than to situations of greater and lesser formality (the formal situations demanding the use of the elaborated code; more informal ones, the use of the restricted code). Nevertheless, access to both codes is similar in its effect to the mastering of a repertoire of registers. There is undeniable disempowerment in not being able to use both the restricted and the elaborated codes, or in not being able to recognise which code is more appropriate in different social situations.

10.2.2 Register

Register varieties are defined according to their social and occupational origins; for instance, we can speak of a religious register, a register of advertising, or a formal register. The term is a useful abstraction which serves to correlate patterns of distinctive linguistic features with the dimensions of their immediate context or situation. Registers may be identified and defined in terms of three dimensions: **field** (broadly speaking the subject matter of the text, **tenor** (the social roles filled by the people taking part and the personal relationships between them) and **mode** (the channel or medium of communication, that is primarily spoken or written). These three dimensions of register will be discussed in detail in Section 10.3; at this stage only two points need to be made:

- Although it is convenient for the purposes of analysis to separate the three dimensions of field, tenor and mode, the division is an artificial one. All three dimensions operate simultaneously; they are mutually constraining and mutually determining. A change in one dimension, for example from a spoken mode to written mode, will have the effect of producing greater formality and distance in the tenor and a selection of different lexis and grammatical structures in the field. Text analysis exercises usually attempt to keep two of the three dimensions 'constant', varying only the category under analysis, but we must bear in mind that 'real' language always incorporates all three dimensions.

- If one has some acquaintance with a type of register, it may be possible to predict a number of its linguistic features and to identify some aspects of the non-linguistic context in which the text is situated (for example the use of *aforesaid* will almost certainly indicate a legal register). Mostly, however, register analysis must be kept relatively open-ended, particularly since what is expected and considered appropriate in a particular register may change over the course of time. For example, guidelines for **Plain English** (i.e. the use of simple, direct, clear and unpretentious language in legal and official documents and in medical, technical and business usage) are now being developed in many English-speaking countries. Moreover, we must keep in mind that the categories of description, for instance describing tenor as formal or informal, are based on the two extremities of what is, in fact, a continuum. Not only can the actual text select features of formality from any point within the possible spectrum, but 'inappropriate' choices can also be deliberately made, usually for a parodic or humorous effect.

The two categories of dialect and register intersect in a number of ways. In many language communities there is strong division of labour between dialects, with only the High variety (standard and prestige) or the Low variety (colloquial and local) being considered appropriate for use with certain registers. This situation is known as **diglossia**. The term **code-switching** is often applied where register differences are associated with a number of completely separate languages, for example English and Welsh in Wales, or English, Chinese, Tamil and Malay in Singapore.

10.3 Dimensions of register: field, mode and tenor

10.3.1 Field

The dimension of register which is most readily associated with occupational varieties is that of field, typically defined by the text's subject matter and closely identified with lexis. Field-specific vocabulary may be exclusive to that occupation, for example *byte, floppy disk, laptop* and the acronym *PC* in computer technology; *dialect, phoneme, lexis,* in linguistics; *purl and garter stitch* in knitting. Common core words may take on specific meanings in different registers; for example *mouse* in computing; *movement* (of a sonata) in music; *cover, pickup* in contemporary music; *action, clause, appeal* in legal discourse. As well, compounding possibilities may be extended, as for example in computing terminology from *hardware* to *software* and *liveware,* and particular collocations may become associated with certain fields, as in the use of *prestige residence* in real estate advertising. It is largely through the recognition of field-specific lexis or jargon that we are able to identify the topic of a text. The use of jargon among members of the same occupation is convenient; it provides a short-cut, an economical and precise norm, a common ground for speakers bound together by their interests or profession. It would be difficult, if not impossible, to learn to play a game of tennis without knowing the terms *deuce* and *let,* or cricket without understanding what is meant by *leg before wicket* or *cover drive.*

However, the word 'jargon' has become 'loaded' with strong negative connotations and is often described pejoratively as *doublespeak* or *gobbledegook.* This is partly because it excludes those people who are not part of the 'in' group, and partly because of its associations with such registers as advertising, 'officialese' and 'bureaucratese', and with political and economic discourse. Here we find language being used to mislead and obfuscate, as in the military use of *collateral damage* and *ethnic cleansing* to mean killing people. Some of the many words to denote the discontinuation of employment range from the colloquial and unpretentious *fire* and *sack* to such obscure euphemisms as *downsizing, involuntary separation, career change opportunity, efficiency gains* and *work-force imbalance correction*. Jargon has much in common with **slang**. Although they differ in so far as slang is used in spoken, colloquial, non-technical environments, while jargon is typically found in written, formal and technical language, both are often used deliberately to include and exclude, and to either create or minimise interpersonal distance.

Lexical differences are the most obvious features of language which identify the field, but many grammatical differences are also characteristically associated with different registers. Imperative clauses are typically found in instructional registers, passive clauses in scientific texts, present tense verbs in headlines. Moreover, different fields tend to select different patterns of complementation in NPs, clause subordination as against coordination, and particular rhetorical structures (e.g. the tripartite pattern as in *signed, sealed and delivered* is typical of legal discourse). Field is characterised by habitual correlations of lexis and grammatical patterns that people who are acquainted with a particular register come to expect and associate with it.

Nor is it only through the subject matter that field is identified. The field may be only partially verbalised, used mainly to accompany some ongoing non-verbal activity, for example *I'll just toss this in and then we're off ..., Yeah, let's take it from the top and one and two and ...*. The entire discourse situation, that is, every aspect of the context in which a communication takes place contributes to the final shape of the language associated with it. Whereas a recipe will identify the field of cooking, the language involved in the process of actual food preparation will differ from the language of both the recipe book and a restaurant review of the same meal; the language used in an operating theatre will differ from that used to describe the same procedure in a textbook on surgery; playing a game of basketball will call for a different use of language from that used to reflect upon the same game at a later stage.

It is because our choice of language is affected not only by the subject matter, but also by what we are 'doing' through language and by the pupose for which we are doing it that the concept of field is difficult to apply to casual conversations. Conversation is characterised by rapid switching of topics covering a number of fields and by a shared context. The primary purpose of most casual conversation is 'phatic' (see Sections 9.2.1 and 10.4.1) and this function is better described by the dimensions of mode and tenor than by those of field. Note that in an interview, although it has the surface appearance of a conversation, the situation is different. Interviewees are 'kept on track' by the interviewer: turns are usually formally allocated and the topic restricted. In the Fourplay interview (Appendix F), apart from one brief digression dealing with the band's name, all discussion is limited to the topic of contemporary, 'popular' music-making, and there is a very high proportion of field-specific lexis and grammar consistent with this topic (e.g. *pickups, gig, moshing, do rock, played big crowds*).

10.3.2 Mode

Mode is the dimension of register which accounts for the effects on our linguistic choices of the medium in which language is transmitted and received. For most speech communities, now as ever, the primary choice has been between speech and writing. Smoke signals and drum messages have been used in a limited and secondary fashion, transmitting short, specific messages over smallish distances; the sign languages used by the deaf (while a primary code and highly developed and extensively studied) are outside the scope of this book.

Speech always precedes writing ontogenetically and phylogenetically, that is, it is primary in the development of each individual person and in the history of each language. Writing is always secondary. From stone tablets and inscriptions to its use in the contemporary electronic media, writing suggests the prior existence of speech. Although, or possibly because, almost every human being, even the highly literate, uses speech more frequently than writing, writing has, in every speech community, the greater prestige. This is partly because writing must be specially learnt and is often not accessible to all, and partly because of its association with the standard dialect and consequently with registers highly valued by society, such as legal writing and scientific discourses, and the language of education and government. As well, writing is revered because it has conquered the 'tyranny of distance', both in time and in space; because of its relative permanence written works can still be read hundreds or even thousands of years after their creation. Sound transmission (e.g. by telephone and radio) and sound recording are relatively recent phenomena, but their development has altered our perception of what actually goes on in speech, and has led linguists at least to consider spoken and written texts in terms of difference rather than relative prestige.

The linguistic features that distinguish speech and writing most strongly reflect the effect of one variable, the presence or absence of the addressee. Typically, speech is associated with the presence of an addressee, writing with the the absence of an addressee. This factor has a number of important corollaries:

(i) **Immediate feedback** If the addressee is present, the speaker need not be as explicit and careful with lexis or grammar, as the addressee can circumvent misunderstanding by providing immediate feedback (e. g. a raised eyebrow or other body language, **backchannelling** in the form of *Oh yeah, uh-huh, um*, or explicit questions). Vague words like *thing, thingamajig* are used, as the speaker does not need to be pedantically precise. The addressee in turn is helped by the presence of intonation and body language. The absence of these in writing is poorly compensated for by punctuation. The immediate environment shared by speaker and addressee encourages the use of deixis: the speaker can physically point to something in the room, and words like *today* and *here* will be interpreted in the appropriate context.

(ii) **Lack of preparation time** In face-to-face speech situations, speakers generally do not have time to prepare their contributions carefully, and must think 'on their feet'. Not surprisingly, pauses, hesitations and 'fillers' (*er, um, you know, I mean, sort of, like*) are commonly produced. The lack of time available for planning and reviewing also leads to false starts, where the speaker loses track of the original construction or decides to change direction in mid-sentence.

(iii) **Strategies of speaker/addressee interaction** Conversation, which is not the only but certainly the main use of speech, is by definition dialogic. The speaker and addressee alternate roles, taking turns to speak, both initiating turns and responding to them, and 'yielding the floor' to one another. Turn-taking procedures are observed, with turns often allocated by name or implied by eye-contact or postural changes (although overlaps do happen). 'Unfilled' pauses may be misconstrued as yielding the floor and the speaker may be interrupted (another reason for the use of 'fillers' like *er* and *um*). Adjacency pairs are followed through (e.g., a question demands an answer, an offer an acceptance or rejection) and the presence of the addressee is additionally acknowledged in other ways, with *you know*, *eh* and tag questions. Consequently, the spoken mode, at least in casual conversation, tends to create dynamic, open-ended texts, contrasting with the static, closed, monologic character of most written textxs.

(iv) **Informality** Speech in the immediate presence of one or a few addressees tends to produce informality, although an increase in the size of the audience reverses this tendency. Some linguistic signs of informality in speech are contractions (*I'll*, *you'd*), omission of the subordinator *that* (e.g. *I know you'll like this*), and the use of phrasal verbs and sentence-final prepositions. More informal and attitudinal lexis is typically used in speech than in writing (e.g. degree adverbs such as *really* and *absolutely*, and 'hedges' such as *kind of*, *sort of* and *more or less*). It is interesting to observe how the unexpected absence of the addressee may affect our language, as when we are required to leave an answering machine message on the telephone. Many speakers are thrown into a mild panic which results in the increased formality of that message (e.g. we may choose to say *purchase* rather than *buy* or *get*). This effect is similar to the increased formality found in most writing, where, except in very personal instances such as in personal notes and letters, the audience is undifferentiated or unknown and the writer must predict the needs of his/her addressees by being more explicit and precise, and consequently more formal. Writing tends furthermore to be more impersonal than speech – especially official writing. It is interesting to note, however, that, in fact, it is only in writing that one has the option of completely obscuring one's own person: an author of a novel or a participant in the Internet chat rooms can even pretend to be a different gender.

(v) **Rhetorical structure** Because typical speech is dialogic and spontaneous, we tend to organise it chronologically (e.g. *and then I said, and then she said and ...*). Clauses are strung together using simple coordinators *and* and *but* and there are no clear sentence boundaries. Written language, by contrast, tends to be organised not chronologically but logically, consequently using a different rhetorical structure. Very complex NPs are more common in writing (see the discussion of nominalisation and lexical density later in this section). In the absence of intonational means for indicating information focus (see Section 8.1), writers may make use of constructions such as the cleft sentence or existential sentence. Speech processing factors may also have an influence: extraposition is common in speech because speech processing favours right-branching constructions, that is, those that place long content-heavy items of complex information at the end of the utterance. Written language, since it can be reviewed any number of times, is not so bound by this need.

(vi) **Functions of speech vs writing** The ease and rapidity of speech transmission make it particularly suitable for several functions that we shall discuss in more detail in Section 10.4.1 below. Most important of these is the phatic function, that is oriented to the establishment and maintenance of interpersonal contact. The use of interjections (*ouch, oh,* etc.) is quintessentially expressive; many are difficult to render in writing (e.g. *hmm? psst?*). Speech also has greater affinity with the poetic resources dependent on sound, such as alliteration – many advertisements and political discourse exploit this – as do we all when in the grip of spontaneously expressed overwhelming feeling. *He is such a pompous, pretentious, pontificating, pedantic prig* was once produced by one of the present writers much to the amusement of all present. Writing, on the other hand, is best suited to communication of complex, detailed material, which may demand considerable planning and restructuring and which may include material not capable of being transmitted orally at all, such as maps, tables, graphs, lists of figures, scientific formulae. It is well suited also to transmission of anything which must be remembered and recorded with utmost precision. Written material can even circumvent the constraints of linearity – dictionaries, glossaries and such, as well as computer hypertext documents, while written in a certain order, may be dipped into at will as the need arises.

Some material is composed exclusively in and for either the spoken or the written medium, that is, either spontaneously spoken to be heard face-to-face and immediately as in casual conversation, or written to be seen only, such as telephone directories, dictionaries and medical prescriptions. However, 'mixed modes' have existed for as long as writing has been more or less freely available. TV news and interview introductions are pre-written to be read aloud, while the dialogue in plays and novels, and much poetry, is written to be read 'as if heard spoken'. Lectures are a good example of a mixed mode; they must provide precise information, but will not do so effectively without a degree of interpersonal contact: eye contact, spontaneous comment from the lecturer, responses to questions from the students. As well, lectures usually make use of both pre-prepared visual materials such as maps and overheads, and of spontaneous writing on the blackboard.

   The traditional division of the means of language transmission into spoken and written, aural and visual, is subverted by the modern media. Telephone conversations use an aural medium, with the addressee present but not face-to-face. Most people become familiar with the problems this combination presents when having a telephone conversation with young children. Even adults have to be conscious of the need for constant backchannelling (*um, indeed, quite, uh-huh*) to ensure that the speaker does not think that the addressee has gone away or fallen asleep. On the other hand, 'conversations' on the Internet, while written, take on many characteristics of the spoken mode, developing compensatory devices for the absence of the voice and intonation.

We conclude our discussion of mode by noting an important feature characterising the written mode, its use of **nominalisation**. In spoken language it is usual for actions to be expressed by verbs, actors by pronouns or common nouns, and clauses loosely connected by simple coordinators and subordinators, such as *and, but* and *because*. In written language, by contrast, many verbs, adjectives, coordinators and subordinators are converted into nouns or 'nominalised'. For example the coordinator *but* may be turned into the noun *exception* and the subordinator *because* into the noun *reason*. The resultant nouns can then be extensively pre- and postmodified, forming often complex NPs, which are then connected by the verb *be* or other semantically empty verbs into copulative structures. The process is very useful to a number of formal written registers as it allows for neat and precise 'packaging' of a great deal of detail. However, heavily nominalised sentences are often much harder to process and may require a number of readings. Additionally, and importantly, nominalisation helps to create a text which does not have to specify personal responsibility; that is, the NPs in the subject position may stand for abstract ideas or complete events rather than people acting upon the world. The NPs in the object position representing the people affected by the actions of others tend to disappear altogether. Thus nominalisation may become a powerful tool for obfuscation of certain 'facts' and for promotion of particular ideological perspectives. Consider the choice of *the need to pursue the efficiency gains projected in order to* ... instead of *We had to sack some of the staff.*

    Texts with extensive nominalisation exhibit higher **lexical density**, that is, they have a higher proportion of open class words: nouns, verbs, adjectives and adverbs. A number of tests, such as the Fog Index and the Flesch Readability Score, use the notion of lexical density to judge the difficulty of different texts. Many computer programs include grammar checks incorporating lexical density scores. Their usefulness is, however, dubious as they are able to determine neither the actual effect of the high lexical density in a particular text, nor whether these are appropriate to the register of the text concerned. What is acceptable and appropriate in a science report or a philosophical treatise will not be appropriate or effective in a children's textbook.

The following example of a highly nominalised text comes from the journal *Science* (11 Sept 1998):

> *Improved judgement is now influencing the quality of research conducted on health effects of airborne particulate matter.*

The object NP (*the quality* ...) consists of 12 words and features a good deal of embedding. Twelve of the 17 words in the sentence are open class, 6 being nouns and 2 verbs (one of them non-finite). A spoken version of the same sentence might run something like this:

> *We can now do better research on how small particles in the air which we breathe affect our health, because we now know better what kinds of these particles are relevant.*

There are still 6 nouns, but only 16 of the 31 words in the sentence are open class. There are 6 verb phrases, and the longest NP is 5 words. Notice also the introduction of the human actor, *we*.

Because nominalisation enables us to produce an impersonal tone, and the number of abstract nouns makes the text appear more impressive, such texts have become the norm in much bureaucratic and official writing, exposing these to criticism as gobbledegook and to much humorous parody. We shall end this section on a lighter note:

> *It is our collective intent to communicate to others our desire that they should experience considerable elevation of mood on the occasion of the recommencement of a relatively arbitrary cycle of time measurement and a continuation thereof for its duration.*

The above sentiment comes from a University Challenge programme screened on ABC-TV in 1989. It means, in short, *We wish you a Happy New Year*.

The differences between the spoken and written modes that we have discussed in this section are summarised below:

Mode

Spoken	Written
context and background factors	
• primary – both individuals and languages develop speech before writing	secondary – must follow speech
'natural'	learnt
no equipment required	specific equipment necessary
• taken for granted, 'devalued'	prestigious, highly 'valued'
• aural	visual
organised in time	organised in space
transmitted over small spaces only until the 20th century development of telephones, sound recording and electronic media	transmitted over considerable space and time
transient	permanent
spontaneous	prepared
• addressee typically present	addressee typically absent
dialogic	monologic
dynamic, interactive, open-ended	static, closed
immediate feedback	delayed feedback, if any
context-bound	context-free
presence of intonation and body language	punctuation and layout
• best suited for phatic exchanges and spontaneous, cooperative, immediate development of ideas	best suited for complex material development of ideas allows planning, revision, inclusion of maps, graphs, diagrams, figures and formulae
language characterised by	
• problems due to pressure on the speaker: pauses, fillers (*er, um*), hesitations, breakdown in sentence organisation, repetitions, interjections and discourse markers (e.g. *oh, well, yeah*)	
• strategies of addressee involvement: first and second person pronouns interrogative tags, imperatives, interrogatives, 'markers of sympathetic circularity', (e.g. *I mean, you know, sort of, like*)	less audience-involving third person pronouns declaratives

Spoken	Written
language characterised by [continued]	
• syntactic features – lack of clear sentence boundaries 'minor' sentences clause complexity coordination • lexical features: deictic reference informal, vague lexically sparse slang, clichés, idiomatic expressions hedges and emphatics e.g., *sort of, really*	clear sentence boundaries complete, 'major' sentences phrase complexity subordination precise reference more formal, precise lexically dense heavily nominalised

10.3.3 Tenor

In Section 10.2 we identified the tenor dimension of register in terms of the relationship between the participants in a given situation. Although there is considerable intuitive awareness that we all modify our 'tone of voice' according to the situation, the meaning of an utterance is commonly thought to be determined by the field characteristics alone. Yet no meaning is complete, perhaps even possible, without our knowledge of the features accompanying its presentation: the pitch, volume, tempo of the delivery will allow us to 'read between the lines' sensing the writer's anger, delight, excitement, or intended irony. In fictional writing these are often expressed explicitly, (as in *she snarled/snapped/said warmly ...; her voice rose/trembled...*). The physical stances of the speaker and the addressee, as well as the degree of physical contact between them (including eye contact), will also contribute to the overall 'meaning' of the communication. Most societies have clear expectations about the amount of personal space appropriate in different social situations and recognise that invasion of this with personal stance, gesture or volume of voice are indications of differing power relationships between the participants. Complete neutrality of tone is impossible: the closest thing to it would be a written text in which impersonal constructions and unemotive vocabulary are used to give the impression of professional behaviour, objective rendering of facts or emotional distance. The verbal and non-verbal behaviour of the participants is influenced by their identity both personal and as determined by their social and professional status (called functional tenor by some linguists), by what they hope to achieve through the communication and by various features of the setting. This dimension of register needs to be learnt, initially during our early years of socialisation, and throughout life as we take on additional 'roles'. Children are encouraged to extend their 'tenor' repertoire with directives such as *Say thank you*; *Wait your turn to speak*; *Do not speak to your mother like that*; *Take that cheeky expression off your face*. Many professionals have an explicit code of ethics: doctors, lawyers, teachers learn to behave appropriately as part of the tools of their trade, to establish and maintain professional 'distance' both physically and verbally.

The crucial motivating factor in the dimension of tenor is distance, which is also in mode, where it has a straightforward, physical manifestation, and field, (e.g. where use of jargon is appropriate if both parties share professional knowledge and inappropriate if used as a means of excluding some participants from access to the information imparted). Distance in tenor is created by unequal, non-reciprocal power relationships (socioeconomic, class, professional), by differences in age and gender, by the frequency of contact and degree of emotional involvement. Physical distance affects relationships as well, accounting in part at least for the increased formality of written mode and of telephone messages. A larger audience likewise increases the distance between the speaker and those addressed.

The linguistic features of tenor are characterised by greater or lesser formality, which itself can be achieved primarily by differences in explicitness, in directness, and in the use of terms of address. Let us consider each of these in turn.

(i) Linguistic markers of explicitness At the most formal end of the formality continuum we tend to assume the existence neither of shared knowledge between us and our audience, nor of a shared value system; that is, we work on the presumption of distance and power as against familiarity and solidarity. There is a strong relationship between formality and explicitness. Phrase and sentence construction tends to be complex and intricate; enunciation and handwriting (or typed presentation) careful and precise; and the words are selected for precision and emotional neutrality.

At the most informal end of the formality continuum the opposite prevails. Reduction rules in every way, in the casual quickly written note, in less clear enunciation (*yeah, yep, gotta*), in the prevalence of contracted forms. Less care is taken in the selection of grammatical constructions and lexis. Slang, swearwords and emphatics (*really, great, cool*) are used to add colour.

(ii) Linguistic markers of directness   Distant formal relations call for a higher degree of both positive and negative politeness (with positive politeness being defined as explicit use of politeness markers such as *please* and *thank you* and negative politeness involving strategies designed to 'save face'). Social distance will generally occasion the use of less direct grammatical constructions and the avoidance of exclusionary, possibly offensive lexis like slang, especially in those situations which have inherent in them a degree of possible confrontation. An opportunity to escape politely from an undesirable situation can be offered by use of pre-structures (e.g. *Are you doing anything tonight?* or *Will you have some spare time this arvo?*). It is usually understood that such 'pre-structure' questions are likely to be followed by an invitation or a request. Thus the addressee can be prepared for the situation and has a chance to respond politely, without either party 'losing face'. Requests and orders may be less aggressively expressed by avoiding the imperative mood in favour of the declarative or interrogative. For example, a request to shut a door can be expressed as *Could you shut the door if you don't mind?* or *I think we should shut the door – there's a lot of noise outside.* In fact we are so attuned to having to make politeness inferences that even a simple statement such as *Gosh, it's really noisy here* will normally produce the desired result.

Potentially confronting situations can be further toned down by using the past tense, negative polarity and tags as in, for example:

> *I was wondering whether you'd mind giving me an hour of your time this afternoon?*
>
> *You couldn't lend me ten bucks till Monday, could you?*

In addition, hedges such as *perhaps*, in the following example, may be used to mitigate the potential brusqueness of an utterance by creating an impression of lesser certainty.

> *Perhaps we could get together tomorrow at 10 and discuss this matter further.*

(iii) Pronouns and terms of address The most obvious linguistic feature of tenor difference is created by the differential use languages make of pronouns and terms of address. Many languages express respectful, intimate or dominant relationships through their pronoun systems: singular second person is used to address children, intimates and social inferiors, second person plural in other cases. (Similar modulations are still detectable in Shakespearean English, but are no longer possible in most English dialects, the Quaker use of *thou* being an exception.) In communities where such pronominal differences exist, it is possible to gauge the progress of one's relationship quite explicitly because one cannot begin using the singular form until explicitly invited to do so. French has a special verb *tutoyer* to refer to the practice of using the singular pronoun. Many languages use patronymics (e.g. Russian) and other special honorific markers (e. g. Japanese) to signal tenor relationships. In all languages it seems to be important to avoid the direct use of the second person pronoun in more formal, less reciprocal relationships. In Russian the term for *they* instead of *you* was used by the serfs in face-to-face encounters with their social superiors. In English it would be considered extremely rude to use the vocative *you* in conjunction with the imperative, for example *You, pick this up.* One of the reasons the use of inclusive *we*, especially among nurses and primary school teachers, (e.g. *We are skittish today, aren't we?*) is the polite avoidance of the second person pronoun.

The systems of address terms that we find in the languages of the world are used to make clear the addressee's professional and social status, their gender and kinship relationship with the speaker. The more formal and distant the relationship, the more specific the terms, for example *Your Honour, Your Grace, Your Royal Highness, Auntie, Mr/Mrs/Miss/Ms, Dr Smith, Sister Mary, Professor Smith*. Until recently even in English, one could not begin using first-name terms until invited with a casual remark such as *Do call me Jane, none of this Dr business*.

Most names can also be systematically altered to indicate a loving intimacy and playfulness, or a brusque dismissiveness. Consider such variants as *Peter, Petey, Peterkins, Ped/Pedro, Pete* and *Jane, Janey, EJ, Elizabeth Jane Smith!* Inappropriate use of first names can be an effective strategy for disempowerment, as in the case of a male boss addressing a recently employed female as *Jane,* while being addressed by her non-reciprocally as *Mr/Dr X*. Other notable disempowering strategies can reduce adults to the status of children, as in the well-documented use of *boy* in American English when addressing an adult male African American, and the use of *girl* by a male office manager to a female and possibly older staff member (e.g. *Would one of you girls type this up for me?*).

We conclude this section by observing a process that has been occuring in late twentieth-century English that some have called 'informalisation'. In other words, many of the markers of private, personal and informal discourse are spreading into the more public spheres, strangers are being addressed by first name by receptionists and sales personnel, official correspondence is written 'as if spoken', a criminal lawyer interviewed on the radio says *Yep* and *You gotta see it this way*. This development has both advantages and disadvantages. Informal language seems to reduce distance and make participants interact on more equal terms. However, the sense of intimacy that is thereby created may produce a false sense of security, making it harder for us to prosecute our case if necessary. The differences between formal and informal modes discussed in this section are summarised below:

Tenor

Most Formal	Most Informal

context and background factors

• public discourse written mode; monologic large audiences, 'public' setting field: professional, official language constitutes the whole communication	private discourse spoken mode; dialogic small audiences, intimate setting field: everyday, conversation language accompanies other activity
• relationship between participants based on power: unequal, distant relationships difference in professional role, age, gender and social standing	relationship between participants based on solidarity: reciprocal, close relationships, similarity of social class, age, gender
low frequency of contact and emotional involvement taught by explicit instruction/ professional induction in later life	high frequency of contact and emotional involvement 'natural' behaviour

language characterised by

• explicitness lexis: classical, abstract, polysyl- labic (e.g. *tolerate*)	reduction lexis: colloquial, concrete, mono- syllabic (e.g. *put up with*), vague words (e.g. *thingamajig*), deictic reference slang, clichés connotative, emotive swearing, 'attitude' words, (e.g., hedges and emphatics)
precise reference professional jargon denotative, neutral	
'full' forms of 'phatic' expression and discourse markers: *Good morning, Good bye, Quite so* syntax consistent with written mode: complex phrases; intricate, carefully planned complete sentences	reduced 'phatic' expressions and casual discourse markers: *Hi, 'Bye, Yep, OK* syntax consistent with spoken mode: shorter phrases; clause connection by coordination; ellipsis (e.g. *Another coffee? You OK?*)
phonological precision	phonological reduction and abbrev- iation (e.g. *'em*)
careful layout and handwriting	informal punctuation (e.g. exclama- tion marks, dashes)
dialogue: formal, explicit alloca- tion of turns and floor holding/ yielding strategies	dialogue: less careful, interruptions and overlaps

language characterised by [continued]	
Most Formal	**Most Informal**
• indirectness/politeness requests/orders: mood choices – declarative, suggestions. past tense, negative polarity, interrogative tags	direct expression imperative and interrogative common
pronouns: inclusive – *we* impersonal *Would madam like to ...*, *Guests are requested to ...*, *It is desirable that ...*,	*you* more personal expression of opinion, stronger expression of obligation, (e.g. *you must, want you to ...*)
• terms of address title + surname titles – professional, kinship, gender	first name only, often reduced nicknames, diminutives, etc.

10.4 Further dimensions: functions and genre

10.4.1 Functions of language

In addition to the three dimensions of register (field, tenor and mode), the overall purpose for which the text is intended plays an important role in what aspects of language are selected and emphasised. In 1960, in his Closing Statement to a Linguistics and Poetics symposium, Roman Jakobson claimed that all verbal behaviour is goal oriented and proposed six different functions, or 'orientations' of language. Three of these, the primary orientations towards the 'I', the 'you' and the 'it', had been previously proposed by the psychologist Karl Bühler. Jakobson called these the **expressive/emotive** function (where language is primarily used to express the speaker's feelings), the **conative** function (where language is used to get the addressee to do what the speaker wants) and the **referential** function (where language is used to convey information about the world around us). Jakobson's other three functions were the poetic, the metalingual and the phatic. With the **poetic** function, the primary orientation is towards the form of the message that is, the focus is on the message 'for its own sake' (as in the playful uses of language found in proverbs, mnemonics, slogans, advertisements and, of course, poetry). When language is used to refer to itself, to elucidate the message (much of the present book), we have the **metalingual** function. Finally, the **phatic** function has as its primary aim the establishment and maintenance of personal relationships; that is, its orientation is towards social contact, as in small talk, exchanges about the weather and ritual expressions like *How do you do?*.

Jakobson's six functions of language provide a useful adjunct to the three dimensions of register, and apply across the whole spectrum of verbal communication. For example, the expressive/emotive function is dominant in lyric poetry, but also in the more mundane expressions of the speaker's feelings, such as interjections and swearing. The conative function is predominant in serious scholarly arguments as well as in propaganda and advertising. In our daily language interactions with young children we use the referential function (e.g. *These puppies won't grow very big; Dachshunds are really quite small dogs*) and the poetic function – not only in the form of poems and nursery rhymes, but also in the use of alliteration, rhyme, rhythmic and figurative language, which are used in many early childhood 'learning experiences' and games. Consider, for example, the alphabet song and the character, Count, in the children's programme Sesame Street. We resort to the metalingual function, not only in the disciplines where we need to explain language with language, for example linguistics and philosophy, but also in our answers to our children's questions: *What's that? It's a dog, it's a dachshund. What's it mean? What's a dachshund?* and so on. And we train quite young children in the use of the phatic function when we teach them to say 'Hello' and to wave 'Tata'.

While most speech events have one dominant orientation, there may be a number of secondary, less central aims as well. For example, whilst the primarily persuasive aim of advertising is reflected in the conative function, the need to inform as well may be reflected in the referential function, and the need to attract attention and shape the message so that it is easy to remember is reflected in the poetic function.

10.4.2 Genre

Before leaving this chapter and proceeding to text analysis proper in Chapter 11, we must briefly introduce another term. One area where the functional approach has become particularly prominent has been in the context of **genre** theory. Genre is an ancient term, referring as it did in classical Greek to the division of literary works into the three categories of poetry, drama and epic. These divisions were regarded as fixed and 'natural', and seem to correspond, to a large degree, to the three 'basic' functions of language, that is, expressive/emotive, conative and referential respectively. During the twentieth century the concept of genre gradually migrated from the field of literature and stylistics to the area of register analysis and sociolinguistics, and in particular to its potential applications in all areas of education. Genres are now considered to be culturally based, evolving and adapting to the different, changing needs of the society in which they are institutionalised, and the term applies to various communicative events from all walks of life, no longer only to such literary forms as the novel, the ode or the tragedy, but also to non-literary forms such as recipes, reports and lectures.

A genre is a publicly recognised communicative event, and each society gives specific names to the genres and sub-genres that it regularly uses. Although the actual features of each genre vary to some extent and may change over a period of time, the users of a particular genre have certain expectations with regard to the structure ('staging') and the linguistic features which are likely to be prominent in it.

Consider, for example, the 'recipe' genre. We all recognise that recipes must contain at least two important sections, a list of ingredients and the method or procedure. As well, it is usual for us to expect a recipe to have a (probably deliberately enticing) title and to provide such additional details as the intended number of servings and the appropriate accompaniments. It is typical for the title, appropriately, to be placed first, followed by the list of ingredients, the method and the other details in that order. It is usual for us to expect that recipes, whose primary function – like that of all instructional genres – is conative, will make extensive use of sentences in the imperative mood and of elliptical constructions and other abbreviations (see Chapter 9).

While each society may, as part of its communicative activities, make use of a large number of registers, varying as they do along the continua of mode and tenor, and the virtually unlimited number of potential field differences, it seems likely that there are institutionalised in any community a much smaller number of generic possibilities. On a macro scale we can describe, for example, the genre of the report. A report can be constructed in many of the possibilities offered by the three register dimensions; we have school reports, business reports, reports on various aspects of science, and most of these can be spoken or written, extremely formal or reasonably informal. Our socialisation into adulthood rests largely on our ability to know how 'things are done' in our society, and one important aspect of this is our ability to recognise and operate a range of genres.

Exercises

See end of the next chapter.

11 | Text analysis

In the many different areas where text analysis is now practised, such as pragmatics and sociolinguistics, stylistics and literary studies, two main directions are taken, usually concurrently. These can be described as the 'top-down' approach and the 'bottom-up' approach. The top-down approach focuses on larger considerations, beginning with a broad category such as a particular communicative genre or function (e.g. an advertisement, or 'persuasive' texts in general), or an aspect of social context (e.g. whether women use language differently from men, or how age affects certain aspects of language use) or a broad 'field' (e.g. religious language, the language of biology, or the way we 'write' history). The bottom-up approach begins with linguistic features themselves, such as the discourse particles *well, you know* or the simple present tense. The use of these features in different social situations is then described. For example, *well* and *you know* are typically used in informal, spoken situations, while the simple present tense is often used to make generalisations, as in the report genre.

11.1 'Top-down' approach

As an example of a 'top-down' analysis let us consider the genre of headlines. How do we expect headlines to be constructed? What contextual dimensions of headlines can we describe and how will these affect the selection of specific linguistic features found in headlines? That is, given the 'bundle' of situational factors, and our acquaintance with headlines as a prominent genre in our society, can we describe the linguistic features that are typically associated with it?

The mode of headlines is always written, and the tenor and

field depend on the particular instance. The overall effect of a headline depends on many things, in particular the poetic features which help it to attract and retain our attention, 'to entice the reader into the story without giving the whole game away' according to one Sydney editor. As well, many non-linguistic features need to be considered, including print size, colour and type, and general layout. The constraints of limited space have led to the development of a range of linguistic features: various types of ellipsis and abbreviation, special punctuation conventions and the use of short words whenever possible. In the area of grammar, headlines prefer reduced sentences; often, in fact, NPs only are used. Ellipsis of closed-class words (e.g. determinatives and prepositions) and of the verb *be* is also favoured and ambiguity may arise as a result. Consider, for instance, *Eye drops off shelves*, and the old World War II gaffe *8th Army push bottles up Germans*, where the identity between the plural noun suffix *-s* and the verbal suffix *-s* produces an additional interpretation. In punctuation and lexical choice the twin aims are again to reduce space and to increase impact. Commas are used to suggest a variety of grammatical relationships: asyndetic coordination, (e.g. *Study finds sex, pregnancy link*), apposition (e.g. *Driver, 85, guilty*) and direct speech (e.g. *Crime increase, polls show*). An exclamation mark is a visual shout. Question marks and inverted commas (when not used for marking direct speech) imply speculation or doubt and distance the paper from the views expressed within the inverted commas.

Turning to lexis we find that short, punchy, vernacular and colloquial words are preferred and there seems to be a penchant for metaphor, especially metaphors of battle (*clash, feud, blitz, war*) and religion (*mercy, vigil, crusade*), and other somewhat sensationalist words. For example, prices *plunge* and *soar*, *shock* and occasionally are *slashed*. Politicians *quit, quiz* and *slam* each other and *scrap* their appointments or policies. Every fire is a *blaze* or an *inferno*, every investigation becomes a *probe* and every disagreement a *row*. Somewhat archaic words are also often used, for example *vow, pledge, unveil* a tax plan, *shun, helm*. These words are short, vernacular and hyperbolic; they have a strong emotive effect, often reinforced by their aural overtones (alliteration, for example) and by 'poetic' play-fulness. Various rhetorical devices: synecdoche, metaphor and allusion make headlines often obscure and difficult to under-stand (as well as delightful and intriguing), and consequently they are often an especially difficult genre for foreign learn-ers of English. Consider the headlines *Lebed targets Russia's 'sick old man'* and *Sacked Lebed – now a cornered tiger* which ap-peared side by side in one newspaper. Lebed means 'swan' in Russian and the *sick old man* is not only a direct reference to the Russian leader, Boris Yeltsin, but also an allusion to the common metaphor for Russia at the turn of the twentieth century – the 'sick old man of Europe'. Thus a full under-standing and enjoyment of these headlines is extremely context- and culture-dependent.

Headlines are not written by the journalist responsible for the article, but by a special headlines subeditor, and reflect not only our cultural expectations of the genre (i.e. the most effective way of packaging a lot of information into a small space) and the editorial policy of the paper or journal in which they appear, but a great deal of individual creativity as well.

11.2 'Bottom-up' approach and checklist

For the 'bottom-up' approach we would like to offer the following checklist of lexical, grammatical and other features which should be taken into consideration when describing any text. An examina-tion of such features, at least those which seem to be relevant for the text concerned, is an important first step in any text analysis. Whilst this approach often brings accusations of mere 'train spotting' or 'butterfly collecting', one is often repaid with in-teresting and unexpected insights. It is also an easier approach for students often totally untutored in any detailed and ob-jective language analysis, who are otherwise likely to make unwarranted and subjective assumptions about the text be-fore them. All the items mentioned below (with the exception of commonly known terms, such as 'innuendo') have been discussed in the relevant chapters throughout the book (Parts A and B). The notions behind the grammatical tests suggest-ed in Section 1.5, such as substitution and movement, are still useful at this point of text analysis. For example, consider the potential effect of moving a particular word elsewhere in the sentence, or of substituting a verb for a heavily nominalised construction, or of substituting a less emotive word for an emotionally charged one in a highly persuasive text. Such strategies will underline the effect of the original item, and will consequently allow us to make a better informed choice.

Checklist

Lexis

Word class: open/closed

Does any class seem over- or underrepresented? Some implications here include:

- A preponderance of adjectives and adverbs, suggesting a descriptive or evaluative text.
- A high incidence of nouns, relating to nominalisation and lexical density.
- Pronouns, especially the conative use of *you*, expressive *I*, impersonal *it*, inclusive/exclusive *we*, lack of first and second person pronouns in impersonal texts.
- Phrasal verbs, typical of informal, spoken language.

Core lexis/non-core lexis

Some items to consider here are:

- Simple, short, vernacular (informal tenor) vs ornate, long, Latinate (formal).
- Archaic, obsolete, dialect words.
- Field-specific or 'technical' vocabulary, jargon, acronyms.
- Collocational restrictions, especially if 'broken', as in the e. e. cummings poem, Appendix A.
- Different types of discourse particles and interjections (mode).

Connotative/denotative lexis

- Connotative, for example 'loaded', biased, emotive lexis, (also called 'purr' and 'snarl' words by some linguists).
- Vogue/'buzz' words, clichés, euphemisms, 'doublespeak' and gobbledegook.
- Slang, swearing and taboo words, innuendo.
- Superlatives, persuasive words, hyperbole (tenor and field, such as advertising).
- 'Modal' words, for example attitudinal adverbs such as *unfortunately* and *perhaps*, emphatics/intensifiers, hedges/downtoners.

Lexical sets

- These contribute to cohesion, persuasiveness of a text and help to identify its field.

Grammar

Verbs and VPs

- Simple present *is/am/are* indicate strong modality of certainty, commonly found in texts with a conative function; often used in highly nominalised texts as well.
- Simple present tense also suggests generalisation, as in informational texts, reports; past tense is used in narratives.
- Voice: passive could be used for its impersonal, agentless potential, to alter the information distribution or for cohesion.
- Mood: imperative, interrogative, declarative, exclamative. (Consider the implications for tenor: politeness; conative function; interactive situations, etc.).
- Modal auxiliaries: modality (certainty, obligation); politeness, etc.
- Finite/non-finite: present participles convey a sense of activity, past participles a sense of inertia and passivity, both common in descriptive texts.

NPs

- Complex NPs are characteristic of certain genres, as well as

of written mode (see nominalisation and lexical density).
* Different types of dependents, for example peripheral dependents in apposition, are typical of journalese (e.g. *John Brown, the new MP,* ...)

AdvPs
* Check their position in clause and within VP, especially. (Discussion in Section 11.3.)

Clauses and sentences
* Minor vs major sentences.
* Sentence types: simple, compound, complex. (These may reflect such factors as the age of the writer or the projected audience.)
* Sentence complexity: left-branching structures, where the weight of grammatical structures to the left of the predicate is heavy, are more difficult to process, especially aurally, than right-branching ones, where the principle of end-weight is observed.
* Information structure: active/passive, topic/focus, any 'marked' choices.
* Impersonal constructions.
* Verb/clause types: monotransitive, copulative, for example, and the associated semantic roles, such as actor/patient and so on.

Visual and aural effects

These are responsible for important first impressions.
* Layout of advertisements, recipes, poetry, especially concrete poetry.
* Charts, tables, graphs, and so on.
* Punctuation (especially in informal and conative texts).
* Use of capitals, as found on the Internet, and also such 'creative' uses as the capital letters distinguishing all the dialogue ascribed to Death, a character in the novels of Terry Pratchett.
* Aural effects, such as alliteration, rhyme and rhythm.

Rhetorical effects

* Rhetorical 'devices' and types of comparison, contrast and association (metaphor and simile, synecdoche and metonymy).
* Patterning and sequence of every sort: parallel constructions, balance, repetition and climax. Common in all persuasive texts, they provide a sense of order and achievement. Note in particular the cumulative effect of sequences of two and three items. Interestingly, research on the structure and effect of political speeches finds that speakers are most likely to be interrupted after a triadic sequence, least often after a sequence of two, suggesting that indeed some sense of conclusiveness is associated with the number three. Patterns of threes are very common in all varieties of English.
* In English, the principle of endweight promotes our preference for short items to precede longer ones in lists. Whilst it is considered more polite to mention 'ladies' and 'gentlemen' and the addressee or a third party before the speaker, politeness is sometimes disrupted for reasons of end-weight. Consider *men and women* vs *ladies and gentlemen*, *Tom, Dick and Harry* vs *Harry and I*.
* Allusion and intertextuality (i.e. the relationship between text, and reference to other texts. See Section 11.3 for illustration).

11.3 'Mysteries': a text analysis

The final section in this part of the book will attempt to demonstrate some of the methodology advocated in the preceding chapters. The text used in this exercise comes from an essay entitled 'Mysteries', published in *Crossing the Gap*, a book of occasional essays by the Australian journalist and writer, Christopher Koch. This edited version of the original essay was used as part of the 1990 New South Wales (Australia) Higher School Certificate English examination paper, the students having been instructed to 'explore the effects of the different kinds of language in the given passage'.

We begin with a 'top-down' perspective, noting that this

essay belongs to a well-known genre, with writers like Charles Lamb, William Hazlitt and George Orwell in its tradition. A personal essay is typically a highly polished piece of writing, usually very subjective, its whole purpose being to express the author's attitudes, values and emotions. Personal essays, in contrast with political and occasional topical issues, are not concerned with telling a story, although they may use them, as ours does, to illustrate a point in the argument, or as a point of departure for the author's personal musings. Personal essays may be intensely conative in function, but typically they do not set out to inform or to persuade, merely to reflect upon some topic of interest or concern for the author.

Let us now adopt the 'bottom-up' approach, presenting a detailed analysis of the grammatical structures of the entire text, as well as comprehensive lists of lexical sets, rhetorical devices and other features suggested in the Check List. Since the passage, as it is given, clearly falls into three stylistically separate units, we shall label these A, B and C. A refers to the poem 'Mapooram', B to the Tyrolean myth, and C to the remainder (that is, the body of Koch's essay, including the two lines preceding and introducing Part B). Part C is actually considerably longer in the full text. However, the rest is stylistically consistent with the passage as it stands and the complete essay is far too long for detailed analysis. As there is an obvious difference in tone and style between the three sections, a separate analysis will be presented for each section and the salient features then compared to each other.

Parts A and B have in common a number of important characteristics. The mode of both the 'Mapooram' and the Tyrolean myth is spoken; we are told that 'Mapooram' was 'related by the Aboriginal Fred Biggs', while, as a myth, Passage B would most likely have been composed with oral delivery in mind. The purpose of both is narrative; on their surface they tell a simple story. The textual features of the spoken mode in these passages are the predominance of relatively simple lexis and of the compound sentence pattern. 'Mapooram' uses direct addressee-involving techniques, such as the imperative and interrogative clause types, the personal pronoun *you*, and the three dots to suggest the trailing-off effect common in spontaneous speech. Passage B is somewhat more formal, but for the most part it also uses simple, almost child-like, sentence structure and short, native core-vocabulary words.

The two passages differ in some minor ways: A is verse and B is prose. A has several items of Aboriginal English (e.g. *a clever-feller, sing the tree*), while in B there are a number of lexical items typical of fairy tales. The principal difference between A and B, and the one we shall examine now in some detail, is their handling of the actor/patient semantic roles, which help to create the very different world-views apparent in the two passages. In semantic terms the role of the actor identifies the performer of the action of the verb, the role of the patient identifies one who is directly affected by the action of the verb. Syntactically these two roles are typically represented by the subject and the direct object respectively in an active transitive sentence. The patient becomes the subject of a sentence in the passive voice and the actor is represented as the axis of an optional PP introduced by *by*, the omission of this PP resulting in what is commonly called an 'agentless passive'. In 'Mapooram' there are 12 clauses (both main and subordinate) and 4 of them have *you* as subject, for example *lie down, hear, say, go and find*. The subjects of the other 6 clauses are all introduced in a logical progression from the concrete *wind* to the abstract *Mapooram* (2 instances), to the concrete *tree, rubbing itself,* and so finally to the spirit *Wireengun, the clever-feller*, who *sings that tree* (2 instances). *You* is never represented as the patient; in other words, the *you*, the individual addressee in the poem, and also the generic Everyman it represents, is portrayed as a person fully in charge of his/her own destiny, actively seeking out and comfortably responding to the information about the fantasy world of his culture – the wind making the tree sing, thereby allowing the spirit Wireengun to release/create the Mapooram, 'a song to bring things out, and close things up ...'.

The power relations between Man and the Other are very differently configured in the Tyrolean story. There are 26 clauses in this passage. Because of the position of this passage within the body of the essay, and strong stylistic similarities between B and C, we are assuming that the fairy story is 'retold' for us by Koch in his own words. Of the 26 clauses, 8 active clauses have the herdsman as subject plus 2 passive clauses; 6 others have the herdsman as object. The remaining subject NPs refer to the 'lady' (3), the 'air', 'food', 'wine' and 'fairies' (5), 'everything' and 'no one' (2), and 'the old crone'/'Death' (5). Although the herdsman is commonly represented as subject, he rarely engages in deliberate action: he 'follows'. The relatively high proportion of subject/agent clauses (11/26) associated with the herdsman becomes farcical when we look more closely at the types of actions which are ascribed to our Everyman. The herdsman 'follows' his cows, 'finds' the place enchanting, 'accepts' the lady's offer, 'forgets' his home and family, 'grows' homesick, 'begs to be allowed' to return, 'gets back', is 'asked' where he'd been ... and 'falls dead'. At the same time, he is also consistently presented as the patient, with the other participants 'meeting' him, 'leading' him, 'giving' him food, 'offering' him work, 'allowing' him to return, not 'recognising' him, 'approaching' him, 'asking' him, 'looking' at him, 'taking' him by the hand ... and thereby killing him. At the risk of labouring the point, this is hardly a portrayal of a man of action, a man in charge of his own destiny.

Two other stylistic differences between A and B are worth exploring at this point as they contribute to the overall world view distinguishing the passages. Passage A gives an impression of activity and immediacy in its choice of the present tense and its almost total absence of scene-setting (there are no adjectives and only one adverb, *somewhere*). However, paradoxically, such sparsity and 'presentness' also suggest timelessness and universality of the experience: the time is both right now and always, the actor both 'you' and everyone. The verbs in Passage B, on the other hand, are almost entirely in the past tense, emphasised by several time adjuncts, for example *one day, for a time, after a time, for 200 years*. This is a typically narrative pattern and the distancing effect of the past tense is further reinforced by explicit reference to the world of the Faerie (*unearthly, outer world, different* and the capitalised *Death*). The choice of tenses and lexical sets is primarily motivated by the generic requirements of the two passages, that is, what is expected of them and what tells us that this text is a fairytale. However, in contrast with each other and reinforced by the clause structure dominant in the sections describing the world of the fairies, (i.e. the static, descriptive but inactive copulative, often with ellipsis of the copula, as in *the air was balmy ... the food delicious ...*), this pattern also has a noticeable effect on the balance of power set up in the two passages. In Passage A the 'fantastic' is Wirreengun, a 'he'; the mood choices are the addressee-involving imperative and interrogative; and the Everyman, 'you', is presented as freely and actively participating in the interaction (*you hear, you say, you go*). In B the other players are 'the Lady' and 'the old crone, Death', and, as previously suggested, the subject/object configurations suggest that it is they who hold the balance of power. In other words, in A the fantastic is presented as natural, ever-present, male and freely chosen by the protagonist; in B the fantasy is part of a static, distant, female and unnatural world into which the protagonist stumbles quite unintentionally, and in which he remains through a mixture of self-indulgence and emotional inertia. Like his cows, 'natural' but without real intention, the herdsman enters the Other world, where the fairies are powerful, but also do not appear to have any real intention of 'keeping him in thrall'. Everyman finds that life has passed him by. Using passages A and B as his point of departure, is this then the view Koch argues in Passage C? Not quite. There seems to be considerable skewing of both the proposition and the tone; playing down the pleasant and attractive elements suggested in both A and B. Fantasising is now presented as much more a factor of our inner dream world, as a kind of physical illness, and, importantly, as a conscious deliberate choice on the part of the protagonists.

Passage C differs from A and B in that it is no longer the rather flat, unadorned narrative favoured by those two, but a piece of expository writing which uses a number of different devices of persuasion to advance its central thesis. The guiding metaphors upon which Koch builds his perhaps unwarranted reading of the world-view presented in the opening illustrations are embodied in two literary allusions: one to Shakespeare's 'All the world's a stage', from *As You Like It*, and the other to Keats's 'La Belle Dame Sans Merci', which is explicitly referred to, in the second paragraph of Passage C, by the words *we wake on the hillside*. What further unifies the two allusions and gives considerable force to Koch's message is a whole string of threatening negative sexual images – the 'dissolving' genders of the 'roles' we choose to play on 'some insubstantial stage'; 'some sort of death' which 'empties' us 'of our will to live', and 'drains' us of our 'capacity to love what's real'; 'the fatal loss of time' which we spend 'addicted to perversity', which causes us 'to waste away'. Physically positioned at the centre of this run of images is the paradoxical coupling of 'masturbation' and 'the spirit'.

The argument is based on a false premise. The allusion to Keats is quite unwarranted. The herdsman in the fairytale is not compelled to his actions by any unearthly power, but seems motivated rather by his own complacency; and the appetites described in the Tyrolean tale are not sexual, but rather the much less romantic and passionate food, wine and weather. Sexual interpretation could, perhaps, be foisted by the modern Western reader upon 'Mapooram' through the image of the *tree rubbing itself*, but such a suggestion would need to be substantiated. Why then does Koch use such explicit and profuse sexual imagery where logically there seems no such implication? The answer could be that he does it for the same reason that our car advertisements tend to feature semi-naked nymphets, and our political propagandists cry 'rape' in order to whip up a spot of racial tension. Sexual innuendo is a powerful tool of the professional persuader.

The persuasive nature of Passage C is developed through every potential strand of the text – through the selection of lexis and grammatical structures, through the information packaging and cohesion and the marked, emphatic positioning of attitudinal adverbials, and through the use of a number of specific rhetorical patterns and devices. The latter include synecdoche (*the West*), typical of political journalese; and repetition and parallelism at every level of language structure – lexis, grammar and sound. There are several lengthy lexical sets in the passage. As well as the already mentioned set of words which describe desire as a pathological problem: *addiction, masturbation, perversity, dissolve, drain ... genders ... to long,* there is a 14-item set based on *myth: Fairyland, magic, legends,* a 16-item one based on *illusion: shadows, actors, stage, real, dream ...* , and a 10-item set of words dealing with the dissemination of culture: *stories, video machines, films.* Several basic contrasts are developed and emphasised through lexical repetition: real/magic, children/adults, Christian/pre-Christian, Christianity/scientific humanism, basic myth/ society's new basis and body/spirit. The use of poetic resources such as sound symbolism may also serve to contribute to the overall persuasiveness of Passage C. In his *Cambridge Encyclopaedia of the English Language* (p. 414), David Crystal suggests that the sounds [l] and [m] are strongly associated with sensual, pleasurable experience. Throughout this passage Koch chooses patterns where these sounds predominate; for example in the second sentence of the main text alone, we have *long, time, myth, paramount, magic real, more and more, illusion.* In fact, the frequency of alliterative patterns in Passage C is quite out of the ordinary.

Several other patterns emerge on consideration of the grammatical and informational structures in Passage C. Let us explore two of these: the distribution of subject and topic, and the patterning of modality. Of the 27 clauses in C (considering both main and subordinate clauses in this exercise), *we* appears as the subject and the topic in 4, and as the subject preceded by a coordination or cohesive adjunct in 3 further clauses (*and, but, instead, perhaps ...*). However, in two more clauses the subject is *the West*, a synecdoche for *we*, and 6 non-initial clauses in a long compound asyndetic sentence begin with other lexical variants for *we: our, whose* and *few people.* If we combine the subject/topic patterns with the dominant clause patterns associated with them: transitive (7), intransitive (11), copulative (9), an interesting overlap becomes apparent. The relatively unusual pattern for this text is the transitive, the one clause pattern where one participant is seen as directly affecting another participant. In 5 of the 7 transitive clauses in Passage C the action-initiating participant is *we*, the only others being *this one (message of warning)*, and *masturbation*. The objects of the *we*-initiated actions are *the time when myth was paramount, long hours with our video machines, ancient fables, 'roles'* and so on. *We* is thus grammatically emphasised to represent the participants consciously initiating their own choices, as having and using free will in the return to paganism.

The copulative pattern provides a powerful means throughout Passage C for the stating of facts, as in the following:

> *Fairy stories are messages of warning*
>
> *The penalty is some sort of death*
>
> *We are all actors*
>
> *The West is no longer a Christian society*
>
> *It is plainly not so at all.*

Two existential constructions, the opening *There are many variants* ... and *there is a penalty* ... might be considered as having a similar effect; that is, a new, important piece of argument is placed in the position of informational focus, and the verb *be* additionally suggests that this information is unquestionably, unarguably true.

The last feature we shall examine in the present discussion concerns the unusually prominent role played by the adjuncts in this passage There is scarcely a clause in Passage C which does not contain at least one, often up to three adjuncts. These fall into two broad semantic fields: one dealing with time and the other with modality, that is, the author's assertion of the validity of his evidence and his attempts to structure our perception of it. Expressions like *for the present era, currently, at any moment* and *some time ago* constitute the first group; into the second fall items such as *rarely, perhaps, always, plainly, really* and *tacitly*. What is of particular interest in Passage C is the placement of adjuncts in the clause: a very large proportion are placed in informationally marked positions. Typically, adverbials come at the end of the clause, trailing behind the main constituents, or at the very beginning of the clause, a characteristic position for attitudinal adverbs. In Passage C many adverbials are found in the middle of the verb phrase, between the auxiliary and the main verb where they are very intrusive and consequently attention-drawing. Some examples of this tendency are *were rarely meant, seems currently to long; seem, at least for a good proportion of our time, to be living*. The bluntness of this effect is softened by a seeming tentativeness introduced in the use of hedges, notably *perhaps* (used twice), and of modal auxiliaries such as *may*, and *would*. This manipulation of our certainties is evident also in Koch's use of the agentless passive, of the ambiguously authorial/inclusive *we*, and in his selection of many patterns of the spoken mode (compound sentences, often beginning with *and*, phrasal verbs and interrogatives). All these contribute to our sense of being involved partners in his argument and are characteristic of texts of this genre.

In this section we have tried to demonstrate that, as suggested in Section 11.2, an extensive linguistic description of the stylistic choices available to the writer may repay us generously with unexpected insights. These in turn enable us to arrive at an evaluation of a text which is based on principles which are both less subjective and more transparent than they may have been without the use of such linguistic procedures.

Exercises

The following exercises may be undertaken over a period of time, or in a group situation. They may be as extensive and as comprehensive as time and students' expertise allow and may be returned to at some later stage.

1.   a. With special attention to recipes in Appendix B and part of Appendix C, and any other written recipes you may be able to collect, and using some of the staging and structural details mentioned in Section 10.4.2, make a detailed description of the recipe genre. Notice that the example in Appendix C may be untypical.
b. Vary the tenor and the mode; for instance, get a friend or an elderly relative to tell you a recipe, or transcribe a short episode from radio/TV cooking programmes. (Such programmes often provide free written recipes. Compare

these to your transcripts if possible.)

c. Vary the genres within the general field of food writing; for example analyse a newspaper restaurant review or someone telling you about a meal they enjoyed (or hated). Compare the staging, layout, lexical and grammatical choices.

d) Vary the field but retain the general instructional genre as in a recipe; for example instructions on how to make a quilt cover, or how to play a particular game. What features of the text – lexis, grammar, staging, layout – remain the same? Why?

2. Using the headlines collected for Chapter 9 and any others, analyse these for the generic features outlined in Section 11.1. Compare different papers (e.g. tabloid and broadsheet) or different sections of the same paper.

3. There are two advertisements included (Appendix C and Appendix D). Collect a number of other advertising or promotional items (e.g. political campaign items and municipal notices are often written in the same 'conative/ poetic' way). What are some of the features of persuasive material in general? Repetition of key words, 'poetic' devices, features of involvement (e.g. *you* vs *we*, imperative, interrogative), generalisation and features of spoken mode are some aspects of language to examine.

4. a. Analyse the transcript of the FourPlay interview (Appendix F) for features of mode and tenor (Section 10.3).
    b. Tape and transcribe a short passage from the radio – a call-back programme, an interview or a panel discussion. Compare to a passage from a newspaper/journal on the same topic, or a very similar one.
    c. 'Chat' to a friend, an elderly relative and a distant acquaintance and then write a 'pretend' letter to each person on the same topic. Compare the adjustments in tenor that you make for the different people and the differences of mode in spoken/written interchanges.
    d. Examine a page or so of stage dialogue. (Harold Pint-

er is noted for his naturalistic dialogue. Try any reasonably contemporary playwright.) What features of 'real' dialogue are missing? Why? (Try to imagine the situation in real life, or get a friend to improvise it with you.)

5. Compare a number of different university lectures. Many lectures are taped and could be used for transcription. How do different fields affect the general features of the genre? Discuss also mode-mixing, tenor differences, and the resultant implications on immediate understanding, on note-taking and on memorability.

6. Appendix E is an extract from an article entitled 'Creature Features' written by a research scientist from the Australian Museum for a weekend broadsheet newspaper. What can we determine about its field, tenor and mode? What genre is suggested by its use of the present tense?

Appendix A

anyone lived in a pretty how town

by e. e. cummings

anyone lived in a pretty how town
(with up so floating many bells down)
spring summer autumn winter
he sang his didn't he danced his did.

Women and men (both little and small)
cared for anyone not at all
they sowed their isn't they reaped their same
sun moon stars rain

children guessed (but only a few
and down they forgot as up they grew
autumn winter spring summer)
that no one loved him more by more

when by now and tree by leaf
she laughed his joy she cried his grief
bird by snow and stir by still
anyone's any was all to her

someones married their everyones
laughed their cryings and did their dance
(sleep wake hope and then) they
said their nevers and slept their dream

stars rain sun moon
(and only the snow can begin to explain
how children are apt to forget to remember
with up so floating many bells down)

one day anyone died i guess
(and no one stooped to kiss his face)
busy folk buried them side by side
little by little and was by was

all by all and deep by deep
and more by more they dream their sleep
no one and anyone earth by april
wish by spirit and if by yes.

Women and men(both dong and ding)
summer autumn winter spring
reaped their sowing and went their came
sun moon stars rain

Appendix B

Recipe

Fantastic caramel cream rice pudding

90 gms butter (must be unsalted)
¾ cup lightly packed soft brown sugar
2 cups cream
1½ cups milk
1 cup rice (short or long grain)
about ½ cup extra cream for top
cinnamon or nutmeg for dusting

1. In a heavy saucepan melt the butter and sugar over medium heat and stir until sugar is dissolved.
2. Increase heat to high and gradually stir in cream and milk.
3. When mixture reaches boiling point stir in rice, cover saucepan and cook over low heat about 35–40 minutes. Stir every 10–15 minutes until most of the liquid is absorbed and rice is creamy.
4. Spoon the remaining cream on top of rice and sprinkle with nutmeg or cinnamon as preferred.

Serves 4. (Don't skimp on the cream and butter. This is <u>not</u> a healthy pud).

Appendix C

Seaview advertisement
(Note: the advertisement includes
the recipe)

SERVE the
moroccan lamb pink,
and the SEAVIEW
Cabernet Sauvignon red.

An afternoon enjoying some of
the best things in life. Old friends,
the great outdoors, some top food,
and of course a Seaview.

Everyone agreed it was a 'red'
kind of day, so we served a Seaview Cabernet Sauvignon with
lunch.

And more than once, its rich,
ruby plum colour and its soft taste
were given generous nods of ap-
proval.

After our feast, a short siesta
gave us the strength to tackle a
gentle bushwalk, and then all too
soon the time came to pack the day
away. Until next weekend, any-
way.

Iain Hewitson's Lamb with Moroccan flavours

Firstly whip up a Moroccan
style marinade by whizzing
together, in a blender, a cup
of olive oil, along with 1/2
a bunch of coriander, 1/2 a
bunch of parsley, 1/2 a tsp.
of turmeric, 1/2 a tsp. of cu-
min, 1 tsp. of sambal, 2
tsps. of honey and 2 tsps.
of soy. Then bung in one of
the new cuts of lamb, such
as the rump or topside, and
leave for one hour before
roasting in a very hot oven.
Rest for 5 minutes before
carving into thin slices and
serving with all the juices
and couscous or creamy
mashed potato.

'It's a view worth sharing'
Iain Hewitson

Appendix D

Army recruitment advertisement

You've done your best, now do better.

Finally, your Year 12 results are here. So how did you go?

Whatever your results, it's now time to make plans for the future.

But how do you know whether or not your further studies will give you the edge you need to succeed in a fiercely competitive job market?

Well, when you study through the Australian Army, getting a well-paid, secure job is a certainty.

Whether it's a university degree, technical and trade training, or leadership and management skills, the Army will guarantee you a job when you graduate.

Plus the Army will pay you to study and cover costs like books, HECS fees and equipment.

It's not just your academic skills that can give you an edge either.

In the Army, you gain a new sense of confidence, leadership and discipline. Which are qualities that are always in demand.

Indeed, the civilian work force is always looking for people with the endeavour, attitude and ability only the Army provides.

So if you're looking for a better tertiary qualification, just call 13 19 01 today.

The Army.
The Edge.
13 19 01

Appendix E

Extract from 'Creature Features'

by Tim Flannery, printed in the *Sydney Morning Herald*, Tuesday 30 December, 1997.

Dr Mike Grey, arachnologist, counts the first day of summer from the arrival of the first male funnel-web at his office. A steady stream of spiders crosses his desk year-round, many brought in by members of the public curious about the identity of the spider found in their garden. Male funnel-webs choose summer to wander in search of a mate, bringing the normally reclusive creatures into contact with humanity. Grey, by the way, assures me that he also knows when the school holidays have started, by the vast increase in funnel-webs brought by those enjoying time outdoors.

Dr John Paxton, ichthyologist, has a different method of prediction. Each year, tropical sharks move down the coast towards Sydney as the warm current extends southwards. As well as sharks, it brings tropical fish, tropical pelagic life and even sea turtles. As with so much else in Sydney, the timing of the current's arrival, its intensity and duration varies considerably from year to year. But, when the water temperature reaches 21 degrees C (as it did in the first week of December this year), tropical sharks are likely to have arrived off the Sydney coast.

Paxton believes that some Sydney newspaper editors exhibit their own behavioural changes that mark the arrival of summer. He says he counts summer as having started when he reads his first sensationalist, scaremongering shark attack article. In vain, he points out each December that it has been 34 years since a fatal shark attack occurred in the Sydney area and 60 years since a fatal shark attack off a Sydney surf beach. Such articles used to be annual occurrences before the media understood the importance of sharks. Lately they have returned, prompted no doubt by the 'feeding frenzies' such articles cause at newsagents.

Appendix F

Interview with Sydney band FourPlay

transcribed from radio Triple J, January 1998

Announcer: If you think classical string instruments are incompatible with rock music, you've probably just never been to see the Sydney band FourPlay. They're a *rock* string quartet formed a few years ago when the classically trained performers discovered pickups and traded their Mendelssohn for Metallica and the Beastie Boys. Since then they've played big crowds like the Byron Bay Festival and are on the verge of releasing their first CD of covers and originals. Our Loud* reporter, NM, sought out the band to find out just how you do rock with a cello.

TH: It all started actually as a ... as a classical string quartet. Peter and myself and Chris who isn't here and our old violinist Pip, we were all members of the Australian Youth Orchestra ... and got together and one day we decided to play Purple Haze (which the Kronos Quartet had done) for a friend's 21st and it went down well so we kept doing it and we did other things ... we went into the New South Wales Uni Band Comp and to our own surprise as well as everyone else's we won the New South Wales Uni section and it all took off from there ... [music]

NM (interviewer): I know it sounds like a cliché but ... FourPlay? [all laugh] ... it's got sort of sexual overtones ... tell me about that [giggles]

---

* The Loud Festival was a youth festival of music and the arts held only through the media in January 1998.

LG: Well, we're a highly sexual band ... we just ooze animal magnetism on stage and we just thought it was appropriate [giggles ... all laugh]

TH: [cuts into laughter] well, it was a joke really [all laugh] ... erm ...

PH: I think it's a it's a way of of showing that we we're sort of not your average classical string quartet; you know it's not like a name for a string quartet it's like a name for a a rock band and so it's got a bit of ... it doesn't take itself too seriously ... [music]

NM: Why rock on strings? You ... why ... What's inspired you to do this and I guess step out of what people expect a string quartet to play to doing some really – you know – stuff that heavy guitars and drums and really noisy singers usually perform?

LG: Well why should *they* have all the fun? [all laugh]

PH: Yeah, why not?

TH: We'd always wanted to play in bands and we only play these instruments ... well Peter plays piano as well ... and I can play didgeridoo and things but you know ... you can't it's ... it's not expected to to play to play this music on string instruments and we just thought why not, let's do it ...

LG: and we can scratch ... and we can make noisy things ...

PH: and we can scratch away ... and play ... and use distortion pedals and whatever and sound like a whole rock thing and it's

TH: and use distortion and [indistinct] really great ...

LG: Well, we can certainly get sounds out of our instruments that ... you wouldn't hear anywhere else ... there's a lot of sort of bridge bashing and things like that and I think we do take people by surprise ... [mmm] you know they don't really expect what we're going to come out with ... you know they're certainly not expecting ... distortion wah wah viola ... [music]

NM: Well, what about audience responses? Tell me about some of these? Or ... what do your audiences think of you?

LG: Well, we've had ... head bangers and and and moshers at some of our gigs ... you know that's that's a first ... what else? [all laugh]

PH: We get a really good reaction from most of the crowds

... we cross a a diverse spectrum ... people at at just really kind of rock gigs really like the music 'coz they you know they know a lot of the stuff we play and they enjoy it because we get into the music and we don't kind of make it austere and what they think of as classical – it's a rock performance so they get into it ...

TH: I think that our teachers were a little less impressed [all laugh] although ... they've been very supportive ... but it does ... play around with your technique... to get up on stage and muck around ... so ... yeah [laughs] I think they enjoy the music but ... less impressed by what what we are doing to ourselves and our instruments ...

NM: Well ... that's it ... I mean you treat your instruments pretty meanly ... how do they stand up ... how do your instruments stand up?

LG: Well. I know that I have to rehair my bow more often because every time I play Beastie Boys about 6 bow hairs will ... sort of ... fly off [laugh]

PH: Yeah yeah that's right

TH: I've actually got a special bow which I ... I use for Four-Play which is a fibreglass bow rather than your delicate eighteenth-century piece of wood – it's a chunk of fibreglass with some horsehairs attached which is totally unbreakable [all laugh] ... it's fun ... it's fun to play ...

LG: You should see what Tim does...

[music]

Announcer: T and PH and LG from the rock string quartet FourPlay going out with a Jeff Buckley cover. They were speaking to Loud reporter NM. And here's a song they were doing early on in the piece.

[music]

Appendix G

'Mysteries'

An extract from the essay, 'Mysteries', in *Crossing the Gap: A book of Occasional Essays* by Christopher Koch, first published 1987

> *Go out and camp somewhere. You're lying down.*
> *A wind comes, and you hear this 'Mapooram'.*
> *'What's that?' you say. Why that's a Mapooram.*
> *You go and find that tree rubbing itself.*
> *It makes all sorts of noises in the wind …*
>
> *A Wireengun, a clever-feller, sings*
> *that tree. He hums a song, a Mapooram:*
> *A song to bring things out, and close things up …*

> *Mapooram*, related by the
> Aboriginal Fred Biggs to
> the poet Roland Robinson.

There are many variants on the basic myth of the visit to Fairyland. In a version from the Austrian Tyrol, it runs like this.

A herdsman one day followed his cows across a hillside, and under a great stone, and so into a cave. There he was met by a lady. She gave him food, and led him into a strange, gentle countryside, where she offered him work as a gardener. He found the place so enchanting that he accepted her offer; and for a time he forgot his home, his family, and the life he had left outside. The air of that place was always balmy, its food delicious, its wine like nectar, and its people of unearthly beauty, since these were fairies.

But after a time the man grew homesick, and begged to be allowed to return to the outer world. He was allowed to do so; but when he got back, everything looked different – and no one recognised him except one old crone. She came up to him and said: 'Where have you been? I've been looking for you for 200 years.' And she took him by the hand and he fell dead; for she was Death.

Fairy stories like this were rarely meant for children, but were messages of warning; and perhaps this one holds a warning for the present era. The West seems currently to long for a return to the time when myth was paramount, and magic real, and to be more and more preoccupied with illusion. We spend long hours with the shadows on our video machines; our stores are full of books on legends and fairy lore for adults; our science fiction imitates ancient fables, and more and more of our films are recreations of myth and fable as well. And we seem, at least for a good proportion of our time, to be living at second hand. We talk constantly of 'roles' and 'images' and 'fantasies'. We are all actors, it seems, on some insubstantial stage, whose identities and even genders, may at any moment dissolve.

But there's a penalty for addiction to illusion, as the stories of the visit to Fairyland have always insisted; and the penalty is some sort of death. We wake on the hillside not only to discover a fatal loss of time, but that our fantasy has emptied us of the will to live; masturbation of the spirit has drained us of our capacity to love what's real. Addicted to Elfland's dream and perversity, we waste away.

The West is no longer – officially at any rate – a Christian society. Few people seem to be asking what sort of society it is, perhaps because it was tacitly agreed some time ago that its new basis would be scientific humanism. But has this really turned out to be true? As far as the counter-culture is concerned – and a good deal of our popular culture as well – it is plainly not so at all; instead, we have a society that's increasingly reaching back to paganism: to worship of the earth, and to the myths and beliefs and values of the pre-Christian world.

Answers to exercises

1a. (1) *friend, friends; leaving* (2) *have, haven't, had, hadn't; been; good, better* (3) *them; are, aren't, were, weren't* (4) *encouraged; simple, simpler* (5) *is, isn't, was, wasn't; being* (6) *do, don't, did, didn't; team, teams*

1b. (1a) No (1b) Yes (1c) *a + guy + wearing jeans* (2a) No (2b) Yes (2c) *to + his former girlfriend*

1c. (1a) Old men and old women may enter (1b) Old men, and women of any age, may enter
(2a) It was to her brother that she sent it from Perth (2b) It was to her brother from Perth that she sent it
(3a) The car salesman from Japan is here (3b) The salesman of Japanese cars is here

1d.

```
S  H          M   Rel        Ax   Dr      H              Pred   P    M      H
( People    (   from     ( the    country)))          (   (   can   become)
NP N          PP  Prep      NP  Dv      N              PredP  VP  Aux    Mv

PCs    M       H
(  quite   lonely))]
AdjP  Adv     Adj
```

1e.

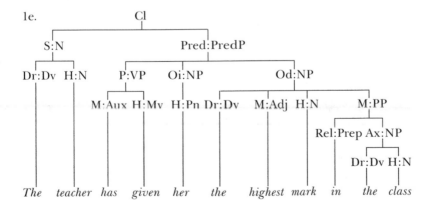

1f. (1) The subject and verb must agree in number (*none* is assumed to be singular – 'not one' – but *have* is plural). The rule overlooks the fact that noun phrases headed by pronouns such as *none*, *some* and *any* are felt by many speakers to be plural.
(2) Prepositions 'govern' the accusative case. (Thus, *between you and me*.) The prescriptive rule overlooks the fact that some speakers have a different rule when a preposition 'governs' a coordination of elements.
(3) Prescriptive grammar would require possessive *their* instead of *them* on the grounds that *being* has a noun-like function, cp. *their absence*. For most speakers *their* would be used only in formal style.
(4) The rule is that which forbids so-called 'split infinitives'. Unlike its Latin counterpart, however, *to ignore* is not a single word.
(5) The rule is that which forbids sentence-final prepositions. The rule is followed only in some formal varieties (*In which room were you hiding?*).
(6) Sentences with ellipsis are acceptable only if the omitted words can be restored exactly (*monitoring* cannot be inserted in the second clause: **than it has ever been monitoring before*). Most speakers ignore this rule when the correct missing form – here *monitored* – can be readily inferred.
(7) It is assumed that there is ellipsis here (of *is*), so the pronoun should be *he* and not *him* (see the rule for (6) above).

2a. (1) verb, adjective (2) verb, adjective (3) noun, verb, adjective (4) verb, adverb, adjective, noun (5) adjective, adverb (6) adjective, adverb (7) adverb, adjective (8) adjective, adverb

2b. (1) *saucepan* N, *knife* N (e.g. *He has a knife*) or V (e.g. *He will knife you*), *bottle* N (e.g. *It's in the bottle*) or V (e.g. *Let's bottle them*), *toothpick* N, *pepper* N (e.g. *Pepper tastes hot*) or V (e.g. *She peppered the steaks*), *spoon* N (e.g. *Do you have a spoon?*) or V (e.g. *Spoon it into the bowl*), *father* N (e.g. *He's my father*) or V (e.g. *He fathered two children*), *son* N, *cousin* N, *mother* N (e.g. *She is our mother*) or V (e.g. *She mothers us*), *aunt* N.
(2) *even* Adj (e.g. *The surface is even*) or V (e.g. *She will even the score*), *slow* Adj (e.g. *Boats are very slow*) or V (e.g. *It slowed to a halt*), *straight* Adj, *narrow* Adj (e.g. *The road is narrow*) or V (e.g. *The road narrowed*), *high* Adj.
(3) *better* Adj (e.g. *Golf is a better game*) or Adv (e.g. *They played better today*), *yellow* Adj, *hardly* Adv, *well* Adj (e.g. *I am not feeling well*) or Adv (e.g. *She sings well*), *poorly* Adj (e.g. *She's feeling poorly today*) or Adv (e.g. *He performed poorly*).

2c *flooming* V (present participial *-ing* suffix; takes *were* as dependent; modified by adverb *dribly*)

dribly Adv (adverbial suffix *-ly*; modifies verb phrase *were flooming*)
gridge N (takes article *the* as dependent)
brod N (takes article *the* as dependent)
plinged V (past tense *-ed* suffix)
strun N (takes article *a*; head of phrase functioning as subject)
vorled V (past tense *-ed* suffix; takes object *them*)
breening V (present participial *-ing* suffix; modified by adverb *frowly*)
frowly Adv (adverbial suffix *-ly*; modifies verb *breening*)
mubbed V (past tense *-ed* suffix; takes object *their niddish toks*)
niddish Adj (adjectival suffix *-ish*; modifies noun *toks*)
toks N (plural suffix *-s*; takes determinative *their* as dependent)
plodgers N (plural suffix -s; takes article *the* as dependent)
pidulous Adj (adjectival suffix *-ous*; 'describes' *plodgers*)
clandishly Adv (adverbial suffix *-ly*; modifies verb *jipped*)
snitchful Adj (adjectival suffix *-ful*; modifies noun *strun*)
strun N (takes article *the* as dependent; modified by adjective *snitchful*)

2d. Open: *peach, will* (N), *mine* (N/V), *fine, hear, mist, undo, bath, green, inn*
    Closed: *that, he, will* (auxiliary verb), *mine* (pronoun) *at, should, both, in*

2e. (1d), (2b), (3a)

2f. (1) *The treasurer has put forward three more suggestions* (2) *We put the rest of the money into an investment account* (3) *A mosquito bit him* (4) *They have noticed it*

2g. (1a) O (1b) PC (2a) O (2b) PC (3a) PC (3b) O

2h. (1) *You* (S) *should heat* (P) *the olive oil* (O) *in a deep pot* (A)
    (2) *She* (S) *seems* (P) *more depressed than ever* (PC)
    (3) *Football* (O) *she* (S) *can't stand* (P)
    (4) *They* (S) *visit* (P) us (O) *here* (A) *every year* (A)
    (5) *Unfortunately* (A) *the best players* (S) *sign* (P) *contracts* (O) *in Europe* (A)

3a. Open task

3b. (1) M, M (2) C, M, C (3) C (4) M

3c. hair: *She has lots of hair* (Mass) ~ *She has a hair in her eye* (Count)
    glass: *Glass was everywhere* (Mass) ~ *Wash your glass in hot water* (Count)

lemonade: *He prefers lemonade* (Mass) ~ *He would like a lemonade* (Count)

paper: *It was covered in paper* (Mass) ~ *She was reading the paper* (Count)

weakness: *He won't tolerate weakness* (Mass) ~ *She has developed a weakness in her wrist* (Count)

3d. (1) D, D (2) I, D (3) D, I, D (4) D, D

3e. (1) e.g. *all the shoes* (2) *the three children* (3) *all her many efforts*

3f. (1) A: *a purveyor (of small goods) (from Turkey)* – it is the purveyor who is from Turkey; B: *a purveyor (of small goods (from Turkey))* – it is the small goods that are from Turkey

(2) A: *the report (of the train disaster) (on Friday)* – it is the report that occurred on Friday; B: *the report (of the train disaster (on Friday))* – it is the disaster that occurred on Friday

(3) A: *some photographs (of the girls) (on the sofa)* – it is the p h o t o - graphs that are on the sofa; B: *some photographs (of the girls (on the sofa))* – it is the girls who are on the sofa

3g. (1) *all those heavy girders* (2) *feather dusters* (3) *irresponsible children who play truant* (4) *John's first drive in the car*

3h. (1) *the <u>family</u>; that pathetic <u>joke</u> about the Irish pilot; the Irish <u>pilot</u>*

(2) *<u>people</u>; the <u>rumours</u> about Tom's lifestyle; Tom's <u>lifestyle</u>; <u>Tom</u>; such <u>indifference</u>*

(3) *every <u>contestant</u> in the quest; the <u>quest</u>; a <u>prize</u> which will be treasured for years; <u>which</u>; <u>years</u>*

3i. (1)
```
       Dr      Dr     H              C
    (  all    the   members    (of the athletics club))
       Dv      Dv    N            PP
```

(2)
```
       Dr        M      H              PD
    (  Mary's  older  brother,   [who excels at chess])
       GP       Adj    N            RCl
```

4a.

Vs	Vo	Ved	Vi	Ven	Ving
comes	*come*	*came*	*come*	*come*	*coming*
sings	*sing*	*sang*	*sing*	*sung*	*singing*
forbids	*forbid*	*forbade*	*forbid*	*forbidden*	*forbidding*
fights	*fight*	*fought*	*fight*	*fought*	*fighting*
lays	*lay*	*laid*	*lay*	*laid*	*laying*
puts	*put*	*put*	*put*	*put*	*putting*
buys	*buy*	*bought*	*buy*	*bought*	*buying*

4b. (1) Ved (2) Ven (3) Ven (4) Ven (5) Ven

4c. (1) Vi (2) Vo (3) Vi (4) Vi (5) Vo

4d. (1) *was* Ved, *hoping* Ving, *hear* Vi, *expected* Vcd (2) *get* Vi, *started* Ven, *'s* Vs

4e. Operator: Non-operator:
    We need not stay   *We don't need to stay*
    Need we stay?   *Do we need to stay?*
    He usedn't to like violent movies *He didn't use to like violent movies*
    Used he to like violent movies?   *Did he use to like violent movies?*
    She dared not travel alone   *She didn't dare to travel alone*
    Dared she travel alone?   *Did she dare to travel alone?*

4f. (1a) regular or habitual present activity (1b) an activity in progress at the time of speaking
    (2a) an event located in the past (2b) an event that was in progress at a past point in time
    (3a) a future event that is presently scheduled (3b) an intended future event

4g. (1a) an event located in the past (1b) a recent event of current relevance
    (2a) regular or habitual present activity (2b) a recent event of current relevance
    (3a) A situation in the past (3b) a situation extending up to the present

4h. (1) It is possible that Mary will visit him after lunch ~ Mary has permission to visit him after lunch
    (2) It can be inferred that he has regular treatment ~ It is required that he have regular treatment
    (3) It can be predicted that they will contact us soon ~ They have an obligation to contact us soon

5a. *It is a musical instrument* vs *She comes from a musical family*
    Here is the foreign embassy vs *Such an idea is foreign to me*
    They mine magnetic ore vs *She has a magnetic personality*
    He likes abstract painting vs *He developed an abstract argument*
    Add up all the odd numbers vs *He has an odd expression on his face*
    It was a moral tale vs *Her behaviour was not very moral*

5b. Gradable: *overweight, sweet, mature, positive*

5c. (1) Adj: predicative complement function; could substitute an adjective such as *healthy*
(2) Adv: adjunct function; could substitute an adverb such as *soundly*
(3) Adv: modifier function; could substitute an adverb such as *impeccably*
(4) Adj: predicative complement function; could substitute an adjective such as *loose*

5d. (1) *Eventually, nearby* (2) *separately* (3) *well* (4) *quickly*

5e. (1) *of* (Prep), *as* (Subord) (2) *although* (Subord), *on* (Prep) (3) *if* (Subord) (4) *that* (Subord), *when* (Subord)

5f. (1) *In addition, fast* (2) *In all honesty, regularly* (3) *At no time, to that place*

5g. (1a) verb (1b) preposition (2a) preposition (2b) verb

6a. (1) Ditransitive: 'She found a reliable guide for him'. Complex transitive: 'She considered him to be a reliable guide'.
(2) Ditransitive: 'They will call a doctor for her'. Complex transitive: 'They will apply the title "doctor" to her'.
(3) Ditransitive: 'They made a model soldier for him'. Complex transitive: 'They turned him into a model soldier'.

6b. *He brought some beer* (Monotransitive); *He brought us happiness* (Ditransitive)
They elected a treasurer (Monotransitive); *He elected himself treasurer* (Complex-transitive); *They elected themselves a treasurer* (Ditransitive)
She seems upset (Copulative)
He told a rude joke (Monotransitive); *He told us a rude joke* (Ditransitive)
They drink regularly (Intransitive); *They drink beer* (Monotransitive); *They drank themselves senseless* (Complex-transitive); *They drank us a toast* (Ditransitive)
He died (Intransitive); *He died a poor man* (Copulative); *He died a painful death* (Monotransitive)

6c. (1) *We* (S) *treated* (P) *them* (Od) *as friends* (Cx)
(2) *They* (S) *sold* (P) *him* (Oi) *a house* (Od) *yesterday* (A) *for one million dollars* (A)
(3) *He* (S) *makes* (P) *me* (Od) *angry* (PCo)
(4) *She* (S) *accused* (P) *them* (Od) *of neglect* (Cx)
(5) *Henry* (S) *seemed* (P) *quite depressed* (PCs) *last week* (A)

(6) *I* (S) *told* (P) *my friends* (Oi) *that it was unfair* (Od)
(7) *You* (S) *should take* (P) *on* (Cx) *some more work* (Od)

6d. (1a) exclam   (1b) interrog   (2a) interrog   (2b) imper   (3a) decl
(3b) imper

6c. (1) phrasal (2) prepositional (3) phrasal (4) phrasal (5) prepositional (6) phrasal (7) phrasal (8) prepositional

6f. (1) *Who can help us?* (2) *Where did Phillip go to college?* (3) *What did he say was worrying him?* (4) *When does the train leave?* (5) *Which bus is he waiting for?* (or *For which bus is he waiting?*)

6g. (1) 'What type of terrible music is played there?' ~ 'How terrible the music is that is played there!'
(2) 'How often is it that I have told you to behave yourself?' ~ 'How often I have told you to behave yourself!'

6h. (1) clausal (2) subclausal (3) clausal (4) subclausal (5) clausal

7a. (1) *that he's a doctor* (NCl/O) (2) *that I own* (RCl/M) (3) *as they used to* (CCl/M) (4) *which pleased the class immensely* (RCl/PD) (5) *if they will offer her the job* (NCl/O)

7b. (1) Restrictive: 'You should ask those particular neighbours who saw the incident'. Non-restrictive: 'You should ask the neighbours; they saw the incident'.
(2) Restrictive: 'The car which he was driving was one which I hadn't seen before'. Non-restrictive: 'He was driving a car; I hadn't seen him driving a car before'.

7c. (1) Cling/Clause/O (2) Cli/Clause/Cx (3) Clen/Clause/PD (4) Cling/Clause/A (5) Cli/NP/M (6) Clen/NP/M (7) Cli/AdjP/C (8) Cling/PP/Axis

7d. (1) 'What he forgot was the time he spent in prison': *when he was in prison* is a postmodifier of *time*; 'When he was in prison he forgot the time': *when he was in prison* is an adjunct.
(2) 'The note was written before they suspected me': *before they suspected me* is an adjunct in the clause *that I had written the note before they suspected me*; 'Before they suspected me I revealed that I had written the note': *before they suspected me* functions as adjunct in the main clause.
(3) 'He admits to his open defaming of them': *openly* is an adjunct

in the Cling; 'He openly admits to defaming them': *openly* is an adjunct in the main clause.

(4) 'He was unwise to speak in an honest fashion': *honestly* is an adjunct in the Cli; 'Honestly, he was unwise to speak': *honestly* is an adjunct in the main clause.

(5) 'It was last week that he saw them': *last week* is an adjunct in the *that*-clause; 'Last week he said that he saw them': *last week* is an adjunct in the main clause.

7e. declarative: -
   interrogative: *We wondered when it would end*
   exclamative: -

   declarative: *He promised that he would be there*
   interrogative: -
   exclamative: -

   declarative: *She asked that she be permitted to join*
   interrogative: *She asked whether it was possible*
   exclamative: -

   declarative: *I assume that you approve*
   interrogative: -
   exclamative: -

   declarative: *We doubt that the concert will go ahead*
   interrogative: *We doubt whether the concert will go ahead*
   exclamative: -

   declarative: *She forgot that it was late*
   interrogative: *She forgot whether she'd ordered a taxi*
   exclamative: *She forgot how late it was*

7f. (1) *He was driving at great speed and very carelessly* (2) *It's an attractive apartment but quite inexpensive* (3) *She likes fast cars and living dangerously* (4) *He is either on drugs or intoxicated*

7g. 1. (a) *Tom and Jerry have escaped* (b) *They escaped and disappeared* (c) *They gave the police and the press a false lead* (d) *We found them trapped but unhurt*
   2. (a) *two or three apples* (b) *a red and white flag* (c) *thunder and lightning* (d) *protesters holding placards and shouting loudly*
   3. (a) *completely and utterly exhausted* (b) *tall or short* (c) *too old for late nights and for wild parties* (d) *fond of Bill and of his friends*

7h. (1) *<Women and men over thirty>* are *welcome*: 'Women of any age, and men over thirty'; *<Women and men>* *over thirty are welcome*: 'Women over thirty and men over thirty'.
(2) *Alsations can be <extremely aggressive and temperamental>*: 'extremely agressive, and temperamental (to any degree)'; *Alsations can be extremely <aggressive and temperamental>*: 'extremely aggressive and extremely temperamental'.
(3) *<Mary and <Bill or Peter>> made this mess*: 'Mary, and either Bill or Peter'; *<<Mary and Bill> or Peter> made this mess*: 'Both Mary and Bill, or Peter'
(4) *Tom plays <indoor cricket and football>*: indoor cricket, and football; *Tom plays indoor <cricket and football>*: 'indoor cricket and indoor football'.

8a. (1) NO (*a major literary figure* = predicative complement, not object) (2) *The troops were ordered by Colonel Carruthers to advance* (3) NO (*last week* = adjunct, not object) (4) *That language is a sign system was established by Saussure* (5) *We were instructed by our supervisor to begin working* (6) NO (*a pauper* = predicative complement, not object) (7) *John is known by us to be a fraud*.

8b. (1) The identity of the assassin is probably unknown (2) The agent is recoverable from the previous clause (3) The agent is inferrable (wind, storm, etc.) (4) The agent is probably identifiable in small print on the sign!

8c. *There is someone absent* (2) NO (3) NO (4) *There was no one hurt in theaccident* (5) NO (6) *There appeared a mysterious figure*

8d. (1) *It was the swimmers who were attacked by a large shark near the pier; It was a large shark that attacked the swimmers near the pier; It was near the pier that the swimmers were attacked by a large shark*
(2) *It was a detailed report that he gave to the police after the accident; It was he who gave a detailed report to the police after the accident; It was to the police that he gave a detailed report after the accident; It was after the accident that he gave a detailed report to the police*

8e. (1) Cleft (*Margaret did it*) (2) Extraposition (*How cold it was was surprising*) (3) Right-dislocation (*The way he behaved was very strange*) (4) None (5) Extraposition (*Who was to peel the potatoes was undecided*) (6) None (7) Cleft (*We set out on a cold morning in June*) (8) None (9) Right-dislocation (*The car she was driving was a Honda*)

Glossary

Absolute One of the three degrees of comparison, contrasting with **comparative** and **superlative** (e.g. *large* vs *larger/largest*).

Accusative case Personal pronouns functioning as **object** are typically in the accusative case (e.g. *She helped **her***).

Active voice Contrasting with **passive**, applies both to clauses and to VPs (e.g. *Mary scolded the kitten* is active, vs the passive *The kitten was scolded by Mary*; *scolded* is active while *was scolded* is passive).

Adjective ('Adj') A part of speech which functions as head of an **adjective phrase**, is typically gradable and denotes a property (e.g. *tall, selfish, dry*).

Adjective phrase ('AdjP') A phrase headed by an **adjective**, which has modifier and complement as possible dependents (e.g. *small, very small, smaller than a mouse*).

Adjunct ('A') An element of the clause which, unlike subject, predicator, object and predicative complement, is readily omissible. Adjuncts characteristically express 'circumstantial' meanings such as time, place and manner (e.g. *when it rains in Liverpool, happily*).

Adverb ('Adv') A part of speech which functions as head of an adverb phrase and may modify a verb, adjective or another adverb. Adverbs are often derived from adjectives via suffixation with *-ly* (e.g. *cleverly, rarely*; 'non *-ly*' adverbs include *here* and *away*).

Adverb phrase ('AdvP') A phrase headed by an adverb as headword, which has modifier and complement as possible dependents (e.g. *foolishly, so foolishly, as foolishly as the others*).

Adverbial clause ('ACl') A type of subordinate clause introduced by a subordinator such as *because, although, until* or *when*, and functioning as an adjunct.

Agreement The correspondence, in terms of grammatical features such as **person** and **number**, between the verb and the subject (compare *She jogs* and *They jog*).

Anaphora The relationship between one item, usually a pronoun, and its antecedent (an expression which facilitates identification of the pronoun-referent). For example *If **your brother** accepts the offer, **he** will regret it*.

Article There are two articles, definite *the* and indefinite *a/an*. They belong to the class of **determinatives**.

Aspect The **progressive** aspect (e.g. *She has read the paper*) and **perfect** aspect (e.g. *She is reading the paper*) are categories of the verb phrase used to express types of temporal meaning.

Attributive An attributive adjective (or adjective phrase) functions as modifier in a noun phrase (e.g. *a **naughty** boy, **noisy** seagulls*).

Auxiliary verb ('Aux') *Be*, *have*, *do* and the **modals** function as dependents of the main verb in a verb phrase. They express tense, modality, aspect and voice.

Back-channelling A term used in conversational analysis; any comment from a listener while the speaker's turn is in progress. This provides feedback to the speaker (e.g. *yeah, indeed, uh-huh*).

Case The system of inflections applied to nouns (**genitive**: e.g. *uncle's*), and to pronouns (**nominative**, **accusative** and **genitive**: e.g. *he / him / his*).

Clause A grammatical unit whose main structural patterns involve combinations of the functions subject, predicator, object, predicative complement and adjunct. The immediate constituents of a clause are normally phrases. A clause may form a whole sentence (e.g. *Jill has a car*) or just a part of a sentence (e.g. *Jill has a car but she prefers to walk*).

Clitic Reduced form of a word attached to another word (e.g. *she'll*).

Closed class A word class with a fixed membership: pronoun, preposition, coordinator, subordinator, auxiliary verb, etc.

Closed interrogative An **interrogative** that is typically used to ask a question for which there is a closed set of answers (e.g. *Were you born in Australia? Yes/No.*), and involves inversion of the subject and operator.

Code 1. In general linguistics, any system of words, sounds, signs that conveys information.

2. In sociolinguistics, any system of communication in a language or a language variety, spoken or written.

3. In the work of British sociologist Basil Bernstein (b. 1924), two different 'orientations' to meaning are proposed. In the **Restricted Code** meanings are presented implicitly, reflecting a more group-based approach to meaning making. The **Elaborated Code** reflects a greater emphasis on the expression of individual identity and is linguistically represented by greater explicitness. The earlier controversial identification of the codes with social classes has now been replaced by recognition that all speakers use both the 'communicative' styles.

Code-switching In many countries it is customary for people to switch from one language or dialect to another depending on the special circumstances of the situation, such as the setting, the subject of the conversation and speakers' roles with respect to each other (e.g. in Singapore many speakers use Malay in everyday transactions, Chinese or Tamil at home, and English as the medium of education and in professional contacts).

Coherence If a text, spoken or written, appears to 'hang together' rather than being a random collection of sentences, it is said to have coherence. Such a text would make sense because it would appear logical and consistent in its development and structure, and would not contradict any of our presuppositions and knowledge about our world.

Cohesion The text-internal organisation of a text: the links and bonds established on the surface level of a text by the use of pronouns, coordinators and subordinators, and lexical patterning, which all combine to give it a sense of connectedness (e.g. *John stayed at home because he felt ill. Consequently he* ...). It is usual to distinguish cohesion from its text-external counterpart, **coherence**.

Collective noun A type of noun referring to a collection of entities (e.g. *herd, crew, crowd*). A singular collective noun may be used with either a singular or plural verb (e.g. *The crowd was/were pushing forward*).

Collocation A habitual association between particular words in a language (e.g. *blond* goes with *hair, butter* is *rancid* not *rotten,* the *mind boggles*). Phrasal verbs are characterised by collocation (e.g. *put **up** a fight, put **in** an effort, put **off** making a decision*). Collocation differs from 'idiom', where the literal meaning is not possible to deduce from the total construction (e.g. *a red herring*).

Common noun The main subclass of nouns, contrasting with **proper nouns** and **pronouns** (e.g. *woman* vs *Evelyn* vs *she*).

Comparative One of the 'degrees' of comparison for adjectives and adverbs (vs **absolute** and **superlative**). Indicated by the suffix -*er* (e.g. *smarter, faster*) or by the adverb *more* (e.g. *more heroic, more sheepishly*).

Comparative clause ('CCl') A type of subordinate clause introduced by *than* or *as*.

Complement ('C') Applied as a general term to elements in the clause which – by contrast with adjuncts – are normally not omissible and are 'controlled' by the verb (objects, predicative complements, and various non-central varieties for which we have used the symbol 'Cx'). Also labelled as 'complements' are dependents in noun phrases, adjective phrases and adverb phrases which – by contrast with modifiers – are 'controlled' by the headword.

Complex sentence Has one or more subordinate clauses embedded within its structure (e.g. ***When** pruning roses be careful, **because their thorns are very sharp***).

Complex-transitive clause A clause containing an object and an objective predicative complement. Also applied to the verb used in such a clause (e.g. *She found him annoying*).

Compound sentence Has two or more main clauses (e.g. *Wear some warm clothes or you will freeze*).

Coordination The relationship between grammatical units of equal rank: clauses (e.g. *He huffed and he puffed*), phrases (e.g. *a knife or a fork*), and words (e.g. *old but solid*). Contrasts with subordination, the relationship between grammatical units of unequal rank.

Coordinator ('Coord') A word (e.g. *and, or, but*) or a pair of words (e.g. *either … or*) that link coordinated elements.

Copula A 'linking' verb taking a **predicative complement** (e.g. *be, seem*). A copulative clause is one that contains such a verb.

Co-reference The relationship between grammatical units which have the same reference (e.g. a pronoun may refer to an identical referent in an earlier or later part of the text, as in *John is tired, because he had a late night*; *Let me tell you this, I had a great time last night*). See also **anaphora**.

Co-text The relevant linguistic environment of which a given item is a part; co-text can be contrasted with 'context' (the entire non-linguistic background and cultural expectations associated with the meaning of a specific text).

Declarative The 'unmarked' mood, as opposed to the interrogative, imperative and exclamative moods. Applied to a type of clause typically used to make a statement.

Deixis The relationship between a linguistic item and an extralinguistic entity (e.g. in *I don't like it*, *I* is related by deixis to the speaker, and *it* to something disliked by the speaker).

Determinative ('Dv') Part of speech with the function of **determiner** in noun phrase structure (e.g. *a, the, that, both, three*).

Determiner ('Dr') A pre-head dependent in a noun phrase may be either a determiner or a modifier (e.g. in *the tallest building*, *the* functions as a determiner and *tallest* as a modifier).

Dialect A variety of a language defined according to the characteristics of the 'user', specifically associated with regional speech, but also with social class, gender and age. Dialects are most easily recognised by a distinctive pronunciation (or accent), but typically also have a distinctive vocabulary and grammar. Dialects are regarded as socially less 'proper' and prestigious than the **standard**, itself originally a regional dialect.

Diglossia In sociolinguistics, a term referring to a situation where two different varieties of a language are used in a speech community, each for a distinct set of social functions. The two varieties are classified as high (H) and low (L). The H variety, generally a standard dialect, is selected for more formal uses (e.g. education, literature, church, and broadcast media) and has greater prestige; the L variety, usually a vernacular, is used in private, more informal settings. Latin was the H variety throughout the early Christian world. English often plays that part in the former colonies of the nineteenth-century British Empire.

Direct object ('Od') A type of clausal complement found in transitive clauses and representing the 'goal' or 'patient' (e.g. *Ted sold **his unit**; Ted sold us **his unit***).

Discourse A term used in linguistics to refer to any stretch of language larger than a sentence, whether spoken or written, and having a logically consistent and unified structure (e.g. this book, this glossary entry, a lecture or a speech). The term is often used as an equivalent of **text**.

Discourse marker A lexical item whose function is to mark off sections of discourse rather than individual sentences or clauses (e.g. *well, now* tend to introduce new or contrasting material). Diverse items such as *firstly, finally, however* are sometimes included in this category, as are also miscellaneous items designed to involve the listener (e.g. *you know, I mean*).

Ditransitive clause Has two objects (e.g. *They sent me a final reminder*). May also be applied to the verb in such a clause.

Ellipsis In grammar, the omission of one or more elements of a sentence or a phrase, where these can be recovered from either the immediate context or the surrounding text, or on the basis of our knowledge of the grammar of English. Ellipsis provides a strong cohesive force in a text and is also commonly used in conversation for speed of response and economy of effort.

Endocentric Constructions such as NP and VP that have a head-dependent structure. Contrasts with **exocentric**.

Exclamative The mood of a clause that is introduced by *what* or *how*, and characteristically makes an exclamation (e.g. *What an impressive debater she was!*; *How impressive she was!*).

Exocentric See **relator-axis construction**.

Field One of the three dimensions of **register**, defined in terms of the topic or subject-matter of the text, what it is 'about'.

Filler Various hesitation forms such as *um, er* which produce a 'filled', non-silent pause.

Finite clause Contrasting with **non-finite**, a clause with a tensed verb (e.g. *He has been nominated*), an imperative clause (e.g. *Get nominated*), or a 'subjunctive' clause as in *They demanded **that he be nominated***).

Functions of language The six funtions of language defined by Roman Jakobson are as follows: expressive/emotive (expressing the speakers' feelings); conative (used to influence the addressee); referential (used to convey information about the rest of the world); poetic (focusing on the form of the message); metalingual (using language to explain itself); and phatic (the use of language primarily for social contact rather than exchange of information or expression of feelings).

Gender The distinction, applied to singular personal pronouns, between 'masculine' (*he, him, his*), 'feminine' (*she, her, hers*), and 'neuter' (*it, its*).

Genitive phrase ('GP') A **relator-axis** phrase in which the relator is the clitic *'s* (e.g. *the dog's*).

Genre Classical Greek theory divided literary works into three distinct genres or types: epic, poetic and dramatic. These three were thought to be archetypal, natural and fixed. In the twentieth-century genre is regarded as a set of conventions which identify the shared expectations of writer and reader, and which change from culture to culture and from one period to another. The term is now applied much more broadly to any structured, purposeful and culturally identifiable language activity (e.g. interviews, buying and selling exchanges, cooking recipes).

Gobbledegook A pejorative term for the wordy, pretentious and confusing use of language, especially as used in much bureaucratic and official writing. The term is particularly associated with the Plain English Movement's campaign to simplify the language of legal, government, business and technical documents, making these more accessible to members of the ordinary public.

Head ('H') The central word in a phrase, which determines its classification (nouns head noun phrases, verbs head verb phrases, etc.), and which may be accompanied by one or more dependents (e.g. *a* **sight** *to see; was* **writing**; *very* **honest**).

Hedge Any words which allow a speaker or writer to soften the impact of what is being communicated, to prevent it from appearing too arrogant or too assertive. Hedge words have a similar effect to that of some modal auxiliaries (such as *may, could*). In academic and other formal texts, common hedges are *almost, somewhat, hardly*; in everyday speech: *a bit, just, practically*. These are sometimes called 'downtoners', contrasting with 'intensifiers' such as *utterly, awfully* and *bloody*.

Hyponymy A sense relation of inclusion. A superordinate term with a more general meaning is called a 'hypernym' (e.g. *furniture*), which can be said to include a number of hyponyms, or more specific terms (e.g. *table, chair, bureau*). These subordinate terms are then called 'co-hyponyms' of *furniture*.

Idiolect A 'personal dialect'; the speech habits peculiar to a particular individual.

Imperative The mood of a clause with the infinitival form of the verb, typical omission of the subject *you*, and characteristically used to issue a directive or make a request (e.g. *Watch your step!*; *Don't be untidy!*).

Indirect object ('Oi') An object which normally precedes the direct object in a **ditransitive** clause, which generally represents the 'recipient', and which can usually be paraphrased with a *to*-phrase or *for*-phrase (e.g. *He sent **her** a red rose*; compare *He sent a red rose to **her***).

Infinitive ('Vi') One of the three non-tensed forms of the verb, the infinitive is used in imperatives (e.g. ***Be** careful!*) and after modals (e.g. *You should **be** more careful*). An infinitival clause is one with the infinitive as predicator (e.g. *They need **to be more careful***).

Inflection Morphological variation of a word to express such grammatical distinctions as number (e.g. *fence ~ fences*) and tense (e.g. *decide ~ decided*).

Interrogative A type of clause characteristically used to ask a question. There are two subtypes: **closed interrogatives** and **open interrogatives**.

Intransitive A clause lacking a complement (object, predicative complement, etc.). Also applied to the verb used in such a clause (e.g. *Kim has fainted*).

Jargon The technical vocabulary of a specialist group (e.g. legal jargon, computer jargon). The term is often used pejoratively because, if used unthinkingly outside its relevant area, or used deliberately to impress or confuse, jargon is, like slang, a powerful instrument for the exclusion of outsiders.

Lexis A term used in linguistics for the vocabulary of a language or a language variety.

Main clause ('MCl') A clause that is not subordinate. *We understand* is a main clause (and simple sentence), *We understand that they may not be agreeable* is a main clause (and a complex sentence), but *that they may not be agreeable* is not a main clause.

Main verb ('Mv') The headword in a verb phrase: dependents are auxiliaries (e.g. *throws*; *was **throwing***; *had been **thrown***).

Metonymy A sense relation based on association (e.g. in journalistic writing *the bar* stands for the legal profession, *the press* for the reporters and others involved in the media, and *10 Downing St*, *Canberra*, and *the White House* all stand for governments, as in *Canberra announced today* ...).

Minor sentences Units of language punctuated as sentences but lacking some of the properties associated with prototypical 'major' sentences. Minor sentences tend to be formulaic (e.g. *Hello, Happy Birthday*), or elliptical (i.e., sentence fragments, such as *See you soon*; *My turn?*; *Back Monday*). The use of minor sentences is motivated by the desire to conserve time, effort (as in everyday casual conversation) and space (as in newspaper headlines).

Modal auxiliary An **auxiliary verb** that expresses **modality**: *may, will, could*, etc.

Modality Meanings, such as necessity, possibility, obligation, etc., expressed by the **modal auxiliaries** and also by some adverbs (e.g. *maybe, certainly*).

Mode One of the three dimensions of register, defined in terms of the medium or 'channel' in which the text is transmitted (e.g. spoken or written, face-to-face conversation, telephone conversation, and so on).

Modifier ('M') A function served by dependents in phrases (e.g. *taller **than him**, a letter **from London***).

Mood The system of clause types: declarative, interrogative, imperative, exclamative.

Nominalisation The process by which a noun or noun phrase is formed from a word belonging to a different part of speech, usually a verb or an adjective. Extensive use of nominalisation is characteristic of writing in contrast to speech and it is especially common in formal writing.

Nominative case Pronouns functioning as subject are inflected for this **case** (*we, she, they*, etc.).

Non-finite clause A subordinate clause with a non-finite verb as the first or only verb: an infinitive (e.g. *I'd prefer **to wait here***), a present participle (e.g. ***Being the only survivor**, she quickly became a celebrity*), or a past participle (e.g. *They keep themselves **hidden from the public gaze***).

Non-restrictive relative clause A relative clause whose content is presented as secondary to that of the larger construction, from which it is separated by intonation in speech or commas in writing (e.g. *Have you met Mr Brown, **who lives in the house on the corner?***).

Noun ('N') Nouns head **noun phrases**, are usually marked for **number** and typically refer to 'things'. The class consists of **common nouns**,

proper nouns and **pronouns**.

Noun clause ('NCl') A type of subordinate clause which may be declarative, interrogative or exclamative, and has a range of functions similar to that of noun phrases (e.g. *She told me **that the relationship was over***; *She asked me **whether the relationship was over***).

Noun phrase ('NP') A phrase headed by a **noun**, and whose dependents may be determiners, modifiers, complements and peripheral dependents (e.g. *this situation*; *visitors from Europe*).

Number The distinction between **singular** and **plural**, associated mainly with nouns (e.g. *box/boxes*, *tooth/teeth*).

Object ('O') The function of a clause element which may, in many cases, become the subject through passivisation (e.g. *Tom opened the letter* ⟶ *The letter was opened by Tom*), which is typically a noun phrase, and which is characteristically associated with the 'patient' or 'goal' of an   activity.

Open class The classes of nouns, verbs, adverbs and adjectives are 'open' in so far as they readily admit new members.

Open interrogative An **interrogative** clause introduced by a *wh-* expression such as *what, who* or *when* and used, in the typical instance, to ask a question having an open set of answers (e.g. *What is your address?*; *When is the exam?*).

Operator The function served by auxiliaries (plus main verb *be*, and 'possessive' *have*) in four 'operations': negative contraction (e.g. *They haven't arrived*); inversion (e.g. *Have they arrived?*); emphatic polarity (e.g. *No they HAVEN'T*); and post-operator ellipsis (e.g. *Sue has arrived, but they haven't*).

Participle A non-tensed form of the verb. The two subtypes are present participles (e.g. *bringing, responding, being*) and past participles (e.g. *brought, responded, been*).

Part of speech A word class, such as verb or preposition.

Passive voice Contrasts with **active voice**. A type of clause whose subject represents a 'patient' or 'goal' rather than the 'actor' (e.g. *The kitten was scolded by Mary*). Also applied to the verb phrases in such clauses.

Perfect aspect The **aspect** expressed by auxiliary *have* in combination with the past participle. A situation is, characteristically, presented as resulting from the completion of an earlier event or state of affairs (e.g. *Many visitors **have seen** the Egyptian exhibition*; *She **had marked** all the essays by Monday*).

Peripheral dependent ('PD') An element with a parenthetical character, either a type of adjunct in a clause (e.g. *He failed to show up, **which surprised no one***) or a type of modifier in a noun phrase (e.g. *Tom Jones, **the singer**, is Welsh*)

Person There are three person distinctions associated with personal pronouns. First person and second person pronouns are generally used for the speaker and addressee respectively – alone or with others (e.g. *I, us, mine*, etc.; *you, your*, etc.), while third person pronouns are used for others (e.g. *her, they*, etc.).

Personal pronoun A subclass of pronouns (*he, us, their*, etc.) to which the category of **person** applies.

Phatic communion A term coined in the 1920s by anthropologist Bronislaw Malinowski and subsequently used by many linguists (see **functions of language**). It refers to the use of language primarily for the establishment and maintenance of social contact rather than for the exchange of information or achievement of other goals.

Phrase A grammatical unit intermediate between word and clause, which may be either a head-dependent construction (e.g. *fluffy toys; might decide*), or a relator-axis construction (e.g. *to the ocean; the club's*).

Plain English Movement In the late twentieth century a number of campaigns in the UK, USA, Australia and Canada pressed for the use of simple, direct, clear and unpretentious language in all public domains, especially in legal and official documents and in medical, technical and business usage. Many of these countries now have an official Plain English Policy.

Plural number Used when a noun refers to more than one entity (e.g. *trees, children*).

Predicate ('Pred') The section of a clause apart from the subject which communicates something about the subject.

Predicative complement ('PC') The function of an element in a **copulative clause** or a **complex-transitive clause**, typically in the form of an adjective phrase or noun phrase, and expressing a property or role (e.g. *He is **thoughtless**; We consider him **thoughtless***).

Predicator ('P') The function of a **verb phrase**.

Preposition ('Prep') Part of speech that functions as **relator** in a **prepositional phrase** (e.g. *under, at, with*).

Prepositional phrase ('PP') A type of **relator-axis** phrase in which a **preposition** serves as the relator (e.g. *over the moon, before noon*).

Progressive aspect The **aspect** expressed by auxiliary *be* in combination with the present participle. An activity is, characteristically, presented as incomplete or in progress (e.g. *The wind **is howling**; They had **been picking** cherries*).

Pronoun ('Pn') A type of noun used for **anaphora** or **deixis** (e.g. *he, it, we, this, which*). Not compatible with an article (e.g. **a she*).

Proper noun A type of noun that is characteristically used as a proper name (e.g. *Christopher, France*)

Register A variety of language defined according to the characteristics of the situation in which it is used (e.g. religious register, the register of advertising). Registers are analysable into the three dimensions of **field, tenor** and **mode**. An earlier term, still preferred by some linguists, is 'style'.

Relative clause ('RCl') A subordinate clause usually introduced by a relative pronoun (e.g. *the person who introduced us*; *a movie that you must see*), and typically serving as modifier in a noun phrase.

Relator-axis construction A phrase or clause whose relator serves to relate the other constituent – the 'axis' – to the larger construction (e.g. *under the mat*; *when the taxi arrives*). Contrasts with head-dependent construction.

Repertoire In sociolinguistics particularly: the range of varieties of language available to individual speakers or writers, enabling them to perform particular social roles (e.g. Jane Smith is a mother, singer, doctor and hospital administrator and adjusts the specifics of her language according to the needs and demands of each of these 'roles').

Restrictive relative clause A **relative clause** that typically 'restricts' the meaning of the head noun. Compare *Cars are a nuisance* and *Cars which use lots of petrol are a nuisance* (*cars which use lots of petrol* refers to a smaller set than simply *cars*).

Sentence ('Se') The largest unit in grammar. May be **simple, complex** or **compound**.

Simple sentence A sentence which has the form of a single clause (e.g. *He took it*). Not **complex** or **compound**.

Singular Singular **number** is used to refer to a single entity, by contrast with plural number (e.g. *flower* vs *flowers*).

Slang Non-standard colloquial language associated with various often highly localised subgroups within a society and especially with non-conformist subcultures (such as teenagers). Slang is characterised by its transience and is considered by some to be offensive. Originating in the specialised vocabulary of the underworld (e.g. thieves' cant, criminal argot, flash talk), slang contributes to the sense of solidarity within a group and consequently, like jargon, may be used deliberately to confuse and exclude non-insiders.

Standard The variety of a language most widely accepted and understood in its community. The standard is the medium of instruction, especially to second-language learners, of written documents and of the mass media.

Subject ('S') A clause element that typically precedes the verb (e.g. *Her father has borrowed it*), inverts with the operator in interrogatives (e.g. *Has her father borrowed it?*), is associated with nominative case (e.g. *He has borrowed it*), and 'agrees' with the verb (e.g. *He has/They have borrowed it*). A subject is typically in the form of a noun phrase and refers to an 'actor' and/or 'topic'.

Subordinate clause ('SCl') A clause embedded within the structure of another clause. May be **finite** (noun, relative, adverbial or comparative), **non-finite** (infinitival, present participial or past participial) or **verbless**.

Subordinator ('Subord') A word functioning as **relator** in a subordinate clause (e.g. *if, that, since*).

Superlative One of the 'degrees' of comparison for adjectives and adverbs (vs **absolute** and **comparative**). Indicated by the suffix *-est* (e.g. *fairest, slowest*) or by the adverb *most* (e.g. *most reckless, most prudently*).

Synecdoche A sense relation where a part of something comes to represent the whole (e.g. *lend me a **hand**, a **roof** over one's **head***). Also called 'meronymy'.

Tenor One of the three dimensions of register, defined as the relationship between the participants, the social roles the are playing and the degree of formality they adopt. The term 'manner' (of discourse) is also used.

Tense The verb contrast between present and past (e.g. *blow/blows* vs *blew*).

Text In linguistics: a stretch of language which is perceived as a purposeful connected whole. A text may be spoken or written, short or long, produced by one person or many, and is created by text-internal **cohesion** and text-external **coherence**. Some linguists use the term text interchangeably with **discourse**.

Transitive A clause having an object. Also, the verb used in such a clause (e.g. *Mary dropped the vase*)

Verb A part of speech with as many as six different inflectional forms, typically referring to an action or activity.

Verb phrase A phrase headed by a main verb, and with auxiliaries as dependents (e.g. *failed, could fail, has failed*).

Verbless clause A clause without a verb phrase, and often lacking other elements as well (e.g. *You should knock three times **before entering***).

Voice The category of **active** and **passive** clauses (and verb phrases).

Some useful references

Bolinger, Dwight, *Language, The Loaded Weapon: The Use and Abuse of Language Today*. New York: Longman, 1980.

Brown, R., and A. Gilman, 'The Pronouns of Power and Solidarity', in T. Sebeok (ed.), *Style in Language*. Cambridge, Mass.: MIT Press, 1960.

Crystal, David, *A Dictionary of Linguistics and Phonetics*, Oxford: Blackwell, 2nd edn, 1985.

Crystal, David, *The Cambridge Encyclopedia of The English Language*. Cambridge: Cambridge University Press, 1995.

Crystal, David, and Derek Davy, *Investigating English style*. London: Longman, 1969.

Eggins, Suzanne, *An Introduction to Systemic Functional Linguistics*. London: Pinter, 1994.

Fowler, Roger, *Linguistic Criticism*. Oxford: Oxford University Press, 1986.

Ghadessy, Mohsen (ed.), *Registers of Written English: Situational Factors and Linguistic Features*. London: Pinter, 1988.

Ghadessy, Mohsen (ed.), *Register Analysis: Theory and Practice*. London: Pinter, 1993.

Greenbaum, Sidney, *The Oxford English Grammar*. Oxford: Oxford University Press, 1996.

Greenbaum, Sidney and Randolph Quirk, *A Student's Grammar of English*. London: Longman, 1990.

Gregory, Michael, and Suzanne Carroll, *Language and Situation: Language Varieties and their Social Contexts*. London: Routledge and Kegan, 1978.

Halliday, M.A.K., *Functional Grammar*. London: Edward Arnold (Hodder), 2nd edn 1994.

Halliday, M.A.K., and Ruqaiya Hasan, *Cohesion in English*. London: Longman, 1976.

Halliday, M.A.K., and Ruqaiya Hasan, *Language, Context and Text: Aspects of Language in a Social-Semiotic Perspective*. Melbourne: Deakin University, 1985.

Huddleston, Rodney, *Introduction to the Grammar of English*. Cambridge: Cambridge University Press, 1984.

Huddleston, Rodney, *English Grammar:An Outline*. Cambridge: Cambridge University Press, 1988.

Jakobson, Roman, 'Closing Statement: Linguistics and Poetics', in T. Sebeok (ed.), *Style in Language*. Cambridge, Mass.: MIT Press, 1960.

Leech, Geoffrey, Margaret Deuchar, and Robert Hoogenraad, *English Grammar for Today: A New Introduction*. London: Macmillan, 1982.

Matthews, P. H., *Oxford Concise Dictionary of Linguistics*. Oxford: Oxford University Press, 1997.

McArthur, Tom, *The Oxford Companion to the English Language*. Oxford: Oxford University Press, 1992.

Quirk, Randolph, Sidney Greenbaum, Geoffrey Leech and Jan Svartvik, *A Grammar of Contemporary English*. London: Longman, 1972.

Quirk, Randolph, Sidney Greenbaum, Geoffrey Leech and Jan Svartvik, *A Comprehensive Grammar of the English Language*. London: Longman, 1985.

Wardhaugh, Ronald, *Understanding English Grammar: A Linguistic Approach*. Oxford: Blackwell, 1995.

Index